CRITICAL INSIGHTS

Philip Roth

CRITICAL INSIGHTS

Philip Roth

Editor
Aimee Pozorski
Central Connecticut State University

SALEM PRESS
A Division of EBSCO Publishing
Ipswich, Massachusetts

GREY HOUSE PUBLISHING

Library of Congress Cataloging-in-Publication Data

Philip Roth / editor, Aimee Pozorski.
    pages cm -- (Critical Insights)
  Includes bibliographical references and index.
  ISBN 978-1-4298-3829-0 (hardcover)
  1. Roth, Philip--Criticism and interpretation. I. Pozorski, Aimee L. (Aimee Lynn)
editor of compilation.
  PS3568.O855Z833 2013
  813'.54--dc23

                                                                    2013006798

ebook ISBN: 978-1-4298-3845-0

PRINTED IN THE UNITED STATES OF AMERICA

Contents_____

Career, Life, and Influence

Critical Contexts

Critical Readings

Resources

About This Volume

Aimee Pozorski

In October 2012, when Philip Roth announced quietly in the French magazine *Les Inrockuptibles* that he was "giving up the novel," the news did not go unheeded by fans and critics worldwide. It took a few weeks for the US press to pick up on this announcement—which appeared at first only in French—but when it did, a public outpouring resulted. "And now, what am I supposed to read?," an Italian reader named Stefania lamented, and many bibliophiles shared her plight.

The news culminated in a November 17, 2012, interview conducted with Charles McGrath of the *New York Times*: "his last" interview, Roth tells McGrath. McGrath reports that Roth's Post-it note of a message—"The struggle with writing is over"—is evidence that Roth has, in fact, put down his pen. He has stopped standing at the keyboard. He has stopped turning sentences around. He is done. He tells McGrath that he has not been at work on a novel since 2010, the year his award-winning *Nemesis* appeared.

However, this so-called retirement does not come so easily to scholars of Roth. Emotionally, it is not easy to learn there will not be another provocative novel to outrage the establishment (although it might be safe to say that Roth truly *is* the establishment). There will not be another novel to anticipate with the same regularity we anticipate a change of seasons or a new day of work. But, our intellectual work is not finished, either. Over the span of five decades, Roth has given us much to ponder, to pore over. Although dozens of monographs on Roth's work and life exist, and hundreds of scholarly essays, there is still much work left to be done.

This volume seeks to contribute to some of those efforts: Composed of thirteen original essays, covering a range of Roth's works from the beginning of his career to the end, the volume positions Roth's greatest novels and journalism against the backdrop of the changing literary, historical, and cultural American scenes. Perhaps as a testament to standard wisdom in some circles, this volume focuses most intently on the final decade of Roth's career—a decade in which Roth published some of his most lasting and compelling work.

The volume opens with my essay "On Philip Roth: Ethics and Elegy after the Holocaust," an argument that seeks to reposition Roth within a global context. Responding to the criticism that Roth's work is insular and narcissistic, "On Philip Roth" argues that he is instead perhaps one of the most ethical and outward-looking writers of the twentieth century.

Following a thorough biography of Roth, this collection goes on to place Roth's writing within critical contexts, beginning with Pia Masiero's "Narratological Quicksands in the Nemeses Tetralogy." In this essay, Masiero interprets the narrating voices behind these difficult novels. Informed by James Phelan's understanding of "dual focalization," as well as the four novels' exploration of time, narration, and the construction of the self, Masiero considers the ways in which this tetralogy deals with posthumous narration in particular.

Following Masiero's theoretical essay, Christopher Gonzalez places Roth's career within a cultural and historical context. In his piece, "A Roth for All Seasons: Historical and Cultural Contexts," Gonzalez looks back to Roth's first book, *Goodbye Columbus and Five Short Stories* (1959) and traces Roth's enduring desire to take his fiction in unexpected directions, right up to his most recently published novel, *Nemesis*. Gonzalez argues here that Roth situates his work both in terms of historical spaces as well as within culture, locating in his narrative "the nexus of history and culture."

Maggie McKinley's essay, "Aging, Remembrance, and Testimony in the Later Fiction of Roth and Bellow," reinforces the cultural and critical ties to Roth's work by reading his later fiction in relation to one of his first and last literary mentors, Saul Bellow. In so doing, McKinley's essay argues that both authors depict the act of looking back with a sense of urgency, particularly in their desire to concretize memory in the form of testimony. In both Bellow and Roth, McKinley sees an acute awareness of their own mortality, each finding life in their recuperative acts of narrative creativity.

Following the opening "Critical Contexts" section of the volume, the "Critical Readings" section offers a variety of perspectives on Roth's fiction from a wide range of experts in the field of Roth studies. Organized from the earliest writings in Roth's career to the final novels (discussed at the end of the volume), this section begins with an essay by Patrick Hayes entitled, "'To Rake Suburban Life over the Barbecue Coals': The Writer as Cultural Critic in Philip Roth's Early Fiction and Journalism." Hayes's article looks beyond the fiction for which Roth is best known in order to focus on Roth's little-known journalism from the years 1957 to 1958—articles and essays Roth published in such outlets as the *New Yorker*, *Chicago Review*, *New Republic*, and *Harper's*. According to Hayes, this journalism reveals not only Roth's early thematic concerns, but also his desire to capture significant cultural changes witnessed in postwar America.

Taking up Roth's best work of fiction from the 1970s, Velichka Ivanova's "Beautiful, Obscure Strangers: Women in *The Professor of Desire*" provides a feminist reading of that 1977 novel, considering in particular the novel's narrative structure and this structure's inextricability with the women's voices throughout. For Ivanova, Roth guarantees that the women's voices in the novel are heard, but only belatedly, and often only in order to contradict the opinions of the narrator, David Kepesh. In this way, she argues, women become unknowable for Kepesh, remaining for him "beautiful, obscure strangers."

Miriam Jaffe-Foger, known for her work on the autobiographical gesture, explicates in her essay "Philip Roth's Autobiographical Gestures" such texts as Roth's *The Ghost Writer* (1979) and *The Anatomy Lesson* (1983) in order to consider "Roth's use of the autobiographical gesture as a novelistic approach." Calling into question, as Roth does, the label "American-Jewish writer," Jaffe-Foger looks at Roth's double move in these narratives: simultaneously drawing on his own life experiences while also fictionalizing his subject matter through the use of an alter ego.

Considering less Roth's individual life and more the historical context in which Roth was writing during the 1990s, Michael Kimmage, in "The Mechanics of History in Philip Roth's American Trilogy," closely reads two historiographical subjects: "the way in which Roth uses the novel to construct historical narrative . . . and the notion of history . . . as destructive, violent and beyond the ken and control of individuals." This historical dimension takes on new weight in Namoi Desrochers's essay on trauma in Roth's *The Plot against America*. In "Coping through Collecting: Stamps as a Means of Facing Trauma," Desrochers uses the literary-critical lens of trauma theory to read the figure of the stamps in the 2004 novel. Through young Philip's relationship to, and ultimate loss of, his beloved stamp collection, Desrochers argues, we can also see his reactions to the uncertainty and upheaval that characterize the historical moment on the eve of World War II in the skewed and alternative American history Roth conjures.

The relative lateness—and simultaneous emotional devastation—of this successful novel in Roth's career also speaks to Deb Shostak's interest in "Late Style in the Later Novels." Shostak's work on the final five novels of Philip Roth—*Everyman* (2006); *Exit Ghost* (2007); *Indignation* (2008); *The Humbling* (2009); and *Nemesis* (2010)—considers the ways in which Roth seems decidedly "un-Roth" in his brevity and dissonance throughout the works. Influenced by Edward Said's study *On Late Style* (2006), Shostak adds Roth to a list of artists that includes Shakespeare, Bach, and Matisse—all expressing a form of "artistic lateness" that offers intransigence and irresolution in the face of mortality.

As Gurumurthy Neelakantan contends in his essay on *Indignation* and *Nemesis*, however, during this stage in his career, Roth has not completely given up on some of his more reparative interests—namely, the "heroic ideal"—that also characterize his earliest fiction. In "Philip Roth's Heroic Ideal in *Indignation* and *Nemesis*," Neelakantan takes up the two books in order to consider the ways in which Roth's characteristic "heroic ideal" evolves in the later novels in order simultaneously to represent old age, debilitation, and death. In witnessing the evolution of Roth's heroic ideal, Neelakantan suggests, we can also see an evolution in the cultural and historical developments in twentieth-century America.

Entitled, "'Just as He'd Feared from the Start': The Treachery of Desire in Philip Roth's *Nemesis*," Victoria Aarons's essay provides perhaps the most fitting final thoughts on Roth's career offered here. In it, she interprets Roth's final novel against the dual backdrops of the domestic polio crisis in Newark, New Jersey, and the Second World War raging in Europe in 1944. For her, the protagonist's attempts to reinvent himself throughout the novel "ultimately will be ambushed by the treacheries of desire in the exposing ironies of the Rothian counterlife." This idea of the "counterlife" has been a perennial favorite in Roth's work, but for Aarons, it takes on its final form in *Nemesis*, as it "is here that 'the terror of the unforeseen' becomes the anxious fulfillment of Roth's protagonist's worst fears about himself."

Culminating, finally, with such resources as a chronology of Philip Roth's life, a complete list of works by Roth, a full bibliography, and information about each of the contributors, this volume seeks to offer a comprehensive guide to the life—but, most emphatically, the work—of Philip Roth.

And yet, this critical, interpretive work must not be considered complete. Of course, readers and scholars of Roth will likely never have the opportunity to put down their pens. There is still too much work left to be done. But we can nonetheless wish Philip Roth all the best in his self-professed retirement—in whatever forms that may take.

Work Cited

McGrath, Charles. "Goodbye, Frustration: Pen Put Aside, Roth Talks." *New York Times*. New York Times, 17 Nov. 2012. Web. 21 Dec. 2012.

CAREER, LIFE, AND INFLUENCE

On Philip Roth: Ethics and Elegy after the Holocaust

Aimee Pozorski

Inarguably one of the greatest living American writers, Philip Roth nonetheless provokes in some readers a kind of fury or revulsion. It's as though his most effective works provide a screen on which to project one's disappointments with the world, with America, with men, with sex, with life. His novels, with their expansive yet carefully wrought sentences—and perhaps more tellingly, their pseudo-confessional style—elicit an answering rant from these readers. A quick tour of recent literary awards indicates the problem.

On October 10, 2012, National Public Radio's Kristen Torres asked a handful of Roth scholars if we were willing to be called at 7:00 a.m. EST the next morning, when the 2012 winner of the Nobel Prize in Literature would be announced. Over the previous ten years, I had often thought Roth might win this award, but it had not been on my radar in 2012, at least not before Torres informed me they were preparing the story just in case. "Will you call me even if Roth does not win the Prize?," I naively asked, believing fully that his failure to win must surely be a story in itself. I should have taken a cue from my own oversight, however, as there was too much anti-Roth sentiment among the judges in Stockholm. According to London bookmakers, his odds of winning were one in sixteen, well behind Haruki Murakami and Mo Yan, the latter of whom ultimately did win. Roth's chances were about even with that noted literary figure Bob Dylan. "Why didn't Roth win?," I asked several friends the next day. One, a colleague from Spain, answered wittily, and a bit bitterly: "The answer, my friend, is blowing in the wind."

In truth, I have discounted Roth's chances of winning a Nobel Prize at least since 2008. That year, Horace Engdahl, at the time the permanent secretary of the Swedish Academy, proclaimed: "Of course there is powerful literature in all big cultures, but you can't get away from the fact that Europe still is the center of the literary world. . . . The US is too isolated, too insular. They don't translate enough and don't really participate in the big dialogue of literature. That ignorance is restraining" ("Nobel Chief Disparages US"). It was difficult not to hear that as a critique of Roth himself, one of the greatest living writers in the United States. Speaking for many Americans, David Remnick, editor of the *New Yorker*, countered with: "If [Engdahl] looked harder at the American scene that he dwells on, he would see the vitality in the generation of Roth, Updike and DeLillo, as well as in many younger writers, some of them sons and daughters of immigrants writing in their adopted English" ("Nobel Chief Disparages US"). And as will be discussed below, Roth's fascination with post-Holocaust Jewish identity and with the multiple sources of American identity make his novels a poor place to look for any alleged provincialism.

However, the Nobel Prize committee is not the only body that discounts Roth. Since as far back as 1969, with the appearance of *Portnoy's Complaint*, there has been a violent backlash against his apparent misogyny and curious blend of self-involvement and self-hatred. In a 1974 interview with Joyce Carol Oates, for example, Roth already was forced painstakingly to distinguish his personal life from his literary project, and his literary project from the public reception of that book: "My public reputation—as distinguished from the reputation of my work—is something I try to have as little to do with as I can. I know it's out there, of course—a concoction spawned by *Portnoy's Complaint* and compounded largely out of the fantasies that book gave rise to because of its 'confessional strategy,' and also because of its financial success" (Roth, "After Eight Books" 85). Early on, readers and critics began, mistakenly, to conflate Roth with his title character, Alexander Portnoy—a creation, he insists, that was not meant as a "confessional" description of his own experiences or fantasies; rather, he has described his fiction as a rebellion "directed far more at my own imagination's system of constraints and habits of expression than at the powers that vie for control in the world" (Roth, "Writing and the Powers That Be" 12).

Nonetheless, Roth's reputation for misogyny, self-loathing, and myopia resurfaced in similar terms when he earned the Man Booker International Prize in 2011. Overshadowing the award was the news that Carmen Callil—one of the three judges on the Booker committee—stepped down in protest of Roth's receipt of the award. More striking than her passive resistance in stepping down, however, is the nature of Callil's vitriolic rant against Roth: "He goes on and on and on about the same subject in almost every single book. It's as though he's sitting on your face and you can't breathe" (Chilton; Jaffe-Foger and Pozorski 82; Royal 21–22). And although Callil seemed to be trying to communicate something of the "closed world" of Roth that might, at times, feel suffocating, what she actually communicated is something far more provocative: A type of sexual fantasy we might in fact see in any number of Roth's books.

Rather than understanding Roth's legacy as isolated, insulated, and ignorant on the one hand, or as suffocating and repetitive on the other, I would like to propose here that, in both style and content, Roth is one of the most globally engaged writers alive today, not only in the American literary tradition, but in the contemporary international tradition at large. The Irish novelist Joseph O'Neill has recently focused attention on Roth's ethical dimension, writing of a moment at the end of *My Life as a Man* (1974) when Peter Tarnopol sees off his "horribly antagonistic wife" and then turns to see "his new girlfriend sitting there, waiting" (O'Neill 90). For O'Neill, the line that follows—"Oh, my God, I thought—now you. You being you! And *me*! This me who is me being me and none other'" (qtd. in O'Neill 90)—reveals in Peter a recognition of "one fundamental, never-ending suit that cannot be settled: that between the self and the other. In question is the ethics of human proximity, with special reference to the conflicts of interest created by the demands of love and/or marriage" (O'Neill 90). While understanding fully the perspective throughout all of Roth's works as "conscientiously male—and Jewish, and white, and heterosexual," O'Neill acknowledges: "That being so, I read all of his work with ethical trust, a trust that remains unbroken even when his constructs do not meet with my imaginative agreement" (92).

I once asked Roth how it felt to be understood by Joseph O'Neill as being so trustworthy, so ethical, so far over "on the side of the good"; he dismissed my enthusiasm by saying, "I don't want to be on the side of the good. I want to be on the side of the *good sentence*" (personal interview, 15 Apr. 2012). One thing about which virtually everyone agrees is the value of the Rothian sentence, but I do not think this precludes an ethical dimension in the work. Although it may seem counterintuitive—after all, his novels are allegedly filled with navel-gazing protagonists obsessed sex and death—his all-encompassing sentence style (that is, a style that finds a way to incorporate every relevant detail into one syntactically compact unit) seems to be the best possible form for his ethical imagination. While his characters are at times unsympathetic and at other times downright loathsome (I am thinking of the range from Alexander Portnoy to David Kepesh to Mickey Sabbath), they are nonetheless, or perhaps for that reason, all too recognizably human.

But then there are the vulnerable ones—the youths who populate Roth's later work, such as young Nathan Zuckerman in *I Married a Communist* (1998), Seldon Wishnow in *The Plot against America* (2004), Bucky Cantor in *Nemesis* (2010); the young men seeking to do what is right, such as Gabe Wallach in *Letting Go* (1962), the younger Philip Roth in *Patrimony: A True Story* (1991)—who all reveal that much more has been on the author's mind during the last sixty years than the good sentence. That is perhaps the greatest irony of Roth's work: Despite five or six decades of criticism decrying his depravity, his work has unceasingly explored what it means to be a *good man*.

Perhaps one reason for this interest in ethics has to do with the time and place of Philip Roth's birth, in Newark, New Jersey, in 1933. As a child, he recalls following the war effort carefully and wondering about the fate of his Jewish relatives during the Nazi expansion through Europe in the 1930s and 1940s. Roth observed in 1974: "Little was asked of an American schoolchild, other than his belief in the 'war effort,' but that I gave with all my heart" ("Writing and the Powers That Be" 9).

Roth's fiction reveals this belief in the war effort even when not depicting soldiers doing battle or condemning the rise of the Nazi Party. In fact, often his project appears to be as closely aligned with the European post–World War II ethicist Emmanuel Levinas as it is with other postwar American writers in the realist tradition. For example, Levinas famously conjectured that in the face of genocidal history and its aftermath, one has a decision to make when confronting another human person, and that decision is either "to speak or to kill." Levinas's words are not to be taken as mere hyperbole. For him, this was very possibly a literal truth as he looked to the death camps as a way of understanding the relationships among people in the world, and their own relationships with a higher power.

Although clearly more fiction than philosophy, Philip Roth's novels present the same kinds of questions as Levinas's famous ethical equation: What do we do when faced with another—with an Other—given his or her radical differences from us? How does one handle the psychiatric or bodily illness of another human being or their radical grief in the face of unimaginable loss? Examples from Roth's oeuvre that most readily come to mind are Mickey Sabbath's grief over the illness of Drenka Balich in *Sabbath's Theater* (1995), Kepesh's devastation over Consuela Castillo's breast cancer in *The Dying Animal* (2001), young Philip's encounters with Seldon Wishnow in *The Plot against America*, and the list goes on.

For the purposes of this essay, however, I would like to consider three examples that cover the entire span of Philip Roth's career, beginning with one of his earliest novels, *Letting Go* (1962), then proceeding to his most recent novel, the Man Booker International Prize–winning novel *Nemesis* from 2010, then looking back again to one of his middle works, *Patrimony* (1991), a memoir he wrote on the occasion of his father's death in the late 1980s. Considering these books from the perspective of ethics after the Holocaust will perhaps shed new light on Roth's other works as well—works that deserve far more credit than they originally earned, given critics' fixation on Roth's representations of sex, which seem in hindsight to be for Roth not pseudo-pornographic, but rather an indication of the visceral way couples relate to one another.

Letting Go

Philip Roth published *Letting Go* in 1962, following his first collection, *Goodbye Columbus and Other Stories* (1959), for which he earned the National Book Award. The novel depicts the intersecting lives of two writers, Gabe Wallach and Paul Herz, who seek to do the right thing. The novel ultimately is about a misplaced sense of responsibility, of the way the two men have of conflating manhood with duty. In this sense, the book's relatively conventional, even old-fashioned style is as confining as the responsibilities that burden both men. As James Atlas argues in his 1982 introduction to the work, "Like Paul, Gabe labors under the conviction that by turning away from what he wants he is somehow demonstrating control over his own life. In a way, this acquiescence to ethical claims is a form of self assertion" (xi). Atlas refers to this sense of control one page later, when he writes: "Manliness again, in the guise of sacrifice" (xii). Roth has explained that, whereas this novel is about the confines young men face and their sense of confinement in the face of duty, *Portnoy's Complaint* is about the opposite—a shattering of the confines of social expectation born out in the vernacular of the late 1960s (personal interview, 25 May 2012).

Given the dual plot of *Letting Go*, focused as it is on one man who marries young and struggles to please his wife while another continues to date amidst a burgeoning career, it would seem odd that it ends with such a focus on the fragility of the lives of small children. Indeed, the scant criticism on the novel, dating back to 1969, seems to take up Roth's indebtedness to Henry James (Posnock); Roth's representations of women (Husband); and Roth's experimental use of narrative and narration (Bauer). However, whereas it is rather easy to see the novel's investment in the masculine struggles of each of the protagonists—the international conflict, the dating scene and married life, the evolution of a career—*Letting Go* in fact ends with the death of a small child on the one hand and the adoption of an infant on the other, and emphasizes, in particular, the effects of these moments on the mothers in the margins of the text.

Over the course of this rather long narrative—written in the style of Henry James and Edith Wharton—Paul marries Libby early on, and, after a back-alley abortion, Libby learns she can no longer have children; meanwhile, Gabe Wallach reluctantly settles down with a single mother named Martha and her two children, Markie and Cynthia.

What is interesting about this novel, which seems dated in many ways, is that—looking back to the early 1960s and its historical proximity to the Holocaust—it features many apparently disjointed scenes involving questions about the survival of a child. At one point, for example, Gabe's father tries to involve him in a conversation with the woman named Faye that his father is about to marry. And the way he does that it is to pose an ethical conundrum: As a physician, would Gabe and Faye save a child through a blood transfusion even if it were against the family's religious beliefs? As Dr. Wallach explains: "This is an intellectual exercise, we're simply working out the kinks in our minds" (497). For Gabe, however, it is no such thing; it becomes almost personal and, on the one hand, seems more to do with his dislike of the woman replacing his deceased mother in his father's life. But the scene is easily ten pages long, and ends nearly with Gabe explaining: "I was only asking . . . what right, as a physician, you would have to allow the death of a child, a patient whose life you could easily save" (501). In a section entitled "Children and Men," Faye discloses one of the predominant themes of the novel: "When they grow up . . . they think they know more than their parents" (503). But, as this chapter points out, and as the rest of the book will proceed to demonstrate, the novel's interest is not simply in the conflict between grown sons and their fathers: It is also about a generation after the Holocaust that seems newly awakened to the responsibilities that men have to protect the children.

In the very next chapter, chapter four of the same section, "Children and Men," the reader learns that Martha's son Markie has fallen to his death while sleeping on the top bunk. The chapter begins benignly enough: "That morning, when Cynthia rolled over, she found that her brother had climbed the ladder of the double-decker bed and crawled into the upper bunk beside her" (504). When she pushed with violence at her brother, coming as she is out of a dream, we learn in one uncharacteristically very short sentence: "He rolled only once and fell from the bed" (504). And then: "There was the thud of his head against the wooden floor, then no further sound. It appeared that Markie was going to sleep right through it; he did not even cry" (504). When she realizes that this moment is not also a bad dream, she "rolled toward the wall anyway and closed her eyes. It was then that she began to scream" (504). In this moment, Cynthia gives voice to Markie's death—an incomprehensible vocalization in the absence of Markie's cry. Quite uncomfortably, several pages later, Cynthia also seems to echo historians of the Holocaust who argue that the only witnesses to the gas chambers were those who died in them. Cynthia reflects: "No one knew what happened. Only Markie, and he didn't know either. He couldn't" (508). Tens of pages later, through Roth's use of shifting free indirect discourse, the narrator provides access again to Cynthia's obsessive thoughts circling back to her brother's fatal fall: "He liked to be tickled, but when it was over and his pants were changed, he would say that she made him do it. She wondered if he had come up into her bunk this morning just to be tickled" (517).

She, a few beats later, however, begins to wonder whether Markie "thought he was going to give her a baby because she wasn't married" (517). Confused about the new relationships between her father and June, on the one hand, and her mother and Gabe, on the other hand, she believes when boys and girls are in bed together, it is solely to make a baby. In one of the most touching scenes of the novel, Cynthia goes to bed the next night, hoping to talk to Markie. She is deeply suspicious of Gabe: "He would probably try to get his hands on Markie too, and drown him; she had better warn her little brother about that" (522). But when she turns to speak, Markie isn't there; he is lying unconscious in the hospital just about to die, and Cynthia reflects: "The sight of his pillow, all ready for his bleeding head, gave her the shivers; it almost made her cry, but she wouldn't allow it to. . . . When she had a baby she didn't want to have a strange baby that she wouldn't even know; she wanted the baby to be her. Little Cynthia. She would have a lot of regard for her baby" (522).

The repetition of the word "baby" here—four times, inspired by the sudden realization of the loss of another small child—opens onto the sixth section of the novel, entitled "The Mad Crusader," where Gabe Wallach begins and ends a quest to make official the adoption of an infant by his two friends, Libby and Paul. He first goes to see the infant, who had been living with Libby and Paul for three months, explaining: "He had not dropped in unannounced, bearing an offering, to work up old grievances. He had come for the satisfactions a new child is said to give. He had expected to be able to look down into the crib and know that all was not wrong in the world, or in himself. But no such assurance was forthcoming" (533). His reverie into his past and present—and the future that is yet to come—is broken by the odd sound of the baby: "Turning, Rachel made a weak nasal sound. It was slight, but human and penetrable; it broke through the thin skin of his reflections. What looked to be the truth poured through: he was imagining in the name of the future what should have been a past; he could have left young manhood, stopped bumbling, whenever he chose" (534). In the presence of an infant who punctuates his reverie about a past that is yet to come, Gabe is suddenly called to arms. He needs Rachel's birth father to sign the adoption papers over to Paul and Libby.

Gabe travels from Chicago, Illinois, to Gary, Indiana—one of the rare midwestern backdrops of Roth's typically Newark-inflected novels—to meet Rachel's birth father, Harry Bigoness, only to come face to face with another child compromised. He follows a noise that sounds like the whining of a "kitten or a puppy" (585) and opens the bathroom door to find a boy strapped to the toilet seat: "When he saw Gabe he let out an agonized scream. He strained to release himself from the seat; he face went from red to white to red again; the odor of the child's feces was overpowering" (585). He learns a beat later that "the odor was from sickness" (585). Once again, this apparently gratuitous scene takes far too long to narrate: Two pages later, the boy is still strapped to the toilet, with Gabe understanding that "he had to pick up the boy. He had to clean him. Flushing the toilet a second time, he carried him from the bathroom. . . . All right, he had been impru-dent—*now* was he happy? But there was no backing out, not if he had gone too far" (587).

It is difficult to understand precisely what Gabe is referring to here when he admits he has gone "too far": He has, to this point, inserted himself into the lives of Paul and Libby to the extent that he is in Gary, Indiana, getting adoption papers signed for their infant, Rachel—an ordeal that turns out to be much more than he bargained for—which has in turn led him to Bigoness's bathroom, unfastening from a toilet an unnamed child covered in filth. Nearly the final quarter of the novel is organized around the vulnerability of a child—a theme that Roth seems to have taken up in various forms throughout his career. The novel ends with a reference to the first birthday party Libby planned for Rachel—so it is a happy ending, in that sense. But there are too many haunting images remaining from the death and sickness of other children. I asked Roth at one point why, in a novel about two male writers who are trying to find their way in the world, he would fixate so on the vulnerability of a child, and the apparently gratuitous death of Markie in the end. He explained to me that it was, for him, the limit point or most extreme situation in which a man bound by responsibili-ty can find himself (personal interview, 22 June 2012). Such extremity, of course, is not unique to *Letting Go*. It is a thread connecting many of Roth's works, straight through to his 2010 novel, *Nemesis*.

Nemesis

Nemesis appeared on October 5, 2010, to very positive reviews. Roth's devastating book about a 1944 polio epidemic in the Weequahic neighborhood of Newark, New Jersey, provoked an interview with BBC's *Front Row* featuring Mark Lawson and inspired an essay by J. M. Coetzee published in the *New York Review of Books*. Discussing the book's title, an allusion to the Greek goddess of retribution, Coetzee's essay reads closely the etymology of the word, suggesting that "behind *nemesis* (via the verb *nemo*, to distribute) lies the idea of fortune, good or bad, and how fortune is dealt out in the universe."

In *Nemesis*, Roth takes on the "lunatic cruelty" of deaths of children during the polio crisis—a most extreme case of how bad fortune can be dealt out in the universe. Bucky Cantor, the novel's antihero, calls these polio-inflicted deaths "a war of slaughter, ruin, waste, and damnation, war with the ravages of war—war upon the children of Newark" (*Nemesis* 132). In some ways, this has been a central problem of the twentieth and twenty-first centuries, as it also carries with it doubts about futurity and injustice in a universe that allows innocent children to die. While the novel is unrelenting in its way, it also captures concerns of our global culture, using polio as but one example of the way wars are visited upon the children.

When Bucky visits the father of his girlfriend, Marcia Steinberg, Dr. Steinberg recognizes polio as "a crippling disease that attacks mainly children and leaves some of them dead—that's difficult for any adult to accept. You have a conscience, and a conscience is a valuable attribute, but not if it begins to make you think you're to blame for what is far beyond the scope of your responsibility" (104). In what remains an omnipresent theme throughout the book, Bucky wonders to himself about the responsibility of a higher power, wishing he could ask: "Doesn't God have a conscience? Where's His responsibility?" (105). Here, Bucky also refers to the double meaning of the word "response"—the ability to respond to children in the time of crisis and the ethical demand to do so. Further making the connection between children and responsibility, the novel draws a connection with the Holocaust in Europe, when Dr. Steinberg advises, in response to Bucky's concern about the safety of the playground he oversees: "I'm against the frightening of Jewish kids. I'm against the frightening of Jews, period. That was Europe. That's why Jews fled. This is America. The less fear the better. Fear unmans us. Fear degrades us" (106).

In a moment of panic while speaking with Kenny, the oldest and biggest boy on the playground, Bucky at once remembers Dr. Steinberg's caution about controlling fear, but nonetheless erupts privately, in his own mind: "Every one of them. Those on the field and those on the bleachers. The girls jumping rope. They're all kids, and polio is going after kids, and it will sweep through this place and destroy them all. . . . The neighborhood is doomed. Not a one of the children will survive intact, if they survive at all" (114–15). The fragmented sentences describing the children—those on the field, on the bleachers, and jumping rope—further reveal the ways in which Bucky fails to articulate the deaths of so many children around him. And despite, or perhaps because of, the health crisis in Newark, Bucky proposes to Marcia in search for some sense of a future.

When Marcia accepts, Bucky understands that he is happy. He suggests that "he was almost able to forget his outrage with God for the murderous persecution of Weequahic's innocent children" (135). With the words "murderous" and "persecution" the narrator of *Nemesis* links God with a fascist dictator—and a historical moment that Bucky would like to escape. Deciding to work at a summer camp called Indian Hill in the Pocono Mountains of Pennsylvania, Bucky senses that he has successfully withdrawn from the murderous impulses of God in a new Eden. He believes that the wealthy children surrounding him "were happy, energetic kids who were not imperiled by a cruel and invisible enemy—they could actually be shielded from mishap by an adult's vigilant attention. Mercifully he was finished with impotently witnessing terror and death" (150).

Here, too, with the words "witness," "terror," "death," erupts the language of traumatic history, the history of the Holocaust. We soon learn that Bucky "was struck by how lives diverge and by how powerless each of us is up against the force of circumstance. And where does God figure in this? Why does He set one person down in Nazi-occupied Europe with a rifle in his hands and the other in the Indian Hill dining lodge in front of a plate of macaroni and cheese? Why does He place one Weequahic child in polio-ridden Newark for the summer and another in the splendid sanctuary of the Poconos?" (154).

The novel continues to pose such unanswerable questions as these—questions at once considering the death of a child, the historical calamity of the polio scare, the murder of children in the camps. In fact, over the course of six pages, polio itself is aligned with Bucky's personal war (171–77). And when he finds out from his grandmother, after calling home from "camp," that in the Weequahic section there were thirty new reported cases of polio; seventy-nine cases reported in Newark in one day; and a total of nineteen dead, Bucky braces himself as he "waited in dread to hear the names. Why cripple children, he thought. Why a disease that cripples children? Why destroy our irreplaceable children? They're the best kids in the world" (191). Soon the outbreak spreads to Indian Hill, where a spinal tap confirms that the promising young Donald Kaplow also has contracted polio. Simultaneously, Bucky wonders: "Who brought polio here if not me?" (224). Such recognition—of the idea that the outbreak of polio at Chancellor playground originated with him—produced in him an incommunicable cry: "All at once he heard a loud shriek. It was the shriek of the woman downstairs from the Michaels family, terrified that her other child would catch polio and die. Only he didn't just hear the shriek—he was the shriek" (225). As with Cynthia's scream in *Letting Go*, this moment puts into the place of an articulate reflection on the crisis an inarticulate, but nonetheless genuine, cry of witness.

If nervousness about the close connection between children and death and an ethical failure to save them is not clear to this point, the connection between polio and the Holocaust is reinforced when he also learns about the quarantine of Newark, which feels strikingly like the ghettos in eastern Europe: the concentration camps that preceded the death camps. According to Bucky's grandmother: The "anti-Semites are saying that it's because they're Jews—that's why Weequahic is the center of the paralysis and why the Jews should be isolated" (193).

Ultimately, it is Bucky's guilt over the failure to act and his self-identity as carrier of the disease that threatens to undo him. Toward the end of the novel, it becomes clear that the story of Bucky's nemesis is told by Arnold Mesnikoff, one of Bucky's former charges on the playground who is, in the present day, married with two children and himself a survivor of polio. When Bucky reveals that he has given up Marcia, and with her a lifetime of happiness, Arnold surmises that he "has to convert tragedy to guilt. He has to find a necessity for what happens. There is an epidemic and he needs a reason for it. . . . He looks desperately for a deeper cause, this martyr, this maniac of the why, and finds the why either in God or in himself or, mystically, mysteriously, in their dreadful joining together as the sole destroyer" (265).

As a martyr, Bucky paradoxically aligns himself with the murderous God he described much earlier in the book; in one of his final conversations with Marcia, he further alienates her by exclaiming: "Look, your God is not to my liking, so don't bring Him into the picture. He's too mean for me. He spends too much time killing children" (260).

From beginning to end, then, Roth's fiction takes up this question of children and responsibility—of an impossible ethics in the face of grief. In so doing, his work points up the ways in which neither historians nor writers nor literary critics seem able to adequately represent the instant of a child's death. In the twentieth century, the death of a child seems so horrific, perhaps, because of all that they have come to represent in our genocidal age: innocence, helplessness, hope for the future, and utter vulnerability. That a person—or, in the case of the Nazis, an entire political party—could imagine systematically killing the most innocent and helpless members of society seems incomprehensible. Further, as Bucky acknowledges here, and Gabe recognized in *Letting Go*, to a "kill" a child also forecloses changes in the future and all of the hope these changes carry with them. That is to say, it also forecloses a narrative of the future.

Patrimony

Although not interested in infancy and childhood in quite the same way as *Letting Go* and *Nemesis*, Philip Roth's elegiac memoir written following his father's death returns to questions about our relationships with others, even in, or especially in, the face of illness and undoing. More sharply than before, it asks us to consider what is this Other? Is it a figure in a narrative? Or is it the body, and all its excrement?

On the surface, Roth's memoir appears straightforwardly concerned with the death of his father in 1989. Entitled *Patrimony: A True Story*, the text promises a reconsideration of the tangible and intangible gifts inherited from one's father or passed down from one's ancestors after death. About fifty pages from the end of the book, however, Roth describes the patrimony he is to inherit—a patrimony that is literally shit in his hands.

Considering the rhetorical connection that modern anti-Semitic texts forge between illness and the Jewish community, *Patrimony* appears as an exemplary case in an emerging canon of the Jewish American memoir about illness that functions not only as a personal story, or even embellished fiction and drama, but also as a political and ethical response to this rhetoric in the wake of the Holocaust.

Surprisingly, fewer than twenty peer-reviewed articles exist on the topic of *Patrimony*, and scholars tend to read it as an experimental genre-bending exercise (Gooblar, Wirth-Nesher) or as taking part in a larger conversation in American literature about fathers, sons, and intergenerational conflict (Iannone, Kahane, Gordon). Although it focuses more on the metafictional aspects of *Patrimony*, David Gooblar's reading is perhaps closest to my own in its focus on ethics; considering also such other autobiographical works as *The Facts* (1988), *Deception* (1990), and *Operation Shylock* (1993), Gooblar claims that: "Roth's introduction of his undisguised self into his books leads to . . . a heightened concern with the ways in which writing inevitably affects others" (32). Gooblar's reading, in fact, allows me to come full circle in order to return to my proposition that Jewish American texts featuring aspects of the writer's own life—especially those that attest in graphic details to sickness and the body—not only account for the author's local intergenerational conflict, but also talk back to, and even appropriate, fascist accounts of Jewish life in order to present an ethical demand that we tend with compassion to the sickness of others.

In other words, Roth's encounter with otherness—indeed, his care for his father during a devastating, emasculating scene in the bathroom—and his insistence that "you must not forget anything" (124, 177, 238; the same phrasing, which sounds very much like Elie Wiesel, appears at three different moments in the book) casts the memoir not simply in terms of his personal grief, but also in terms of a cultural grief, an awareness of the importance of honoring the dead. Beginning with the epigraph, "For our family, the living and the dead," the book reads as much as a refutation of the Nazi project—a project which demands the erasure of history and insists on health and virility at the expense of everything else—as it does a personal encounter with grief following the death of one's father.

Both Andrew Gordon and Claire Kahane have addressed closely *Patrimony*'s notorious "shit scene" before, but I believe it is worth returning to here, as it is, in my mind, the most powerful depiction of the alienating effects of the sick body of another. Roth takes five full pages to narrate the event: His father was concerned that he had not had a bowel movement for an extended amount of time, and, when visiting Roth at his home, excused himself from the lunch table. Roth sets in: "I smelled the shit halfway up the stairs to the second floor . . . Standing inside the bathroom door was my father, completely naked, just out of the shower and dripping wet. The smell was overwhelming" (171). Although Roth's focus is on the smell here—"I smelled the shit halfway up"; "The smell was overwhelming"—Roth's representation of his father as vulnerable, naked, dripping wet, forlorn, humiliated, and of Roth himself as kind, gentle, caring, seems to be a lesson in compassion in the face of difference above all else. "I beshat myself," says the elder twice, the second time reduced to tears. "It's okay," says Philip, "it's okay, everything is okay . . . I won't tell anyone . . . I'll say you're taking a rest" (172–73).

But Roth must set out to clean up the mess. He reflects:

> The shit was everywhere, smeared underfoot on the bathmat, running over the toilet bowl edge and at the foot of the bowl, in a pile on the floor. It was splattered across the glass of the shower stall from which he'd just emerged, and the clothes discarded in the hallway were clotted with it. It was on the corner of the towel he had started to dry himself with. In this smallish bathroom, which was ordinarily mine, he had done his best to extricate himself from his mess alone, but as he was nearly blind and just up out of a hospital bed, in undressing himself and getting into the shower he had managed to spread the shit over everything. I saw that it was even on the tips of the bristles of my toothbrush hanging in the holder over the sink. (172)

In one sense, it is entirely true, as Nancy Miller and Kahane have argued, that the memoir is largely about cleaning up the messes of our fathers, of tidying their lives before or after putting them to rest and then doing the best with what remains. But I hate to stray too far from the fact that this is also literal shit—it has exploded everywhere into Philip Roth's personal space—in his "smallish bathroom . . . ordinarily mine" and even on the bristles of his toothbrush. This is shit, Roth seems to be saying, that could possibly end up in his own mouth. And if the content of the passage alone isn't enough to convey a sense of profound alienation, the repeated sounds of the words themselves are ugly: the plosive /b/ and /p/ sounds of spitting and the hard /c/ fricative sounds of a frequent and annoying cough.

Nonetheless, Roth proceeds:

Where his shit lay in front of the toilet bowl in what was more or less a continuous mass, it was easiest to get rid of. Just scoop it up and flush it away. And the shower door and the windowsill and the sink and the soap dish and the light fixtures and the towel bars were no problem. Lots of paper towels and lots of soap. But where it had lodged in the narrow, uneven crevices of the floor, between the wide old chestnut planks, I had my work cut out for me. The scrub brush seemed only to make things worse, and eventually I took down my toothbrush and, dipping in and out of the bucket of hot sudsy water, proceeded inch by inch, from wall to wall, one crevice at a time, until the floor was as clean as I could get it. After some fifteen minutes on my knees, I decided that flecks and particles down so deep that I still couldn't reach them we would simply all live with. (174)

Roth's use of the conjunction "and" here in the beginning of the passage emphasizes just how much of it there remains to clean up; the emphasis on the crevices on the floor suggest just how deep it lies ingrained. But the image of a son on his knees on the floor in a pile of his father's shit is the most profound for me, as it reveals a necessary humility in the face of what we cannot master—in this sense, his father's illness and own vulnerability—the cancer and the shit that carries it.

In the end, Roth theorizes this episode as a way to come to terms with one's father's life and impending death: "You clean up your father's shit," he says, "because it has to be cleaned up, but in the aftermath of cleaning it up, everything that's there to feel is felt as it never was before. It wasn't the first time that I'd understood this either: once you sidestep disgust and ignore nausea and plunge past those phobias that are fortified like taboos, there's an awful lot of life to cherish" (175). For every bit of emphasis this observation places on Roth's cleaning up his bathroom, however, there is a way in which we can read this as a reflection on everyday life—of encountering the ill among us who are sick and filthy and vulnerable: once you plunge past those phobias, there is an awful lot to cherish.

At the risk of appearing to reduce our often misanthropic Roth to platitudes, I might just end with a reminder that Roth tells us he arrives at this understanding of his father "not because cleaning it up was symbolic of something else but because it wasn't, because it was nothing less or more than the lived reality that it was" (176). In other words, Roth seems to be telling us, when dealing with others' humanity, all we have, at the basest level, is the shit. There is nothing lofty or idealized or platitudinous about that.

And yet, I believe in this moment that Roth is not telling the entire truth about what the shit represents. Counter to previous interpretations offered by such scholars as Gordon, Kahane, and Iannone, among others—and, indeed, against the explanation provided so straightforwardly by Roth—I interpret the text not simply as a memoir of taking care of his father, and not simply as a genre-bending autobiographical account of Roth's father's last years, but rather as a philosophical treatise on ethics after the Holocaust. For Roth's text also shares the philosophical dimensions of his post-Holocaust contemporaries who warn against forgetting; like such thinkers as Wiesel and Levinas, *Patrimony* insists on an encounter with otherness that acknowledges the radical differences that exist among us—especially in the context of illness and Jewishness, which had become linked hundreds of years ago in widely read anti-Semitic texts.

On the very next page, for example, Roth again reminds us: "You must never forget" (177). And while there is little room remaining here to look at a second scene, I might read as a parallel moment the meal Roth and his father share with Walter Herrmann, a Holocaust survivor and author of what Roth later describes as "a pornographic best seller about the Holocaust" (208–20). Here, too, we have a five-page-plus reflection on the basest of bodily functions—and the fact that the author of the pornography is a Holocaust survivor is of no minor significance. After all, this memoir seems to be saying that we need to be a little better at recognizing the full humanity of others—disease and debilitation and all. And, when necessary, you must clean it up—not because the person is your father, but, more importantly, because he's a man.

In this way, Roth's literature calls for an adequate *ethics* of the moment: the ability to pass on knowledge and to act on that knowledge while understanding this impossibility in advance. The belief that we must confront such figures—of an ill father, of children dying of polio, of unnamed children strapped to toilets—is, on the one hand, omnipresent; but these figures also remind us instantaneously that we cannot possibly confront them with the attention they deserve. An example of this inadequate address connects back to Roth's critical reception, and the criticism launched at him for being sex- and shit-obsessed and therefore suffocating. They are missing the point in all of these moments—a point about human frailty and weakness.

This very impossibility lies as the primary concern at the heart of a philosophy of ethics. Levinas's philosophy regarding the other is, in this way, also a standard for reading—a standard that requires us to "face the figure" as we would face another. Philip Roth's fiction asks that we confront the literary face of an infant, of a polio-stricken child, of a man succumbing to death: unsettling images perhaps more traumatic than ethical in their very silence, more disturbing still in their disembodied screams.

Works Cited

Atlas, James. "Introduction." *Letting Go*. New York: Farrar, 1982. ix–xvii. Print.

Bauer, Daniel J. "Narratorial Games in Philip Roth's *Letting Go*: Testing Grounds for a Career?" *Fu Jen Studies: Literature and Linguistics* 22 (1989): 53–69. *MLA International Bibliography*. Web. 26 Oct. 2012.

Chilton, Martin. "Judge Quits over Philip Roth's Booker Award." *Telegraph*. Telegraph Media Group, 18 May 2011. Web. 28 Dec. 2012.

Coetzee, J. M. "On the Moral Brink." Rev. of *Nemesis*, by Philip Roth. *New York Review of Books* 28 Oct. 2010. Web. 28 Dec. 2012.

Gooblar, David. "The Truth Hurts: The Ethics of Philip Roth's 'Autobiographical' Books." *Journal of Modern Literature* 32.1 (2008): 33–53. *MLA International Bibliography*. Web. 13 Nov. 2011.

Gordon, Andrew. "Philip Roth's Patrimony and Art Spiegelman's *Maus*: Jewish Sons Remembering Their Fathers." *Philip Roth Studies* 1.1 (2005): 53–66. *MLA International Bibliography*. Web. 13 Nov. 2011.

Husband, Julie. "Female Hysteria and Sisterhood in *Letting Go* and *When She Was Good*." *Philip Roth: New Perspectives on an American Author*. 25-41. Westport, CT: Praeger, 2005. *MLA International Bibliography*. Web. 26 Oct. 2012.

Iannone, Carol. "Jewish Fathers and Sons and Daughters." *American Scholar* 67.1 (1998): 131–38. *MLA International Bibliography*. Web. 13 Nov. 2011.

Jaffe-Foger, Miriam, and Aimee Pozorski. "'[A]nything but Fragile and Yielding': Women in Roth's Recent Tetralogy." *Philip Roth Studies* 8.1 (2012): 81–94. Print.

Kahane, Claire. "Gender and Patrimony: Mourning the Dead Father." *Differences: A Journal of Feminist Cultural Studies* 9.1 (1997): 49–67. *MLA International Bibliography*. Web. 13 Nov. 2011.

Levinas, Emmanuel. *Basic Philosophical Writings*. Eds. Adriaan T. Paperzak, Simon Critchley, and Robert Bernasconi. Bloomington: Indiana UP, 1996. Print.

___. *God, Death, and Time*. Trans. Bettina Bergo. Stanford: Stanford UP, 2000. Print.

___. *Outside the Subject*. Trans. Michael B. Smith. Stanford: Stanford UP, 1993. Print.

Miller, Nancy K. "Autobiographical Deaths." *Massachusetts Review: A Quarterly of Literature, the Arts and Public Affairs* 33.1 (1992): 19–47. *MLA International Bibliography*. Web. 13 Nov. 2011.

"Nobel Chief Disparages US as 'Too Insular' for Great Writing." *Washington Post*. Washington Post, 1 Oct. 2008. Web. 28 Dec. 2012.

O'Neill, Joseph. "Roth v. Roth v. Roth: The Complexities and Conundrums of Reading Philip Roth's Work as Autobiography." *Atlantic*. April 2012. 86–92. Print.

Posnock, Ross. "Letting Go." *Raritan: A Quarterly Review* 23.4 (2004): 1–19. *MLA International Bibliography*. Web. 26 Oct. 2012.

Royal, Derek Parker. "Paying Attention to the Man behind the Curtain: Philip Roth and the Dynamics of Written and Unwritten Celebrity." *Roth and Celebrity*. Ed. Aimee Pozorski. Lanham, MD: Lexington, 2012. 11–28. Print.

Roth, Philip. "After Eight Books." Interview with Joyce Carol Oates. 1974. *Reading Myself and Others*. New York: Vintage, 2001. 85–97. Print.

___. *Deception: A Novel*. New York: Simon, 1990. Print.

___. *The Dying Animal*. Boston: Houghton, 2001. Print.

___. *The Facts: A Novelist's Autobiography*. New York: Farrar, 1988. Print.

___. *Goodbye, Columbus and Five Short Stories*. Boston: Houghton, 1959. Print.

___. *I Married a Communist*. Boston: Houghton, 1998. Print.

___. *Letting Go*. (1962). Introduced by James Atlas. New York: Farrar, 1982. Print.

___. "Mark Lawson Talks to Philip Roth." *Front Row*. BBC London, 2010. Television.

___. *My Life as a Man*. New York: Holt, 1974. Print.

___. *Nemesis*. Boston: Houghton, 2012. Print.

___. *Operation Shylock: A Confession*. New York: Simon, 1993. Print.

___. *Patrimony: A True Story*. New York: Simon, 1991. Print.

___. Personal interview. 15 Apr. 2012.

___. Personal interview. 25 May 2012.

___. Personal interview. 22 June 2012.

___. *The Plot against America*. Boston: Houghton, 2004. Print.

___. *Portnoy's Complaint*. New York: Random, 1969. Print.

___. "Writing and the Powers That Be." Interview with Walter Mauro. 1974. *Reading Myself and Others*. New York: Vintage, 2001. 3–12. Print.

Wiesel, Elie. *From the Kingdom of Memory: Reminiscences*. New York: Schocken, 1990.

Wirth-Nesher, Hana. "Facing the Fictions: Henry Roth's and Philip Roth's Meta-Memoirs." *Prooftexts: A Journal of Jewish Literary History* 18.3 (1998): 259–75. *MLA International Bibliography*. Web. 13 Nov. 2011.

Biography of Philip Roth_____

Philip Roth first achieved prominence in 1959 with the publication of *Goodbye, Columbus and Five Short Stories*, for which he won the National Book Award. Delineating the conflict between traditional and contemporary morals as manifested in a young Jewish American man's search for identity, the title novella revived an enduring controversy (which had begun two years earlier with Roth's first *New Yorker* story) over whether his satirical treatment of Jewish themes constituted anti-Semitism. That controversy reached a fever pitch with his novel *Portnoy's Complaint*, which created a sensation in 1969 because of its explicit recounting of a young lawyer's sexual autobiography, consisting largely of compulsive attempts to free himself from the strict confines of his Jewish upbringing through incessant masturbation and sexual conquest. Since then, Roth's output has ranged from wild comedy and political satire to examinations of his role as a writer and son and metafictional explorations of the relationship between art and life, fiction and reality, imagination and fact; or, as he has put it, the "relationship between the written and the unwritten world." In an interview with Mervyn Rothstein for the *New York Times* (August 1, 1985), Roth identified his primary theme as "the tension between license and restraint, . . . a struggle between the hunger for personal liberty and the forces of inhibition."

In their late fifties and sixties, some novelists begin to rest on their laurels, but Philip Roth instead produced some of his best works. Among these were the memoir *Patrimony* (1991), *Operation Shylock: A Confession* (1993), and *Sabbath's Theater* (1995), which won the National Book Award for Fiction. Roth's trilogy of modern American life began in 1997 with *American Pastoral*, which covers the Vietnam era; continued in 1998 with *I Married a Communist*, a look at the Red Scare of the 1950s; and concluded in 2000 with *The Human Stain*, a critique of America's obsession with moralizing and political correctness. For *American Pastoral* he earned the Pulitzer Prize in 1998. Over the next decade, Roth's published works included *The Dying*

Animal (2001), *The Plot against America* (2004), *Everyman* (2006), *Exit Ghost* (2007), and *Indignation* (2008). Other works include the short novels *The Humbling* (2009) and *Nemesis* (2010).

Philip Milton Roth was born on March 19, 1933 to Herman Roth and Bess (Finkel) Roth in Newark, New Jersey, where he and his older brother, Sandy, grew up. His father, the American-born son of Jewish immigrants from Galicia, Spain, whose shoe-store business had gone bankrupt during the Depression, was an insurance salesman who had reached the echelons of management despite the openly anti-Semitic sentiments of his superiors. Like his father, Philip Roth faced similar prejudices that marred his otherwise "intensely secure and protected" childhood. His summer vacations at Bradley Beach on the New Jersey shore were sometimes spoiled by gang attacks against Jews, and, even at the almost entirely Jewish Weequahic High School, Roth was sub-jected to violence inflicted by bullies from neighboring, non-Jewish schools. At the age of twelve, he pledged that when he grew up he would "oppose the injustices wreaked by the violent and the privileged by becoming a lawyer for the underdog" His other passion during his youth was baseball, which, he has written, offered him "membership in a great secular nationalistic church from which nobody had ever seemed to suggest that Jews should be excluded."

From 1950, when he graduated from high school, to 1951 Roth at-tended the Newark extension of Rutgers University before transfer-ring to Bucknell University, in Lewisburg, Pennsylvania, to escape the "provincialism" of Newark and discover "the rest of America." But he discovered instead that Bucknell's "respectable Christian atmo-sphere [was] hardly less constraining than [his] own particular Jew-ish upbringing." While at Bucknell, Roth edited the literary magazine, appeared in student plays, and became a member of Phi Beta Kappa. After graduating magna cum laude with a bachelor's degree in English in 1954, he obtained master's in English from the University of Chi-cago the following year. Roth then moved to Washington, DC, where he served briefly in the US Army before he was discharged due to a back injury. Upon returning to the University of Chicago in 1956, he began teaching a full schedule of freshman composition while working toward a doctorate. During Roth's two-year stint as an English instructor at Chicago, he continued to write short fiction, which he had begun doing at least as early as 1955. Among those who read his work at that time was fellow writer Saul Bellow, who recalled that Roth's stories "showed a wonderful wit and great pace" Roth, however, has said that he did not initially take his own writing seriously because "everybody studying English wrote stories."

But Roth's stories often proved to be of award-winning caliber, enabling him to pursue writing and teaching full time. After serving for a brief period as a reviewer of television and film for the *New Republic*, Roth published *Goodbye, Columbus and Five Short Stories* in 1959. In the title novella, the conflicting values of the impoverished, urban Neil Klugman and the affluent Brenda Patimkin, a Jewish American "princess" whose suburban, upper-middle-class lifestyle is satirized mercilessly, doom the couple's relationship. In the opinion of most critics, the book showed great promise and signaled the arrival of an important new writer. "A brilliant new talent," Arnold Dolin wrote for the *Saturday Review* (May 16, 1959), "Philip Roth has looked penetratingly into the heart of the American Jew who faces the loss of his identity. The conflict involved in this choice between two worlds provides the focal point of drama for a memorable collection of short stories."

The earlier publication of one of the stories in *Goodbye, Columbus*, "Defender of the Faith," which appeared in the *New Yorker* in April 1957, had provoked a barrage of charges that Roth's attitude toward his Jewish subjects was anti-Semitic, a controversy that was revived by his unflattering portrayal of the consumerist lifestyle of the Patimkins, which prompted one rabbi to accuse him of presenting "a distorted image of the basic values of Orthodox Judaism." Nevertheless, the majority of critics were impressed by *Goodbye, Columbus*, which earned Roth a National Book Award, an award from the National Institute of Arts and Letters, a Daroff Award from the Jewish Book Council of America, and a Guggenheim fellowship that enabled him to travel to Rome. In 1960 he began a two-year stint as a visiting lecturer at the University of Iowa Writers' Workshop, followed by two years as a writer-in-residence at Princeton University in New Jersey.

Roth's next two books are now generally considered minor works. *Letting Go* (1962), his first full-length novel, focused on the ethical dilemmas of a young Jewish academic at the University of Chicago. Despite the keenly observant qualities of Roth's prose that were unfailingly mentioned by reviewers, *Letting Go* was invariably faulted for its sprawling length and its diffusiveness. *When She Was Good* (1967), which Roth once referred to simply as his "book with no Jews," is also his only novel to feature a female protagonist. Critics were sharply divided over its merits. Josh Greenfeld, writing for *Book Week* (June 4, 1967), ranked *When She Was Good* "among the few novels written about America since World War II that may still be worth reading twenty-five years from now," but a reviewer for *Time* (June 9, 1967) described the female heroine as "theatrically unsatisfying and an ear-jarring bore." Saul Maloff, whose review for *Newsweek* (June 12, 1967) occupied a middle ground, noted: "With unerring fidelity, [Roth] records the flat surface of provincial American life, the look and feel and sound of it—and then penetrates it to the cesspool of its invisible dynamisms. Beneath the good, and impelling it, he says, lies the horrid."

The period between 1962 and 1967, during which Roth lived in New York City and underwent psychoanalysis, marked the longest hiatus in his productivity that he had ever experienced. He characterized that period as one of "literary uncertainty," adding, "I didn't know what the hell to do. What do I write about? Do I pursue these Jewish subjects any further or get rid of them? . . . It was a period of debilitating disorder in my young life." In an interview with Hermione Lee for the *Paris Review* (Summer 1983–Winter 1984), Roth revealed how his disastrous marriage in 1959 to the former Margaret Martinson

Williams (from whom he was legally separated in 1963 and who died in an automobile accident in 1968) had exhausted his emotional and financial resources. He told Lee:

> I needed [analysis] primarily to prevent me from going out and committing murder because of the alimony and court costs incurred for having served two years in a childless marriage. The image that teased me during those years was of a train that had been shunted onto the wrong track. In my early twenties I had been zipping right along there, you know—on schedule, express stops only, final destination clearly in mind; and then suddenly I was on the wrong track, speeding off into the wilds. I'd ask myself, 'How the hell do you get this thing back on the right track?' Well, you can't. I've continued to be surprised, over the years, whenever I discover myself, late at night, pulling into the wrong station.

Roth restored his career during the late 1960s, when he began teaching literature at the University of Pennsylvania, where he remained on the faculty for about eleven years. The 1969 feature film adaptation of *Goodbye, Columbus*, starring Ali MacGraw and Richard Benjamin, coincided with the publication of *Portnoy's Complaint*, which quickly sold 393,000 copies in hardcover. Roth became an instant celebrity and garnered publicity, not only due to the crudity of his humor, which offended some (the book was banned in Australia) and delighted others, but also because the intimate nature of Portnoy's confessional monologue to his psychoanalyst led to considerable prurient speculation about Roth's own personal life. The inordinate amount of attention focused on Roth compelled him to move out of New York City to the Yaddo Artist Colony in Saratoga Springs, New York.

Literary critics, however, were more enthusiastic in their assessment of *Portnoy's Complaint* than the gossipmongers on the television talk-show circuit. Granville Hicks, writing for the *Saturday Review* (February 22, 1969), described *Portnoy's Complaint* as "something very much like a masterpiece." while John Greenfeld, writing for the *New*

York Times Book Review (February 23, 1969), called it a "deliciously funny book, absurd and exuberant, wild and uproarious." Those offended by the book included anti-obscenity crusaders as well as some members of the Jewish community, who felt that the novel was tinged with anti-Semitism. "The charges were several," Roth recalled in an interview with Curt Suplee for the *Washington Post* (October 30, 1983), "and in defense of my accusers, it was only the lunatic fringe who said I was anti-Semitic. The stronger case was that I was lending fuel to the fires of anti-Semites. . . . I don't think it's a matter of a right position or a wrong position. It's two right positions colliding." Ironically, his critics may have unwittingly played a part in the genesis of *Portnoy's Complaint*, as Roth explained in his book *Reading Myself and Others* (1975), by prompting him to pursue the goal "of becoming the writer some Jewish critics had been telling [him he] was all along: irresponsible, conscienceless, unserious." The uproar over *Portnoy's Complaint* did not impede Roth's election to the National Institute of Arts and Letters in 1970.

During the early 1970s, Roth wrote a series of entirely different satirical novels that received mixed reaction and were generally perceived as being less impressive than his other books. *Our Gang* (1971), a parody on the Richard M. Nixon administration that featured a fictional US president named Trick E. Dixon, was described by Dwight MacDonald for the *New York Times Book Review* (November 7, 1971) as "farfetched, unfair, tasteless, disturbing, logical, coarse, and very funny. . . . In short, a masterpiece."

In *The Breast* (1972), Professor David Kepesh has been transformed into a six-foot-tall mammary gland and attempts to reconcile his intellectual and sexual selves. Although he does not succeed completely, his efforts bring him invaluable insights into how to cope with a self-image that is at war with his impulses. Roth once referred to Kepesh as the "first heroic character" he had been able to portray because he went further than other Rothian protagonists in passing through "the barrier that forms one boundary of the individual's identity and experience: that barrier of personal inhibition, ethical conviction and plain, old monumental fear beyond which lies the moral and psychological unknown." (Kepesh reappears, as a professor who moves from the alternate gratification of his mental and physical selves to the achievement of a more integrated way of being, in the 1977 novel *The Professor of Desire*.) "*The Breast* heaves with weighty theme-ideas," Bruce Allen wrote for the *Library Journal* (October 1, 1972), "but it yields nothing firm, lacking any consistent interplay between the serious and the grotesque."

After penning the ironically titled *The Great American Novel* (1973), a baseball satire that one critic dismissed as "a great American bore that's impossible not to put down shortly after you pick it up," Roth authored what many consider one of his finest novels: *My Life as a Man* (1974). Its multilayered story centers on the novelist Peter Tarnopol's attempts to solve his dilemmas by writing "Useful Fictions" about Nathan Zuckerman, a Jewish writer whose life resembles his own. Writing for *Newsweek* (June 3, 1974), Peter S. Prescott referred to *My Life as a Man* as "Roth's best novel" and "his most complex and most ambitious."

Zuckerman became a recurring character, appearing in several of Roth's subsequent novels. In *The Ghost Writer* (1979), a young Zuckerman visits the home of his literary mentor, where he meets a mysterious guest named Amy Bellette whom he believes is Anne Frank resurrected. In a review for the *Washington Post* (September 2, 1979), Jonathan Penner wrote that *The Ghost Writer* "provides further evidence that [Roth] can do practically anything with fiction. His narrative power . . . is superb." *Zuckerman Unbound* (1981) follows Zuckerman as he achieves notoriety with his scandalous novel *Carnovsky* and falls victim to his own bad reputation, which ultimately destroys his love life and his relations with his family. In *The Anatomy Lesson* (1983), Zuckerman, now stricken with inexplicable neck and shoulder pain and mourning the loss of his mother and the decline of his hometown, Newark, decides to abandon writing and become a doctor. Reviewing it for the *New Yorker* (November 7, 1983), John

Updike discovered that "materials one might have thought exhausted by Roth's previous novelistic explorations, inflammations one might have thought long soothed, burn hotter than ever; the central howl unrolls with a mediated savagery both fascinating and repellent, self-indulgent yet somehow sterling, adamant, pure, in the style of high modernism, that bewitchment to all the art-stricken young of the 1950s."

The three novels (*The Ghost Writer*, *Zuckerman Unbound*, and *The Anatomy Lesson*) were published in one volume in 1985 entitled *Zuckerman Bound: A Trilogy and an Epilogue*. Although the epilogue, *The Prague Orgy*, which was considered by many critics to be the best section of the volume, seemed to mark the end of the Zuckerman cycle, Roth resurrected his hero yet again for *The Counterlife* (1986), a stand-alone novel for which he won the National Book Critics Circle Award. William H. Gass declared *The Counterlife* "a triumph" in his assessment of the novel for the *New York Times Book Review* (January 4, 1987) and concluded that it "constitutes a fulfillment of tendencies, a successful integration of themes, and the final working through of obsessions that have previously troubled if not marred his work." Other reviewers were critical of the book's nonlinear storytelling approach. Among the dissenters was Christopher Lehmann-Haupt, who wrote for the *New York Times* (December 29, 1986): "We become so aware of the narrative's duplicity that all that is left to us is the burden of the author's self-consciousness as an artist and a Jew. It's like being trapped between two fun-house mirrors that reflect each other's distortions unto a point that vanishes into absurdity."

During his interview with Curt Suplee for the *Washington Post*, Roth defined the Zuckerman novels as

hypothetical autobiographies. It's very complicated. I have no great brief to make for my life as lived. In fact, it's basically sitting in a chair writing books. It's not very eventful. I don't know what I am—I'm a person who writes. But what excites my verbal life is imagining what I might be, what might befall someone like myself; imagining what kind of person I would be if I were a person. I'm really quite content to be what I am. I never entertained the idea of being a doctor in my life, but writing this book I had to. I don't have to do these things—I have people do them for me.

After writing so many "hypothetical autobiographies," Roth was compelled to pen *The Facts: A Novelist's Autobiography* (1988). A memoir of his first thirty-six years, *The Facts* began as a therapeutic exercise to help him recover from the deep depression he had fallen into after minor knee surgery in 1987. For three months Roth suffered from hallucinations, panic attacks, suicidal thoughts, and other debilitating symptoms, due to the interaction of two drugs he was taking as a result of the surgery. "I thought, something is happening to me; I've got to fight my way out of it," he told Stephen Schiff for *Vanity Fair* (April 1990). "And I would try to write down who I was, to remember who I was." In a review of *The Facts* for *USA Today* (September 2, 1988), William H. Pritchard demurred that "novelists, even when they try to play it straight and pass along naked truths about themselves, clothe those truths in sentences that construct an imagined self instead of handing it over unaltered." In reply to such comments, Roth told Mervyn Rothstein, "I called the book *The Facts*, not 'The Dirt.' I didn't write 'The Dirt.' That's another book."

In the early 1990s, Roth authored books that were strikingly dissimilar in tone, style, and subject. *Deception* (1990) centered on a fifty-year-old married novelist—also named Philip—who records the dialogue between himself and his younger lover, who is also married. The novelist Fay Weldon remarked that *Deception* "reads like a brilliant radio play for a minority audience" in her article for the *New York Times Book Review* (March 11, 1990), while Peter S. Prescott wrote for *Newsweek* (March 26, 1990) that Roth was merely "revving his motor again, his gearshift still stuck in neutral."

In contrast, *Patrimony: A True Story* (1991), which focused on the life and death of Herman Roth, who had died at eighty-six from a brain

tumor in October 1989, was unanimously admired for its "deeply resonant" portrayal of the author's father. "In celebrating his father," R. Z.
Sheppard wrote for *Time* (January 21, 1991), "and by implication the
source of his own character, Roth has not strayed from the long path
he has cut for himself: to dramatize the adventure of assimilation in all
its anxiety, humor, and fertile illusions. As a writer and a son, he has
now dotted the i's and crossed the t's." In 1991 Roth was awarded the
National Arts Club's Medal of Honor for Literature for the body of his
work.

Operation Shylock (1993), which Roth presented as a quasi-au-
tobiographical work, centered on two characters both named Philip
Roth: the narrator—an author suffering from depression who travels
to Israel to attend the trial of a war criminal; and a spy for an Israeli
intelligence agency who is posing as the author. When the "real" Roth
confronts his double, the two begin arguing fiercely about everything
from the Holocaust to the slippery slope of politics in the Middle East.
(Roth's publisher and reviewers called it a work of fiction, but Roth
himself insisted that the story was true, despite many critics questioning the likelihood that Roth had been recruited by the Mossad.) The
novel had a mixed reception from the critics. Paul Gray wrote in *Time*
(March 8, 1993): "Roth has not riffed with quite this comic abandon
since *Portnoy's Complaint*. And the social and historical range of *Operation Shylock* is broader than anything the author has attempted before." In his review for *Newsweek* (March 8, 1993), Malcolm Jones
wrote, however: "If [Roth] intended to replicate the ironic contradictions in the Mideast, he succeeded all too well, exhausting our patience in the bargain. Our lasting impression is of a prodigally gifted
writer searching for ever more complicated and arcane ways to keep
himself amused."

Roth's next novel, *Sabbath's Theater* (1995), revolved around
Mickey Sabbath, a once-notorious New York street performer, now
cheating on his second wife, Roseanna, with a Croatian immigrant
named Drenka. Following Drenka's death from ovarian cancer, the

embittered Sabbath reminisces about their relationship in order to better understand his own wild life. In a review for the *New York Times* (August 22, 1995), Michiko Kakutani called the book "distasteful and disingenuous," and also added that "because Mr. Roth never offers much insight into Sabbath's heart, because he suggests that Sabbath is virtually incapable of sincerity, that even his post-Drenka breakdown may be an act of manipulation . . . the reader is hard pressed to tolerate, much less sympathize with, Sabbath." On the other hand, William H. Pritchard for the *New York Times Book Review* (September 10, 1995) touted *Sabbath's Theater* as Roth's "richest, most rewarding novel." For his effort, Roth won the 1995 National Book Award for Fiction.

In 1997 Roth authored *American Pastoral*, the first book in a trilogy of postwar American life. Narrated by Nathan Zuckerman, the story, which is set during the Vietnam era, recounts the rise and fall of Seymour Irving Levov, known as "the Swede" for his Aryan good looks. Though Jewish, Levov is not as alienated as many of Roth's other Jewish characters; in fact, he becomes first a commanding athlete and later a successful husband and father—someone truly living the dream of the 1950s by assimilating completely into American life. *American Pastoral* earned stellar reviews and won Roth the Pulitzer Prize. In *America* (August 30–September 6, 1997), Sylvia Barack Fishman remarked: "Philip Roth . . . has written a powerful, painful and deeply moving masterpiece that will surprise many readers familiar with his twenty-two earlier books." Mayer Schiller opined for the *National Review* (June 16, 1997) that *American Pastoral* "has everything one could want in a novel. Its rapid-fire insights into the human condition tumble down upon each other. Yet, they are delivered with just the right degree of irony, ambiguity, and humble humor."

I Married a Communist (1998), the second volume in Roth's trilogy, did not fare as well with the critics. Again narrated by Zuckerman, as well as his ninety-year-old high-school teacher, Murray Ringold, the novel relates the story of Ringold's brother Ira, a radio star known as Iron Rinn—who converts to communism during World War II and is later vilified for his beliefs. Betrayed by his wife, Eve, who writes a tell-all memoir about her life with him, Iron Rinn is devastated by the same anticommunist forces that brought down so many Americans in the 1950s. Reviewing *I Married a Communist* for the *New York Times* (October 8, 1998), Michiko Kakutani described it as "a wildly uneven novel that feels both unfinished and overstuffed, a novel that veers unsteadily between sincerity and slapstick, heartfelt melancholy and cavalier manipulation." Robert Kelly, writing for the *New York Times Book Review* (October 11, 1998), was far more complimentary, calling the book "a gripping novel." He continued, "This powerful novel leaves me haunted by the isolation in which each character, not just Ira, stands in history. The book's final page tells of the stars, whose brilliance is matched only by their apartness. A classic image fit to close this new novel by one of the real ones."

The final installment of the trilogy, *The Human Stain* (2000), was a portrait of contemporary American angst. The novel looks at the decline of common sense and civility with regard to sex and privacy in the United States. With Nathan Zuckerman serving as the narrator once again, *The Human Stain* chronicles the life of Coleman Silk, a black professor who has been passing as white for decades. Lorrie Moore, writing for the *New York Times Book Review* (May 7, 2000), called *The Human Stain* "an astonishing, uneven and often very beautiful book." In a review for *Time* (May 8, 2000), R. Z. Sheppard was equally laudatory, noting: "At sixty-seven, Roth has not lost one ampere of his power to rile and surprise. . . . Most novelists wouldn't or couldn't handle the variety of elements that Roth does here. Few have his radical imagination and technical mastery. Fewer still have his daring."

With *The Dying Animal* (2001), Roth revived the character of David Kepesh, who was last seen in the 1977 book *The Professor of Desire*. Though now an old man, Kepesh continues his conquest of young female students. The book was not well received by critics, despite its titillating subject matter. Keith Gessen wrote for the *Nation* (June 11, 2001): "It seems obvious that at this point Roth can do little with sex that he hasn't done already (though he tries in *The Dying Animal*, he tries). This continued fixation is fictionally fallow. . . . Since sex is, in this view, overdetermined, it's like writing about gravity."

In *The Plot against America* (2004), Roth presents an alternate history in which the famed aviator Charles Lindbergh, a notorious anti-Semite in real life, is voted to the Republican Party's presidential ticket and then into the White House, unseating Franklin D. Roosevelt in 1941. Instead of joining the Allies in World War II, Lindbergh signs a pact with Hitler and begins to institute anti-Jewish policies. The novel, narrated by a seven-year-old boy named Philip Roth whose family and home life mirror the author's own, earned mixed reviews. Jennifer Reese wrote for *Entertainment Weekly* (October 8, 2004), "With this fascinating, fertile material, Roth has spun an unconvincing fantasy that falls far short of his finest work. While his depictions of the Roth family's idyllic pre-Lindbergh existence (and Philip's vibrant, eccentric inner life) are detailed and persuasive, he has set them against a cardboard backdrop of a fatally underimagined alternative America." Despite such mixed reviews, the book won a number of accolades, among them the 2005 Sidewise Award for alternate history and the 2005 James Fenimore Cooper Prize in the category of best historical fiction.

Roth chose death as the focus of his 2006 novel *Everyman*, after witnessing many of his friends grow old and die. The story concerns the life, slow decay, and eventual death of the unnamed main character. The events of his life appear out of sequence and are presented as increasingly common and universal as the narrator grows older. Describing *Everyman* as "essentially a medical biography," James Poniewozik wrote for *Time* (May 15, 2006), "It is to Roth's credit that he cannot quite bring himself to write a book as dull and flat as *Everyman*'s concept seems to demand. His style repeatedly breaks its leash, as at the funeral, when the protagonist's brother gives a moving eulogy and his estranged son struggles violently against unbidden grief." That book won him a 2007 PEN/Faulkner Award, making him the award's only three-time winner. Roth was also honored with a PEN/Nabokov Award for lifetime achievement and a 2007 PEN/Saul Bellow Award for achievement in American fiction. In 2007 Roth published *Exit Ghost*, the ninth book narrated by Zuckerman, which finds Roth's alter ego, now aged seventy-one, in search of a New York specialist to perform surgery to treat his incontinence and impotence, and lusting after a well-endowed thirty-year-old short-story writer.

Everyman was to be the first book in a tetralogy whose other titles included *Indignation*, *The Humbling*, and *Nemesis*. In 2008 Roth published *Indignation*, a novel whose main character, the Newark-born Marcus Messner, flees his overprotective father during the Korean War and transfers to Winesburg College, in Ohio, in an effort to emulate the preppy students he sees on the school's catalogue cover. Characterized by reviewer Rita D. Jacobs for *World Literature Today* (November 1, 2008) as a return to "his roots," the book examines the familiar subjects of identity, sex, and death. *The Humbling*, published in 2009, explores the unexpected sexual awakening of an aging stage actor; and *Nemesis*, published in 2010, recounts a polio epidemic in World War II–era Newark.

In 2011, Roth earned the Man Booker International Prize. Several of Roth's books have been adapted as films, including *The Human Stain* (2003) and *Elegy* (2007), which was based on *The Dying Animal*. He is the only author whose novels appeared more than twice on the 2006 *New York Times Book Review* list of the most important works of American literature in the last quarter century, which was based on surveys of writers, critics, editors, and others in the literary world. Among the twenty-two books featured on that list, six were penned by Roth: *American Pastoral*, *The Counterlife*, *Operation Shylock*, *Sabbath's Theater*, *The Plot against America*, and *The Human Stain*.

In November 2012, Roth stated in an interview with the French magazine *Les inRocks* that he had retired from writing fiction. *Salon* later received confirmation of Roth's retirement from his publisher, Houghton Mifflin.

After Margaret Martinson Williams, Roth was married to the distinguished British actress Claire Bloom. The couple, who wed in 1990, had first met in 1965 when they were both otherwise attached and had lived together since 1976. They separated after four years of marriage. In 1996 Bloom published her autobiography, *Leaving a Doll's House*, in which she detailed her turbulent relationship with Roth. (Eve, the traitorous wife in *I Married a Communist*, was generally thought by critics to be based on Bloom.) Since 1973, Roth, who has no children, has lived on his forty-acre farm in northwestern Connecticut.

Source

Current Biography 52 (May 1991): 41–45. Copyright 1991 by H. W. Wilson. Updated Jan 2013.

CRITICAL
CONTEXTS

Narratological Quicksands in the Nemeses Tetralogy

Pia Masiero

Since the publication of his first collection of short stories, *Goodbye, Columbus*, in 1959, Philip Roth has written more than thirty books. In 2000, on the occasion of the publication of *The Human Stain*, Roth looked back on his production and decided to reshuffle the list of his already published books. Since then, Roth has organized his works list (often included at the beginning of his books) under headings that include the names of his most famous characters—Nathan Zuckerman, Philip Roth, and David Kepesh—which correspond to an internal chronology. This authorial choice directs his readers' attention to a specific feature of his literary production, namely the construction of storyworlds around well-defined and recognizable (authorial) masks and (narrative) voices.

More than ten years have gone by since that momentous decision, which has certainly reshaped Roth's oeuvre in changing the trajectory of its (possible) reception. Of the seven fictional books published since, three have found their natural collocation in these newly created groups (*The Dying Animal* (2001), listed under "Kepesh Books"; *The Plot against America* (2004), under "Roth Books"; and *Exit Ghost* (2007), under "Zuckerman Books"), and four have lingered in the limbo of the "Other Books" section up until the publication of *Nemesis* (2010), which spurred another authorial retrospective intervention with the creation of the new heading "Nemeses: Short Novels." In addition to *Nemesis*, the three other books in this tetralogy include *Everyman* (2006), *Indignation* (2008), and *The Humbling* (2009).

This regrouping also comes belatedly, and seems to be an indication that the four books were not there to start with, but took a more defined shape at some moment during the composition of *Nemesis*. "It happened as I proceeded," Roth told Mark Lawson in an interview for BBC Radio 4's *Front Row* and added: "This is my little Lego set." For literary scholars and attentive readers, however, this "boy's delight," as Roth defines it in that same interview, cannot go unnoticed, as it touches the core of the relationship between narrative matters and interpretative stances.

What cannot be ignored is that now—that is, after *Nemesis* and the consequent creation of the new grouping—the placing of these short novels *precedes* our reading experience of them. To those who are skeptical about the importance of paratextual details—and this paratextual detail in particular—I simply say that readers who pay attention to them cannot but read differently from readers who do not. *Not* paying attention implies not attending to a directly formulated and accessible authorial intention conveyed through a first-order illocutionary act, in which Roth *does* something by *saying* something.

But what does this decision signal? Roth might be wondering—both consciously and unconsciously—what will happen to his storytelling after his death. A first answer would thus consider the thematic context of the tetralogy—facing one's destiny, death, mortality, fragility—and assume that Roth may want to take care of his will. As the protagonist of *Everyman* muses, "Writing a will—that was the best part of aging and probably even of dying, the writing and, as time passed, the updating and revising and carefully reconsidered rewriting of one's will" (*Everyman* 62–63). In *Exit Ghost*—the book that stands chronologically between *Everyman* and *Indignation*—an aging Zuckerman wonders what the future of his writing will be once he has lost his grip on memory and remembering. Via Zuckerman, Roth demonstrates he is thinking about the possibility that his world as a novelist might no longer be what it was. What follows, however, will not address the thematic concerns of the tetralogy directly, but will be essentially devoted to the workings of Roth's narratological choices with a special focus on their effects on readers.

Roth's fictional contemplation of the impact of powerful nemeses on his characters is refracted and mirrored in narrative experimentations revolving around violations—the narratological quicksands of the title—of the mimetic code of verisimilitude. What happens when voices are besieged by death and destruction? What happens to words when life is imperiled or gone? In narratological terms: Who speaks from where? The new kid on Roth's narratological block seems to be a narrative voice playing with the reader's mimetic expectations.

In her groundbreaking book *Towards a "Natural" Narratology* (1996), Monika Fludernik has set the stage for a "cognitive and organicist model," (xi) according to which the readability of fictional representations of storyworlds depends on natural—that is, cognitive—parameters. Fludernik's seminal intuition allows her to propose "a narratological conceptualization of the cognitive reading process" (11) that revolves around the readers' projections of familiar knowledge and mostly automatic assumptions regarding textual material. According to this conceptualization, readers apply the same interpretative strategies to their reading that they employ in real-life situations. Fludernik's choice of the controversial word "natural" leads her to redefine narrativity as experientiality. On the textual level, this redefinition implies that "there cannot be any narratives without a human (anthropomorphic) experiencer of some sort at some narrative level," (13) and, on the fruition level, it results in "the evocation of consciousness or with the representation of a speaker role" (13).

Given this framework—which my classroom experience has demonstrated to be very much to the point of what reading is essentially about—the basic Jakobsonian communicative context is the one we as readers tend to apply by default: It represents, so to speak, our reading comfort zone, as it does not require any adjustments to automatic processing gestures. The question guiding my readings of the Nemeses tetralogy—who speaks from where?—condenses our default assumptions concerning the functioning of a storyworld that takes a certain shape according to the voice in charge of the narration (who speaks) and the deictic field (from where) that determines the focalizing perspective. The following analyses will demonstrate how each of the books in the tetralogy require readers to exit their reading comfort zones when they are confronted with textual material that defies naturalizing hypotheses.

Everyman: "There's Nothing Special about My Story"

> Around the grave in the rundown cemetery were a few of his former advertising colleagues from New York, who . . . told his daughter, Nancy, what a pleasure it had been to work with him. . . . And there were his two sons, Randy and Lonny, middle-aged men from his turbulent first marriage, very much their mother's children, who as a consequence knew little of him that was praiseworthy and much that was beastly and who were present out of duty and nothing more. (1)[1]

Everyman begins at the end, with a graveyard scene that acquaints the readers virtually with all the protagonists of the short novel. Well in keeping with the circumstances, people reminisce and the world of the yet unnamed deceased person takes fuller and fuller shape. And yet, once we get past the superficial feeling that everything is offered in a reader-friendly way and begin asking more precise questions, textual data become slippery.

Two items do not fall easily into place: the overriding presence of the deceased person who nonetheless remains without a proper name and the authorial decisions concerning the narrating voice. As for the former, the reader cannot but wonder whether this namelessness has to be linked to the title of the book and whether the singularity and uniqueness of the life we have just been synoptically offered has to be measured against the gauge of representativeness. This hypothesis—death as the great leveler—remains pretty much at the center of the reader's experience of the book, even when an explicit reference—the protagonist's father's shop, "Everyman's Jewelry Store"—is given. As for the latter, the hovering question concerns the narrator's positioning as far as the diegesis is concerned: Are we facing an external or an internal narrator? At first sight, the narrator would seem to know a good deal about the people gathered around the grave. He connects the present with the past: Nancy is "plainly pretty as her mother had been" (4); the sons with the "sensual fullness of their wide, identical mouths, just like their father . . . at their age" (13); he knows what people remember: "Then she remembered his stoical maxim from decades back" (4); and seems to be able to access the characters' minds: "He paused to compose his thoughts so that he could speak sensibly" (5).

And yet, the hypothesis of an external authorial third-person narrator is not completely convincing, as it fails to explain all textual material. "In a matter of minutes, everybody had walked away—wearily and tearfully walked away from *our species'* least favorite activity—and he was left behind" (15, emphasis added). The incidental sentence introduces a first-person plural pronoun that does not run counter to the proposed external-narrator explanation in itself—authorial glosses may, in fact, take this form—but amplifies a number of features that go in the same direction, namely, the *internal* positioning of the narrating voice. On a closer analysis, in fact, a good number of details concerning the people gathered around the grave depend upon verbs and expressions of visual perception hereafter marked with italicized words. About Howie, "it still *appeared as if* he could run a football through the middle of the line" (5); the two sons are "handsome men beginning to grow beefy and *seemingly* as closely linked with each other as . . ."; Lonny's "entire body began to tremble and quake, and *it looked as though* . . ." (13); Maureen is "a battler *from the look of her* and no stranger to either life or death" (14). The presentation of Maureen—the only outsider—constitutes the most significant evidence of internal positioning. When Maureen is presented as the "only one person whose presence hadn't to do with having been invited," who "introduced herself as Maureen," (2) the introduction has the uncanny quality of seeming to concern the narrator as well; when he describes how "she let the dirt slip slowly across her curled palm and out the side of her hand onto the coffin, the gesture looked like the prelude to a carnal act," his conclusion—"Clearly this was a man to whom she'd once given much thought" (14)—is perspicuous for the absence of any cognitive privilege. The internal hypothesis is furthermore strengthened by what seems to be an emotionally involved reading of the situation: "Any note of tenderness, grief, love, or loss was *terrifyingly* absent from [Randy's] voice" (14, emphasis added).

Our (automatic) efforts at naturalizing narratives are likely to lead us to privilege the hypothesis of internal positioning—and visualize this voice as belonging to someone in the tribe, forgetting tiny, but nonetheless present violations concerning the reading of other minds—over the simplest solution of the external narrator which would nonetheless require us to overlook the insistence on knowledge recovered through visual perception and on the emotionally implicated adverbial choice just quoted; the third alternative, a figural narration, does not seem to be available, because none of the characters presented can be considered a good candidate as reflector since we are never offered a recognizably singular point of perceptual origin. In one way or another, none of the possible solutions can be considered fully satisfactory.

The graveyard scene has presented a portrait in absentia, emerging from outside views attuned to the different familial perspectives involved. As far as readers' expectations are concerned, it is all too natural to expect a (re)telling of the story by the only one who could not tell it in the first scene.

> Though he had grown accustomed to being on his own . . . since his last divorce ten years back, in his bed the night before the surgery he worked at remembering as exactly as he could each of the women who had been there waiting for him to rise out of the anesthetic in the recovery room. (15)

The graveyard scene that opened the book recedes in the background to give way to a differently focalized stretch of narrative—the who-speaks-from-where question we have just tentatively answered returns to haunt us, as a difference in focalization requires a redefinition of the coordinates of the narrative we are reading. The mimetic rule of verisimilitude requires the constant anchoring of the narration of a given event to the moment of narrating; such anchoring helps readers to tune in to the embodied experience of the protagonist by providing the existential coordinates from which the narrated events are looked at. This narrative premise seems to set the stage for a figural narration: an external voice presenting events through the filtering of a recognizable consciousness that readers assume belongs to the same person who has just been buried. The situation, after all, allows an easy transition between the two male personal pronouns as this second one is immediately given health problems, more than one wife, and the "sublime experience" (15) of a private nurse—all ingredients that we have already been told about.

The alternatives concerning the narrating voice of the first few pages are clearly not available here any longer: In offering an inside view on the workings of a mind, figural narratives require the existence of an external authorial narrator. The crucial question that has to be ascertained concerns the *kind* of relation this narrator entertains with the restricted perspective he purports to present: is his presence just a transparent medium, or is it audible? Is all we are offered attributable to the protagonist's remembering? In all respects, this narrative structure is double-layered—the narrator represents a metaphorical backdrop that becomes audible each time the restricted perspective is transgressed. Breaches are to be measured in reference to the deictic field constituted by the precise standpoint the first paragraph (whose opening lines are quoted above) has depicted—the *now* represented by "the night before the surgery" and the *here* constituted by a hospital room.

The (naturalizing) problem with what follows concerns the fact that the anchorage to this moment of recollection is maintained in the first pages and then dissipates. What had been put forward as the target of that remembering—the women "waiting for him to rise out of the anesthetic"—soon becomes a much vaster project—a personal biography that has "by this time become identical with [his] medical biograph[y]"

(80). Even if this would be easy enough to naturalize given the present moment—after all, didn't the Everyman of the homonymous allegorical play go through a reckoning of his life while facing death?—readers are nonetheless liable to get lost in the maze of shifting deictics, and an ambiguous interplay between narrating voice and internal perspective.

The ambiguity depends on two jarring trajectories. On the one hand, the presence of the narrator is both signaled by typical quotational signals—"Would everything be different, *he asked himself*" (97)—and by overt narratorial intrusions—"This ordinarily even-tempered man struck furiously at his heart like some fanatic at prayer" (158). On the other, the focusing on the protagonist is at times so intense as to disrupt the usual referential pattern: "He did not want them to cover his father's face. . . . I've been looking at that face since I was born—stop burying my father's face!" (60). Here, in a highly charged emotional moment—his father's funeral—the protagonist's naked *I* surfaces. The most glaring narrative intrusion still far ahead, the temptation would be to consider the third person account just a confession in disguise—a distancing effect that a representative of our species may want to resort to while facing such a challenging predicament as the umpteenth surgical operation. This hypothesis would furthermore be corroborated by the surfacing of second-person addresses—"True, he had chosen to live alone, but not unbearably alone. The worst of being unbearably alone was that you had to bear it—either that or you were sunk" (102)—and by what I called the maze of shifting deictics. "He was remembering *now* her brief period as a track star" (77, emphasis added); "There was an absence *now* of all forms of solace" (129, emphasis added). Now when? The answer is not simple, because the first, original recollection opens up on other embedded recollections, creating a recognizable pattern: The protagonist remembers remembering, and we lose track of the Chinese box of memory in which we are enclosed. Two more issues may furthermore haunt the reader: How is it that, after a final paragraph break has (probably) consigned the narrative back into the hands of the third-person narrator whose voice opened the book, the description of his last hours does not contain a single reference to his endeavor to remember? Conversely, why does the very paragraph inaugurating the figural narrative omit any reference to the way his talking to his parents' bones had "made him feel buoyant and indestructible" (181)? Roth seems to want to fragment narratologically what life has already broken.

Indignation: As Marcus Lay Dying

Indignation inaugurates the alternation that will be confirmed in the following two short novels, as it is built around the retrospective account of the protagonist's life in his own voice. In stark contrast with *Everyman*, which has no chapters, only a long narrative flow interrupted by paragraph breaks, *Indignation* offers the reader a table of contents at the beginning of the book. Here the reader is presented with the key to naturalize what he or she is going to read. The bulk of the book—more than two hundred pages—consists of the chapter "Under Morphine"; the second and final chapter—just seven pages—echoes, chiasmus-like, the first, "Out from Under." And yet, in spite of being told about the circumstances of the telling, readers fall prey to one of Roth's subtle games, and they forget. The liability to forget depends, first of all, on the distribution of textual material. The book opens with a chronological notation linking the global historical arena with the protagonist's existence: When "the agonies of the Korean War began" (1), Marcus enters Robert Treat, a small college in downtown Newark. The question of who speaks is immediately settled, as the first-person pronoun welcomes us immediately. First-person contexts are generally easier to naturalize, as the typical pattern around which they are structured—retrospection—is recognizable as "imitat[ating] the temporal continuity of real beings" (Cohn 144). The retrospective slant, already implicit in the past tense, is, furthermore, very soon explicitly referred to: "I look back at those seven months [before college] as a wonderful time" (7). The specification of the where and when of this present tense is, however, deferred for another fifty pages:

What happened next I had to puzzle over for weeks afterward. And even dead, as I am and have been for I don't know how long, I try to reconstruct the mores that reigned over that campus and to recapitulate the troubled efforts to elude those mores that fostered the series of mishaps ending in my death. (54)

Readers are taken aback by this revelation—another demonstration, if one is needed, that we are essentially impervious to paratextual suggestions. As the revelation of the present of the narration is not a last-minute plot twist, the reader has to cope—while reading—with the issue of literalness struggling between two explanatory frames. The first, natural, has the narrator speak, as the title goes, "Under Morphine"; the second, unnatural, has the narrator speak from an unspecified (and unspecifiable) condition of postmortality. This second alternative is founded on Marcus's saying, "I am dead," and not, "I am dying." By the end of the book, the apparent violation is redressed with a perfectly sensible explanation the third-person narrator in charge of the telling in the final chapter provides: "Now he was well and truly dead, out from under and far beyond morphine-induced recollection" (226).

The issue that interests us here is not so much the eventual resolution, but Roth's choice, first, to offer the readers the (paratextual) key; and second, to proceed with fifty-odd pages of unspecified retrospective recollection before the protagonist announces, "I'm dead"—in contrast with the very title of the chapter—and eventually disambiguate it all almost two hundred pages later. It is worth stressing that, of the three books that are divided into chapters, *Indignation* is the only one that presents a table of contents. This paratextual peculiarity would seem to corroborate Roth's intention to play with readers' expectations and assumptions, to manipulate them through a deft handling of the order of presentation of textual material. Crucial differences notwithstanding, this choice reminds us of Zuckerman's telling us he dreamt a realist chronicle in *American Pastoral* and of readers' forgetting.[2] Title chapter notwithstanding, readers realize that the first fifty pages are to be filed under the heading "under morphine" *only after* page 54. The announcement and its specification both require readers to readjust their interpretative strategies and wonder about authorial intentions. Narrative grounds turn out to be slippery here, too. Elizabeth Tallent wonders: "What do dead narrators offer that live ones don't?" (7). We might speculate that Roth wanted to explore the stakes at play once an impossible utterance is posited, to see whether a dead narrator allowed different, new effects. It is rather significant that Roth has Marcus describe his condition of postmortality by questioning the notions of *now* and *here* that are the necessary ingredients to define the embodied experience of a self around which narrative lives are (mimetically) built—"Even now (if 'now' can be said to mean anything any longer), . . . alive as I am here (if 'here' or 'I' means anything)" (54–55). Once the deictic field—the *now* and the *here*—cannot be defined any longer, what kind of narrative is possible? What happens to the interrelated notions of self and time? Postmodern texts do not shun the predicament and revel in fluid selves and times that the disruption of the deictic field warrants. With *Indignation*, Roth, who has never been keen on postmodern poetics, seems to espouse the opinion of Jacques Derrida, who maintained that "the condition for a true act of language is my being able to say 'I am dead'" and yet "'I am dead' has a meaning if it is obviously false" (qtd. in Macksey 155). First Roth deploys the disruptive force of this act of language, only to falsify it, giving it a perfectly verisimilar explanation.

A partial consequence of this game readers have to cope with is deictic ambiguity. Here readers are forced to consider the possibility of an overlapping of story and discourse in what James Phelan calls dual focalization, which takes place when "the narrator's focalization contains the character's" (118). The whole book—final chapter excluded—is built around two levels of awareness and perception simultaneously present. The very first lines of the pivotal page 54—"What happened next I had to puzzle over for weeks afterward"—condense this duality: so-to-speak "dead" Marcus "continues to puzzle over" (55), as narrating *I*, on his experiencing self "puzzl[ing] over" (54) what happened.

Dual focalization is a way to represent re-thinking and re-seeing, which is much in keeping with what may be deemed Roth's Nemeses project—to contemplate narratological ways to represent threshold situations and require the reader to dwell on uncertain narrative ground.

The Humbling: "The Most Difficult Act There Is"

The kind of problem that readers face with *The Humbling* (2009) is of a different nature. Returning to a telling in the third person that is strictly focalized on the protagonist, *The Humbling* does not pose particular problems as far as the transmission of information is concerned. Well in keeping with what happens in both *Everyman* and *Indignation*, the book closes after the death of the protagonist and the narration sheds the strict focalization to detail what cannot be narrated from an internal perspective. The third-person narrator is thus audibly present in the final paragraph and here and there during the narration of Simon Axler's depression, his transformation (as the title of chapter 2 goes), and his final demise. The third-person narrator provides chronological notations, perceptual coordinates, using his cognitive privilege very sparingly—so much so as to let the protagonist's deepest feelings emerge with the first-person pronoun in quoted interior monologues that are stripped of narrational filtering. This kind of narrating voice is very similar to the one we have met in *Everyman*, the possibility of its being homodiegetic excluded.

How does *The Humbling* thus participate in issues of naturalization that characterize its fellow books? I suggest that the quicksand readers face in the third installment of the tetralogy concerns the Rothian macrotext; I would go as far as to say that *The Humbling* busts the Rothian novel. Book reviewers are unanimous in declaring *The Humbling* a flop. According to Michiko Kakutani, "Mr. Roth recounts [the] events in an offhand manner, as though he were simply going through the motions of ticking off plot points on a spindly, ill-conceived outline"; Alex Clark deems it trite and "pointlessly crude," made up of "sentences that are dismayingly free of Roth's characteristic humour and mischief," which "pile up in a shakily fabular framework but never manage to . . . foreground its larger intentions." It is rather difficult to disagree with these takes on the book, unless one looks for "larger intentions" somewhere else.

Let us start here, too, with paratextual details. As I have said, before becoming part of a larger group, *Everyman* and *Indignation* when first published were listed at the end of the group titled "Other Books." Understandably, *Nemesis*, the book that apparently provoked Roth's rethinking and suggested the title of the new group, immediately made it in the Nemeses section. Mysteriously, *The Humbling*, which should have been listed together with *Everyman* and *Indignation*, at the end of the "Other Books" group, does not appear anywhere in the paratext. This may be certainly explained as an editorial mistake; and yet the absence of the book creates an uncanny effect around it. Playing this interpretative game, we may conjecture that *The Humbling* exists *only* within the context of the Nemeses tetralogy as a representation of the humbling of its author. The book begins with a peremptory "He had lost his magic"; the third-person narrator immediately offers the key to understanding the existential situation of the protagonist. Simon Axler, a once gifted and renowned actor, has to face the tragic awareness that "his talent [is] dead" (1). What he hopes is simply a bad period turns into the excruciating awareness of irreversible loss. His bafflement is total and takes the form of an endless musing in an effort to name that which has destroyed his confidence and explain the "inexplicable" (11).

Bluntly put, what would Roth write if he had lost his magic? What would the critics label as a humiliation? As reviews attest, it would be precisely *The Humbling*. The still-missing "last act" is putting up the act of being finished, destroyed by literary critics. Roth plays "the role of [his] own demise" (5) as he contemplates a writer's worst nemesis—writing without being able to write any longer—and exorcises it by committing a writerly suicide. "You seem to yourself and to everyone around you paralyzed and wholly ineffectual and yet you can decide to commit the most difficult act there is. It's exhilarating. It's invigorating. It's euphoric" (14). What about considering these words, used by a young hospitalized woman to describe suicide, as depicting Roth's own suicidal endeavor? "The most difficult act there is" for a famous and renowned writer could certainly be taken to be writing a book whose "ugliness is unique" (Jones).

Simon Axler manages to kill himself only because "finally it occurred to him to pretend that he was committing suicide in a play" (139). The note he leaves says, "The fact is, Konstantin Gavrilovich has shot himself" (140). The fact is that Gavrilovich has shot himself with the result of killing Simon Axler. The fact is that Simon Axler has humiliated himself with the result of humbling Philip Roth. All his career long, Roth has made clear in countless situations—via Nathan Zuckerman in most explicit ways—that a writer's understanding of the world passes through his writing about it. Here Roth wants to ventriloquize the crossing of the ultimate border and face death and humiliation instead of death and fame. In his blog, Jonathan Jones ponders Roth's feat: "He has something even when he has nothing. He is the most courageous writer alive, and this is another brave move in a career that still packs surprises, albeit nasty ones. Perhaps a new life as a horror writer beckons. Or is this the end?" Well in keeping with the other books of the tetralogy, readers face a question difficult to answer—another (genial) way to contemplate death and interrogate it.

Nemesis: "How Lives Diverge"

Significantly, just like *Indignation*, the other first-person narrative in the tetralogy, *Nemesis* begins by connecting history with an individual existence, or, to be more precise, with a community. The peculiarity of the first pages of the book concerns precisely the presence of this *we* that guides our way into a new storyworld that is threatened by the impending doom of a polio epidemic. In the catalog Uri Margolin lists on *we* narratives, *Nemesis* seems to belong to case (4): "A single member of the class utters all tokens of 'we' in a given stretch of discourse [providing] non-group members with an account of what befell the group."

Readers do not negotiate these pages easily. First of all, the *we* fails to produce an *I*, as would be typical of these narrative situations; secondly, one wonders about the cognitive privileges of the narrating voice. If, on the one hand, the presence of the past tense warrants the knowledge deriving from the passing of time, there is not—as yet—any hint to explain how the homodiegetic narrator knows, for example, that "the kids sloshing away the slime reminded Mr. Cantor of how he'd had to clean up after killing a rat . . . when he was ten years old" (17). The issue of knowledge worsens when, starting from page 19, we plunge into a ten-page-long narrative stretch detailing Bucky's familial setup and his upbringing in Newark with forays into his mind—"However irrational the thought, Mr. Cantor felt as though he had let [his grandfather] down" (26)—and into his grandmother's mind, too: "[She] heard him weeping as she'd never known Eugene to weep before" (27).

When the story of that tragic summer is resumed, the first-person-plural pronoun is nowhere to be seen, and Bucky's inner thoughts, motivations, and assumptions are up front. We seem to have entered a section where a third-person narrator tells the story according to a strictly focalized perspective showing the typical features of this kind of narrative situation. There is nonetheless a jarring detail that continues to remind us of the initial presence of the narrating *we*, namely, the unrelenting reference to the protagonist as "Mr. Cantor," the name stemming from the perspective of the kids looking up at their gym teacher. "The next morning was the worst so far. Three more boys had come down with polio—Leo Feinswog, Paul Lippman, and *me, Arnie Mesnikoff*. . . . The sirens that he and Dr. Steinberg had heard the evening before could well have been from the ambulances speeding them to the hospital" (108–9, emphasis added). And here we are, ninety pages after the last occurrence of a reference to the first-person-plural narrator, the "'we' sayer explicitly refers to himself/herself . . . as participant in the narrated events by means of 'I'" (Margolin). The neutral beginning of the sentence—"three more boys"—renders the appearance of the *me* very surprising. And yet, what is more astounding is that the revelation of the identity of the *I* behind the plural *we* does not change the course the book has taken: In the very same paragraph in which the narrator eventually comes out of hiding, proper name included, there is an immediate lapse into a third-person perspective foregrounded in the objective pronoun *them*, which will be rigorously maintained for the other thirty pages of the chapter in which the *I* remains a ghostly presence adumbrated in the hammering repetition of Mr. Cantor's name. In the second chapter, which leaves Newark behind for the Poconos, not a single reference to the *we* or the *I* is detectable, not even the flimsy onomastic trace embedded in the appellation *Mr.*, which is also shed to give way to a much more straightforward *Bucky*.

Nemesis too, therefore, explores the effects of confusing the line of transmission of information and complicates for the reader the answer to the basic question concerning who speaks from where. Apparently returning to a third-person internally focalized narrative, we go through the momentary lapse from the menace of being stricken by polio according to the protagonist's moment-by-moment experiencing of it. Our Arnie is mentioned together with the names of other kids Bucky feels he has fled in leaving Newark, but returns in the aptly titled chapter "Reunion" with the apparent key to naturalizing the book:

> I ran into him in 1971. . . . After our first emotional street meeting, we began to eat lunch together . . . and that's how I got to hear his story. I turned out to be the first person to whom he'd ever told the whole of the story, from beginning to end, and . . . without leaving very much out. I tried my best to listen closely and to take it all in while he found the words for everything that had been in his mind for the better part of his life. . . . The fact that I had been one of the kids hanging around Chancellor that horrible summer . . . made him bluntly candid in a self-searing manner that sometimes astonished me. (241, 245–46)

The excerpt purports to offer a naturalizing hypothesis: Bucky Cantor has been obsessed with the events of that tragic summer for his entire life; this obsession has fixed each single thought and feeling and word punctuating the thoughts, choices, and dialogues with uncanny distinctness; Arnie is the recipient of this highly emotionally charged (auto)biographical account and he tells it in his own turn. And yet, narratological quicksands are not dispelled here, either, because the information Arnie gives defies being reconstructed as a mere report of what Bucky tells him. Obsession on Bucky's part and attention on Arnie's part notwithstanding, the quantity of detail is too great for any real person to remember: We witness here an example of "mnemonic overkill" (Cohn 162), which has definitely to be filed under the nonmimetic heading. An open question hovers over *Nemesis* as well: Is the naturalizing hypothesis strong enough to explain the second chapter, "Indian Hill"? Is this to be taken as an example of what Henrik Skov Nielsen calls the "impersonal voice" that renders first-person contexts comparable to third-person contexts?

Conclusion

Narratologically undecidable issues reflect the thematic concerns of the tetralogy; nothing requires more illusionism than imagining the final threshold: The precariousness of human existence is refracted in the precariousness of narrating voices that turn out to be both embodied and disembodied, recognizably human and ghostlike. All protagonists of the tetralogy happen to be born around the same time as Roth; their lives, like Roth's own, mostly belong in the past. The books are centered on nostalgic, angered, baffled, past-oriented tales; in the whole tetralogy there is nothing in the present tense but Marcus's "I am dead." The present tense of Roth's writing asks us to attend this most difficult linguistic and existential act with him—a veritable exorcism to "confuse death" (*Everyman* 75), an act of resistance in the shape of writerly *as-if*s. The voice of the author is not posthumous yet.

Notes

1. Unless specified, the quotations in each section come from the book under analysis.

2. For a detailed analysis of these textual dynamics see Masiero "Nothing Is Impersonally Perceived" and *Philip Roth and the Zuckerman Books* 145–53.

Works Cited

Clark, Alex. "Books: *The Humbling* by Philip Roth." *Guardian*. Guardian News and Media, 13 Nov. 2009. Web. 9 Jan. 2013.

Cohn, Dorrit. *Transparent Minds: Narrative Modes for Presenting Consciousness in Fiction*. Princeton: Princeton UP, 1978. Print.

Fludernik, Monica. *Towards a "Natural" Narratology*. London and New York: Routledge, 1996. Print.

Jones, Jonathan. "Is *The Humbling* the End of Philip Roth?" *Jonathan Jones on Art Blog. Guardian.* Guardian News and Media, 5 Jan 2010. Web. 8 Jan. 2013.

Kakutani, Michiko. "Two Storytellers, Singing the Blues." *New York Times*. New York Times, 22 Oct. 2009. Web. 8 Jan. 2013.

Lawson, Mark. *Front Row*. 27 June 2010. BBC, Radio 4.

Macksey, Richard, and Eugenio Donato, eds. *The Structuralist Controversy*. Baltimore: Johns Hopkins UP, 1972. Print.

Margolin, Uri. "Telling Our Story: On 'We' Literary Narratives." *Language and Literature* 5.2 (1996): 115–33. Print.

Masiero Pia. "'Nothing Is Impersonally Perceived': Dreams, Realistic Chronicles and Perspectival Effects in *American Pastoral*." *Reading Philip Roth's* American Pastoral. Ed. Velichka Ivanova. Toulouse: PU du Mirail, 2011. Print.

___. *Philip Roth and the Zuckerman Books: The Making of a Storyworld*. Amherst: Cambria, 2011. Print.

Phelan, James. *Narrative as Rhetoric: Techniques, Audiences, Ethics, Ideology*. Columbus: Ohio State UP, 1996. Print.

Skov Nielsen, Henrik. "The Impersonal Voice in First-Person Narrative Fiction." *Narrative* 12.2 (2004): 133–50. Print.

Tallent, Elizabeth. "The Trouble with Postmortality." *Threepenny Review* 1 (2005): 7–9. Print.

A Roth for All Seasons: Historical and Cultural Contexts_____

Christopher Gonzalez

In his introduction to the 2010 installment of *The Best American Short Stories*, Richard Russo recalls Isaac Bashevis Singer's answer to a question about the purpose of literature. Singer, according to Russo, proclaimed, "The purpose of literature is to entertain and to instruct" (qtd. in Russo xiv). Russo then explicates Singer's grand pronouncement throughout the remainder of the introduction, fixating on the idea that the order of words was a clue to what Singer had meant by "entertain" and "instruct," concluding that, because Singer mentioned it first, entertainment is a significant, though often maligned, component of literature.

Interestingly, one of the things brought to the fore by this notion of literature-as-entertainment is the necessity of an audience for an entertainer. When we think of entertainers, we think of actors, athletes, artists, and, of course, writers, among others. For those who are blessed with the talent, skill, and serendipity to engage audiences en masse, the difficulty often comes in *maintaining* the audience's interest. No one is interested in the superstar athlete who has overstayed his welcome only to become a pale shade of his former self, or the Oscar-winning actress who now can only be found in straight-to-DVD flicks. A career in finding (and keeping) audiences is no simple matter.

Philip Roth, then, must surely be a case study in how to keep an audience once you find one. His career arc traverses through the literary spotlight for half a century, and he has garnered every significant literary prize and award except the Nobel Prize for Literature. Indeed, the sheer breadth of Roth's work across the span of years has yielded rich engagements with history, culture, narrative form, and, of course, audiences. From his first book, *Goodbye, Columbus and Five Short Stories*, in 1959, to his most recent novel, *Nemesis*, in 2011, Roth has continually taken his craft in unexpected directions that have yielded scintillating narratives. Many of Roth's books have notoriously challenged his readers. While his Jewish heritage has generally provided a potent ingredient within his many narratives, Roth typically situates his works along two thematic trajectories: historical time-spaces, and the interconnections of culture.

Using innovative narrative strategies that willfully present audiences with challenges at both the level of narrative form and content, Roth locates his narrative worlds (or storyworlds) at the nexus of history and culture. As Jeffrey Rubin-Dorsky, in characterizing Roth's relationship to his audience, notes, "It is often the case with Roth that succeeding novels respond to, answer, even rebut, preceding ones, if for no other reason than to decenter his audience: performance followed (and often outdone) by counterperformance, the author slipping through his reader's grasp just as he or she tries to take hold" (96). But I take Rubin-Dorsky's point a step further by claiming that Roth's decentering of his audience is not done for its own sake. That is to say, Roth has a larger design in decentering (or destabilizing) his audience, as I intend to sketch below.

Indeed, this chapter seeks to map out the major trends in Roth's work as they relate to these two thematic trajectories vis-à-vis audiences. Specifically, certain moments in world history loom large in Roth's oeuvre, such as the post–World War II period in the United States, the sexual revolution, the Nixon administration, American Jewish and Israeli Jewish relations, and a fictive weaving of the author's own life history as a writer-celebrity. His later works have seamlessly brought together the historical moment of the late twentieth century with alternate/historical fiction, upon which Roth brings his own personal history (both real and imagined) to bear. In addition, this chapter will demonstrate how Roth's works continue to be relevant for contemporary audiences. Though his work has consistently challenged his audiences, I argue that these challenges in turn have allowed Roth to shape and nurture audiences over the course of his writing career. Significantly, these challenging reading situations have not only expanded audience expectations of so-called Jewish American writing; Roth's writings have also helped open spaces for other writers to explore narrative design with fewer constraints. The presentation of innovative storyworld design that takes on important aspects of history and culture, one that pushes audiences in uncomfortable yet productive ways, may ultimately be Roth's greatest legacy to American letters.

Challenging Narrative Designs

One of Roth's strengths is that he ingeniously creates challenging reading situations for his audience. These challenges, often presented to audiences via the form and content of Roth's narratives, suggest a confident writer whose devotion is first and foremost to the design of the storyworlds he creates. Authors are invested with the power to create their fictions, but it is a power that is often limited by what audiences are willing to entertain; in Roth's writing specifically, challenges of form and content may be best understood by thinking in terms of the cognitive obstacles presented to readers of his writing.

In this instance, cognitive effort on the part of the reader is not an indication that a narrative is difficult to understand or willfully abstruse, as in the case of the work of some postmodernist authors who make a conscious and concerted effort to create a narrative that is hard to understand. Such is not the case with Roth, an author who is noted for his impressive and meticulous prose style. For instance, cognitive effort, as I am using the term, points to Roth's blending of his fictional worlds and his actual, biographical world. Because he consistently blurs the margins of these worlds, readers and critics are almost always compelled to divine what in his fiction are figments of pure imagination and what are shadows cast by the author's life.

When audiences are not grappling with what is fiction in Roth's work and what is not, they are often presented with thematic content that challenges their ethics in some significant way. The vehicles of such challenges often come in the form of the most commonly divisive areas of human discourse, namely, politics, religion, and sex. Roth's frank depictions and treatments of potentially sensitive issues are what have often rankled audiences—particularly in the Jewish community and in the critical community as well. For example, early in his career, the Jewish community openly castigated Roth for his portrayal of Jewish Americans in his fiction. He was subsequently labeled a "self-hating Jew," a term Roth has been forced to grapple with for most of his career and which has, ironically, provided the impetus for many of his books.

In fact, Roth's relationship with the Jewish community highlights a burden many ethnic writers must contend with when composing fiction. There are always constraints placed on an author with regard to his or her ethnic or racial group. Representation is ever a battleground for minority groups in the United States. That is to say, certain groups of people constantly struggle to dismantle stereotypes, and those within the community with the power to construct positive representatives or markers of identity in their creative and artistic endeavors are pressured to do so. When authors go against this tacit charge, they incur the ire of the leaders of their communities.

Roth, for his part, has always seemed destined to ignore this constraint faced by ethnic authors, by writing precisely whatever he wants with little regard for whether his fiction is deemed challenging or offensive. Rather than limiting the scope of his narrative canvas, Roth has stretched his canvas in service of whatever particular needs his fiction may have. The resulting artistic freedom has enabled Roth to challenge himself through the design of his storyworlds with the confidence that his work will ultimately find a willing audience. Through the years, Roth has cultivated and shaped a highly devoted audience that in turn has provided him with the venue for pushing his craft in ways that suit him and not according to the demands of the publishing market, critics, or the Jewish American community.

In many ways, we can understand Roth's overarching narrative design impulse as always seeking to destabilize the reader. He often achieves this through the cognitive processes and ethics of the reader.

While a concentration on narrative aesthetics by an author often smacks of self-indulgence, in Roth's writings form and content cohere holistically. Timothy Parrish has made a similar observation:

> As always for Roth, the act of writing and the fact of being a Jew are intertwined. Thus Roth's formal strategies are not deployed merely to deconstruct themselves as fictions that are separate from life or even to engage in contemporary philosophical debates concerning the nature of the self. Rather, they represent a carefully worked out imaginative response to the contradictory identities that his experience as a Jew who is also an American has enforced upon him. (576)

Roth uses audiences' knowledge and experience against them, as it were. For instance, readers have the tendency to keep separate what is fiction and what is actual. Publishers also incorporate signposts to the reader that indicate whether a book is a novel, or a memoir, or non-fiction. Readers have grown accustomed to these and other signposts in order to orient their approach to any given text. Roth uses these instilled reading strategies against readers in an effort to reorder or recalibrate their understanding of identity, America, or history. *The Plot against America* is an excellent example of how Roth takes a historical record of verifiable fact (in this case, the development of the United States as we know it to be) and creates an alternate reality in which famed aviator and antiwar activist Charles Lindbergh wins the 1940 presidential election over Franklin D. Roosevelt. The novel's narrator, Philip Roth, looks back at this singular event:

> When a stranger who did wear a beard and who never once was seen hatless appeared every few months after dark to ask in broken English for a contribution toward the establishment of a Jewish national homeland in Palestine, I, who wasn't an ignorant child, didn't quite know what he was doing on our landing. My parents would give me or Sandy a couple of coins to drop into his collection box, largess, I always thought, dispensed

out of kindness so as not to hurt the feelings of a poor old man who, from one year to the next, seemed unable to get it through his head that we'd already had a homeland for three generations. I pledged allegiance to the flag of our homeland every morning at school. I sang of its marvels with my classmates at assembly programs. I eagerly observed its national holidays, and without giving a second thought to my affinity for the Fourth of July fireworks or the Thanksgiving turkey or the Decoration Day doubleheader. Our homeland was America.

Then the Republicans nominated Lindbergh and everything changed. (4–5)

This novel works on many assumptions, not the least of which is that its readers will recognize the contrast between Roth's created storyworld and the actual historical record. The contrast is manifest within the mind of readers as they continually draw comparisons between the fictional and actual historical record. The cognitive mechanism elicited is the ability of humans to employ counterfactual thinking—to imagine the possible results of certain decisions made and what the consequences of those results might be. Once Roth introduces the monumental difference in the 1940 presidential election in *The Plot against America*, readers are placed in the position of reading the product of Roth's own counterfactual thinking (i.e., the novel) and their own counterfactual thinking for what might have happened if Lindbergh had actually become president. Further, Roth creates characters that bear his name and the names of his actual family members. The result is an interesting weaving of fictional elements that has significant roots in the actual world. As Ginevra Geraci remarks of the uses of history in *The Plot against America*:

Historical buildings and mementos such as commemorative stamps, a pewter letter opener reproducing Mount Vernon, the Declaration of Independence, the US Constitution, the myth of the conquest of the West constitute the problematic ideological backbone of the novel and all contribute to the refigurational process through which history is fictionalized in order to be investigated and understood. In the specific case of alternative history, this process is not only instrumental in illuminating past events and relationships, it is also a tool for disclosing future possibilities that are buried in the past, an instrument for looking into the nature and the scope of those possibilities. (Geraci 191)

A similar reading situation occurs in *Operation Shylock* (1993). In this novel, Roth not only places a fictional version of himself within the pages of his writing, he places a "fake" version of Philip Roth who impersonates the "real" Roth in present-day Israel. Significantly, both of these Philip Roths are fictional characters, even if one of them appears to be the real-life author. *Operation Shylock* makes use of actual people such as Israeli novelist Aharon Appelfeld and actual events such as the trial of former Nazi concentration camp guard John Demjanjuk. With a little help from Roth himself in interviews where he insinuated that the events of the novel actually took place, the defining critical feature of the novel is its ontology. In the novel's epilogue, Roth writes:

Soon enough I found myself wondering if it might be *best* to present the book not as an autobiographical confession that any number of readers, both hostile *and* sympathetic, might feel impelled to challenge on the grounds of credibility, not as a story whose very *point* was its improbable reality, but—claiming myself to have imagined what had been munificently provided, free of charge, by superinventive actuality—as fiction, as a conscious dream contrivance, one whose latent content the author had devised as deliberately as he had the baldly manifest. I could even envision *Operation Shylock*, misleadingly presented as a novel, being understood by an ingenious few as a chronicle of the Halcion hallucination that, momentarily, even I, during one of the more astounding episodes in Jerusalem, almost supposed it might be. (330)

Though the narrator appears to be the biological Philip Roth, he is actually a character in the storyworld. But the challenge here is to recognize that there is a distinction between the two, even if it is a hair's breadth of difference.

Thus, Roth is ever at narrative play in his writings, whether the play originates from formal design elements or creative engagements with history. Through his narrative play, Roth has been able to continually push his own storyworlds into new and interesting areas while at the same time keeping his audiences from ever becoming too comfortable. It is as if, by constantly reinventing both himself and history, Roth's narratives are positioned to take readers down new paths.

Challenges in Roth's Storyworld Design

Throughout his writing career, Roth has emphasized the craft of authorship in his stories. This metafictional quality of his writing has led some critics to examine Roth himself by mining the clues to be found in Roth's fictional writers, such as Peter Tarnapol and Nathan Zuckerman. Zuckerman especially has led many to draw parallels between this fictional writer and his creator. And while many of Roth's protagonists are artists of some sort, in that they create things in which they see artistic merit, Zuckerman is arguably Roth's most significant achievement (in terms of the creation of characters). Roth's audience has traced Zuckerman from his appearance in *The Ghost Writer* (1979), through his authorial dalliances in *American Pastoral* (1997) and *The Human Stain* (2000), to his apparently final appearance in *Exit Ghost* (2007). Consequently, Zuckerman has continually grown as a complex, multilayered character who at times is narrator, protagonist, or creative writer.

Roth's use of Zuckerman certainly bears further scrutiny, though many scholars have investigated this character from a variety of perspectives. Yet one of the issues I wish to raise is the level of complexity that accompanies the effort of *reading* Zuckerman, as Pia Masiero's recent study on the topic, *Philip Roth and the Zuckerman Books: The*

Making of a Storyworld (2011), admirably demonstrates. Masiero delineates her justification for a narratological examination of the Zuckerman books:

> The choice of approaching the subject through the analysis and the consequent amplification of narratological details is internally sustainable because Nathan Zuckerman is himself an author. Roth projects onto his favorite alter ego the burdens and pleasures of authorship; that is, of the actual making of fictional worlds to be engaged in and apprehended by an audience. This implies a constant to the art of fiction; metanarrative commentaries are, in fact, stepping stones in the process of Zuckerman's looking for and finding his own distinctive voice as a writer. Furthermore, all of these details represent the textual junctures in which the readers' repatterning of their working frame is most active. (11)

Masiero's study illuminates Zuckerman's complexity not only in terms of his creation (via Roth) but his own narrative explorations of himself and the world as he experiences it.

As a character who is a significant aspect of the storyworlds he inhabits, Zuckerman goes through the same process of storyworld reconstruction in the audience's mind as they read the narrative blueprint. As David Herman argues, readers are constantly updating the storyworld as more information accretes in the reader's mind. "In trying to make sense of a narrative," Herman maintains, "interpreters attempt to reconstruct not just what happened—who did what to or with whom, for how long, how often and in what order—but also the surrounding context or environment embedding existents, their attributes, and the actions and events in which they are more or less centrally involved" (14). The highly complex process of creating a mental model of a narrative world is often taken for granted, but all readers do this to varying degrees.

Also, Herman points to the difficulty in updating storyworlds as readers encounter new information: "Narrative understanding requires determining how the actions and events recounted relate to what might have happened in the past, what could be happening (alternatively) in the present, and what may yet happen as a result of what already has come about" (14). Though Herman is specifically describing a self-contained storyworld, the difficulties of updating the storyworld are compounded when the overarching storyworld traverses multiple books published over the course of decades. Thus, the more Zuckerman appears in Roth's fiction, the more complex he becomes and the greater the challenges presented to dedicated readers of Roth's fiction. In turn, Roth's writings have necessarily evolved over the course of years. On this matter, Derek Parker Royal, in his examination of *The Human Stain*, notes:

> Such an emphasis [on the subject of death] is a *relatively new phenomenon* in Philip Roth's fiction, especially when contrasted with the themes in such works as *Goodbye, Columbus and Five Stories* (1959), *Portnoy's Complaint* (1969), *The Breast* (1972), *The Professor of Desire* (1977), and *The Ghost Writer*. In these novels the author privileges Eros over Thanatos, the very focus that, for better or for worse, established his reputation as a serious novelist. (128; emphasis added)

To be sure, one of Zuckerman's striking features is that, because he has appeared as a significant character in eight of Roth's books, audiences have witnessed him change over time—watched him move from the lascivious upstart writer in *The Ghost Writer* to the aging man in *Exit Ghost*. As Royal suggests, there is a noticeable telos to Roth's oeuvre, and to his featured narrators such as Zuckerman and David Kepesh, that is uncommon in American literature.

Of course, audiences presented with new information as they read later Zuckerman novels must update what they thought they knew of Zuckerman. And those readers who read a novel such as *The Human Stain* without reading a prior Zuckerman novel are deprived of important details that have shaped Zuckerman, and by extension, Roth. The

Nathan Zuckerman who can only puzzle out Coleman Silk's downfall through his imaginative writing is far from the man who fantasized about Anne Frank in *The Ghost Writer*. This is an important point that is not to be missed. Zuckerman, as a character, transcends the bounds of whatever story in which readers find him. Though he is encountered one book at a time, Zuckerman looms just beyond the edges of the books that cannot possibly contain him. He is more than a character or narrator; he is the connective tissue of an important part of Roth's career. In summarizing Roth's answer to the question of what Nathan Zuckerman allows Roth to do as a writer, Larry Schwartz puts it succinctly but powerfully: "Roth's response speaks directly to the idea of artistic freedom" (67). Moreover, Roth has demonstrated that he has the wherewithal to put his idea of artistic freedom into action within the narrative worlds he creates—something that the majority of authors are unable to bring to fruition. Perhaps all writers have an idea of artistic freedom; few of them, however, are poised to follow through.

Another of Roth's challenges to audiences comes in the form of inserting a fictionalized version of himself into his fiction. While Zuckerman is sometimes seen as a stand-in or alter ego for some aspect of Roth, his fictional doppelganger further blurs the line between the fictional and the actual. In the "Roth books," in which a character named Philip Roth plays an important role, readers are immediately confronted with the question of how much of the character is the actual Roth. The creation of a fictional version of himself forces the reader to make sense of this overlap between character and author, and this narrative design element necessitates that the reader continually make comparisons between the two Roths. What may be viewed as playfulness on the part of the author also can be construed as a notice to the reader that Roth makes few concessions to his audience.

But why is this of particular relevance to understanding the significance of Roth's creative use of himself in the pages of his stories? Other contemporary writers such as Martin Amis, Paul Auster, Dave Eggers, and Kurt Vonnegut Jr. have written themselves into their fictive worlds. So Roth's own efforts are not especially innovative, after all. Still, it is important to remember that it is not simply the introduction of a narrative device where significances lies, but rather how the device is styled within the author's storyworld. Roth as a fictional character, like Zuckerman, is enriched the more he appears within the pages of Roth's books. On parallel tracks, the two Roths have developed over the years but not necessarily in similar ways, despite their ostensible "merger" in *Operation Shylock*.

Related to this alternate Philip is Roth's penchant for reimagining history. So, not only are there alternate Philip Roths, there are alternate realities in which those Philips exist. These realities are not just the type of worlds one expects in fiction, but rather they are worlds that hinge on specific events in real-world history. In his most recent novella, *Nemesis* (2010), Roth conjures the polio outbreak of 1944 in the setting of his childhood Newark, New Jersey. Though readers know that the breakthrough of the polio vaccine thwarted the threat of the polio virus, *Nemesis* manages to create a world where this seeming inevitability of a cure for polio is in doubt. Bucky Cantor's world of strength and athletic prowess is threatened by the ravaging effects of polio and its destructive potential in his community, and ultimately on himself.

In *Indignation*, Roth takes the "forgotten war" (i.e., the Korean War) and parallels the sexual and personal awakening typical of college-age students with the butchery of war. Marcus Messner is confronted with both in *Indignation*, and Roth further challenges the audience with a late-in-the-book revelation that suggests all the things the reader has experienced up to that moment are nothing more than Marcus's morphine-induced remembrances of his life, all while he lies dismembered on a Korean battlefield. And in *The Plot against America*, Philip Roth (as a character) struggles through an alternate history of America wherein Lindbergh becomes president and, thanks to his support for Nazi ideology, enacts an insidious pogrom of Jewish Americans. In this particular novel, the reader is invited to inhabit this counterfactual thinking and wonder what was possible under certain circumstances.

Roth has shown in his fiction that what seems certain or inevitable could easily have turned out horribly wrong. Through such inventive storyworlds, Roth illuminates for readers current realities and recorded history.

Cultural Contexts

In addition to challenging audiences at the level of narrative design, Roth, perhaps notoriously, has challenged his audience at the level of culture. Because Roth's ascent as a writer followed other notable Jewish American writers such as Bernard Malamud, Isaac Bashevis Singer, Chaim Potok, Saul Bellow, and Henry Roth, among others, certain expectations were placed on Roth by audiences and critics. However, Philip Roth countered all expectations by dealing frankly with topics that were deemed taboo in literary fiction, such as sexual liberty, less-than-ideal representations of Jewish parents and their children, and outright excoriations of politics in both America and Israel. Consequently, Roth was taken to task for his engagements with these subjects in his fiction. But to his credit, Roth has always been a writer who retains sole discretion over what he writes. Rather than accede to pressure from his critics, Roth thwarts their expectations even more.

Benjamin Schreier has attempted to recast the dominance of a historically recognizable Jewish subject in Jewish American literary studies. Using Roth's fiction as a case study—and specifically *Goodbye, Columbus and Five Short Stories*—Schreier essentially takes on the scholars of Jewish literature who suggest there is an intangible, tacit quality that makes certain works of literature inherently Jewish. Schreier argues:

> It is not that Roth's characters do not want to be Jews; it is that they do not know how to describe themselves as Jews. And it is not that Roth's books are not texts of Jewish identity or identification; it is that they are just as forcefully countertexts of Jewish identity or identification—countertexts that displace categorical Jewishness from the presumably secure site where we expect to recognize it. (107)

In other words, Roth's narratives cannot be read in light of established paradigms of Jewishness in literary criticism. Rather, his narratives destabilize habituated understandings of Jewish American literature—as well as representations of Jewish identity—as they cry out for new, defamiliarized processes for engaging with the Jewish subject in fiction. I support this claim, for ethnic American writers tend to operate within well-established ways of thinking about these groups of Americans, and further, these writers struggle *against* these powerful ways of viewing identity in the United States precisely through the narratives they design and create. As Schreier's argument implies, an author such as Roth must be the one to counter prevailing notions of Jewish identity through his texts rather than to wait patiently for broader conceptions of ethnicity to manifest overnight.

Next to the topic of Jewish identity, Roth's treatment of sex is one of the defining features of his fiction. The large majority of his books feature libertine characters and narrators that showcase the sexual nature of their personalities for audiences. Roth takes matters that often go unmentioned, thanks to America's puritan roots, and places them on the equivalent of America's dinner table for all to partake. For instance, in his first major work, *Goodbye, Columbus and Five Short Stories*, Roth displays the reality that the children of Jewish immigrants were no longer dealing with the same issues as their parents. The consequences of assimilation on Jewish parents and their children come to the fore in Roth's first book, and evidences his initial foray in depicting the challenge of a burgeoning sexual awareness in second- and third-generation Jewish Americans. Neil Klugman, the narrator of the novella *Goodbye, Columbus*, is caught between the traditions of his Jewish identity (represented in his mother) and the consequences of assimilation (represented in a woman he believes he has fallen in love with, the alluring Brenda Patimkin). Neil is amazed at Brenda's shift from Jewish culture to the all-American WASP family. While Roth's portrayal of Neil as a son suggests that Neil is no longer beholden to the norms and customs of his parents, Neil is equally apprehensive about the ease with which Jewish Americans such as Brenda can cast aside their heritage. Moreover, the sexual relationship between Neil and Brenda, motivated by the sheer lust and sexual attraction generated by these two college-age youths, brings them to the realization that the relationship is untenable.

In part because of the severe criticism Roth received in the wake of *Goodbye, Columbus and Five Short Stories*, complete with the denunciation that he was a "self-hating Jew," Roth released the now infamous *Portnoy's Complaint*. If Roth had only hinted at controversial subjects in his first book, he removed all doubt with the introduction of Alexander Portnoy. The relatively gentle representation of Jewish family life in America in *Goodbye, Columbus* is magnified exponentially in *Portnoy's Complaint*. Alexander Portnoy is transformed once he discovers the pleasures of masturbation in the section titled, "Whacking Off" (17). He cannot keep from self-abuse, and many of the outrageous scenes early in the novel occur when Alexander tries to masturbate without being caught by his parents. "Did I mention that when I was fifteen I took it out of my pants and whacked off on the 107 bus from New York?," Alexander confesses (78). He pleasures himself with a piece of liver he "violated behind a billboard on the way to a bar mitzvah lesson" (19)—liver his family would go on to cook and eat, unaware that Alexander had literally "fucked" the family dinner (134). *Portnoy's Complaint* arguably reaches its crescendo with the appearance of Mary Jane, called "The Monkey," a nymphomaniac. Yet even in this paean to libertine pleasures, Roth makes use of a narrative device in order to account for Alexander's hedonistic and confessional narration: The novel reveals that it is Alexander's narration to a therapist named Dr. Spielvogel, who names Alexander's condition with what turns out to be the novel's title.

Portnoy's Complaint is a significant turning point in Roth's career, because it marks the first moment that Roth willfully engages with his audience in ways that he knows will move them in an emotional, visceral way, if not outrage them altogether. From this novel on, Roth nabbed the sort of creative freedom that few authors have attained. For instance, in what are now known as the "Kepesh books" (*The Breast, The Professor of Desire,* and *The Dying Animal*), Roth brings together the intellectual literature professor with the unrestrained sexuality Roth introduced in *Portnoy's Complaint.* David Kepesh, a recurring protagonist like Nathan Zuckerman, also develops in complexity over the course of the Kepesh books. This in-your-face sexuality permeates Roth's fiction.

But as noted already, from his initial salvo with Jewish culture in *Goodbye, Columbus and Five Short Stories,* Roth has continually written beyond the limited scope of the ethnically identified author. There is often a problem with such a designation, when an author is aligned with or is a representative of a liminal culture or group. Such authors are often seen as representing or speaking for the group in which they have membership, or it may be that they are charged with the task of educating audiences about the nuances of their culture. Like it or not, this is an unfair constraint that is typically placed on ethnic American authors. This is exactly the constraint with which Roth has struggled from the inception of his writing career.

Conclusion

Few authors have had such a prolific career while making so few concessions to his audience as Philip Roth. Rather than attempt to navigate his course as an author according to the prevailing winds of the purchasing market of the publishing industry, Roth has unambiguously devoted his writing to following his own imagination when shaping the storyworlds of his books. In turn, he has push his own artistry in ways that invigorate his craft, so much so that even after more than fifty years, Roth continues to be one of the most significant American authors. Critics speak of Roth's career in terms of early, middle, and late periods. Throughout these periods, and holistically as well, there is an ever-changing Roth whose work has never grown stale. As Singer pronounced, the purpose of literature is to entertain. Roth has certainly entertained his audiences, evidenced by his continued best-selling author status. His work continues to be awarded the highest accolades, in part because Roth is not the type of author one might pejoratively label a "one-trick pony." Rather, through the years, Roth has morphed as a writer and taken many narrative risks. As a matter of fact, it is fair to say that there is not just one Roth. Just as Roth himself has cloned and transmuted his own identity and woven it into the narrative fabric of his fiction, his audience can easily observe the various manifestations of Roth the writer by simply taking in the impressive legacy of his fiction that has yet to reach its terminus.

Works Cited

Geraci, Ginevra. "The Sense of an Ending: Alternative History in Philip Roth's *The Plot against America*." *Philip Roth Studies* 7.2 (2011): 187–204. Print.

Herman, David. *Story Logic: Problems and Possibilities of Narrative*. Lincoln: U of Nebraska P, 2002. Print.

Masiero, Pia. *Philip Roth and the Zuckerman Books: The Making of a Storyworld*. Amherst, NY: Cambria, 2011. Print.

Parrish, Timothy. "Imagining Jews in Philip Roth's *Operation Shylock*." *Contemporary Literature* 40 (1999): 575–602. Print.

Roth, Philip. *Novels 1993–1995*: Operation Shylock *and* Sabbath's Theater. New York: Library of America, 2010. Print.

___. *The Plot against America*. New York: Vintage, 2004. Print.

___. *Portnoy's Complaint*. 1969. New York: Vintage, 1994. Print.

Royal, Derek Parker. "Plotting the Frames of Subjectivity: Identity, Death, and Narrative in Philip Roth's *The Human Stain*." *Contemporary Literature* 47.1 (2006): 114–40. Print.

Rubin-Dorsky, Jeffrey. "Philip Roth and American Jewish Identity: The Question of Authenticity." *American Literary History* 13.1 (2001): 79–107. Print.

Russo, Richard. "Introduction." *The Best American Short Stories 2010*. Ed. Richard Russo. New York: Houghton, 2010. xiii–xix. Print.

Schreier, Benjamin. "The Failure of Identity: Toward a New Literary History of Philip Roth's Unrecognizable Jew." *Jewish Social Studies: History, Culture, Society*. 17.2 (Winter 2011): 101–35. Print.

Schwartz, Larry. "Erasing Race in Philip Roth's *The Human Stain*." 7.1 (2011): 65–81. Print.

Aging, Remembrance, and Testimony in the Later Fiction of Roth and Bellow_____

Maggie McKinley

The act of looking back has long played a role in the fiction of both Philip Roth and Saul Bellow. From Alexander Portnoy's retrospective confessions in Roth's *Portnoy's Complaint* to Artur Sammler's nostalgia-tinged criticisms of modern society in Bellow's *Mr. Sammler's Planet*, some of these authors' most famous (and infamous) protagonists devote a significant amount of energy to the act of reminiscence. Yet what sets this retrospection in Roth and Bellow's later fiction apart from that in their earlier works is the increased urgency with which their protagonists seek to turn their recollections into a more concrete form of testimony. In Bellow's *Ravelstein* (2000), for example, the experience of loss and sense of impending mortality trigger the narrator's decision to write Abe Ravelstein's biography, which becomes both a celebratory and mournful testimony to the past. In Roth's *Exit Ghost* (2007), Nathan Zuckerman faces the losses of old age by channeling his grief and frustration into the script for a play that will be his final artistic endeavor. And in Roth's *The Humbling* (2009), aging protagonist Simon Axler finds himself unable to play the roles that defined his theatrical career, and instead uses his lover Pegeen as a canvas upon which to create and perform a new narrative, one that ultimately mourns everything he has lost.

The similarities across these texts are often striking, and their analogous emphases on creative acts as personal testimonies seem to be a direct invitation for a comparative study. Yet while Roth and Bellow have been spoken of together in the past (largely as a result of their categorization as Jewish American authors), and while scholars have noted the increased focus on age and aging in each author's recent fiction, few have examined the ways in which the representations of aging—specifically the relationship between aging and creativity—overlap in their latest works.[1] This essay demonstrates how examining Bellow's

Ravelstein alongside two of Roth's most recent novels can not only enhance our awareness of the thematic similarities across these particular works, but can also advance our understanding of the ways aging is represented and experienced in contemporary American society. In her study of aging in contemporary fiction and culture, Sylvia Henneberg has observed that literature can help us recognize aging not simply as a "personal drama" but as a "responsibility that requires certain kinds of action and certain kinds of art" (121). With this in mind, I argue here that both Roth and Bellow use the figure of the aging male protagonist in their later works to demonstrate how the experience of aging generates an increasing sense of responsibility to fashion creative testimonies. These testimonies—spoken, written, and performed—become personal and artistic legacies that serve a number of purposes, allowing each protagonist to reflect on his personal history, bear witness to lives of others, and come to terms with the realities of aging and mortality.

In this mutual focus on the creative impulses associated with old age, Roth and Bellow make a unique contribution to American letters. Many scholars within the field of age studies have repeatedly observed a longstanding tendency in American culture to either depict aging as a process of physical, emotional, and intellectual decline, or not depict it at all.[2] The later fiction of both Roth and Bellow, by contrast, presents us with protagonists who face the more complex physical, emotional, social, and gendered struggles that come with age. Neither author neglects the adverse effects of aging, as the creative acts in Bellow's *Ravelstein* and Roth's *Exit Ghost* and *The Humbling* are often triggered by some form of late-in-life crisis, a reaction to both physical ailments and an internalized ageism that leaves their characters feeling inferior and socially extraneous. Yet though both authors address (sometimes tragically, sometimes comically) the various pitfalls and disadvantages of growing old, they also locate in aging a newfound force of creativity that is spurred by the act of remembering, while it also stimulates self-discovery in each protagonist's life.

Although I have selected three works of fiction that I believe most particularly and clearly invite such a reading, it should be noted that both Roth and Bellow have engaged with the theme of aging in a number of their earlier novels as well. For instance, in *The Anatomy Lesson* (1983), *Sabbath's Theater* (1995), *The Dying Animal* (2001), and *Everyman* (2006) Roth develops protagonists who struggle with the various changes brought on by age, from the physical (arthritis, impotence, chronic back pain) to the social (declining careers) to the emotional (the death of loved ones) and intellectual (an increasing preoccupation with mortality). Likewise, in works such as *Mr. Sammler's Planet* (1970), *Humboldt's Gift* (1975), and *The Actual* (1997), Bellow also introduces aging characters who struggle to find their value in society. In fact, the image of what Bellow calls the "*homme d'hors usage*" ("man out of use") makes its way into more than one of his books, appearing first in *Sammler* and then again thirty years later in *Ravelstein*; in both cases, it is used by the protagonists themselves as a self-assessment. Thus, we might view the three works discussed in detail below as an even more integral part of the oeuvres of both Roth and Bellow, as they both echo themes taken up in earlier works while deepening their engagement with the intersection of age, identity, memory, and creative testimony.

Ravelstein, Bellow's final published novel, might actually be read in its entirety as an extended testimony to its fictional namesake.[3] Abe Ravelstein is a respected professor of philosophy, somewhere in his mid-sixties during the period of time covered by the novel, and, when we meet him, suffering through the later stages of AIDS—thus facing the social stigma and personal struggles of both aging and illness. Aware of his rapidly declining health and impending death, Ravelstein has charged the novel's narrator (who never formally introduces himself by name, but whom Ravelstein refers to simply as "Chick") with the task of writing his biography after he has died. In light of this, the novel becomes both a tale about the events leading up to Ravelstein's death and about Chick's role as biographer; likewise, it becomes not only a testimony to and about the life of Ravelstein, but

Chick's written testimony to his own life as well. It is a collaborative creative effort through which both men speak, and in which both men's personalities and personal struggles are rendered on the page.

As Chick notes, Ravelstein has never been wary of sharing his views and beliefs, yet as he speaks of himself to Chick later in life and especially during his illness, he finds in his own narrated testimony a new kind of purpose. Ravelstein continues to extemporize as he always has, reviewing his own life's experiences not as a means to dwell too long in the past, but to look toward the future—though this forward-looking dimension of his spoken testimony is often directed at Chick's future, rather than his own. That is, his oft-repeated maxims and reflections on everything from mortality ("Nothing is more bourgeois than a fear of death," he instructs Chick (4)) to individualism ("You must not be swallowed up by the history of your own time," he says (82)) are designed to be enlightening and instructive to his friend and biographer, who Ravelstein knows will live on after he is gone. In the same light, Ravelstein's request that Chick write his biography after he has died is not self-serving, but part of the responsibility he feels to continue to be present in some way for his friend, even after his death.

Still, Ravelstein himself finds his spoken testament to his own life to be personally beneficial as well, as it allows him to use his past experiences to reflect on his present self. While the novel depicts its subject's physical decline in the wake of his illness, it simultaneously emphasizes his intellectual enthusiasm, mental acuity, and ongoing desire for self-discovery. In this way, despite the constant allusions to death, the tone of the narrative is rarely grim (a detail which, despite other similarities between the authors' late fiction, sets *Ravelstein* apart from some of Roth's later work, including *Everyman* and *The Humbling* in particular). As his health declines, for instance, Ravelstein becomes increasingly preoccupied with the definition and manifestation of love, telling Chick "over and over again what love was—the neediness, the awareness of incompleteness, the longing for wholeness" (95). Ravelstein himself admits that he "would never have expected death to be such a weird aphrodisiac," and seems almost bemused by the fact that his illness, accelerated by his advanced age and ravaging his body, still manages to teach him more about himself (143). Thus, Ravelstein's contribution to this collaborative narrative is regenerative in that it allows him to tap into new understandings of his own life and articulate his own beliefs, while it also provides him with a purpose beyond himself, as he feels it to be increasingly necessary to share his beliefs and experiences with Chick.

As readers, however, we also know that Ravelstein's words are coming from beyond the grave, and that it is Chick who is retelling his story and, in a way, appropriating the voice of Ravelstein. In doing this, Chick is simultaneously narrating his own life and identity through this remembered relationship with his friend and mentor, his recollections of Ravelstein almost always triggering some form of self-reflection. His act of creativity, then, becomes not only one that honors Ravelstein, but that allows him to look inward and bear witness to his own life. Even more significantly, perhaps, is the fact that the biography he has been commissioned to write eventually becomes a life-sustaining task. During a vacation with his wife after Ravelstein's death, Chick falls victim to a near-fatal infection, but even at death's door, he says, "I seemed to believe that I wouldn't die because I still had things to do. Ravelstein expected me to make good on my promise to write the memoir he had commissioned. To keep my word, I'd have to live" (221–22). *Ravelstein* thus makes the narrating or preservation of another's memory through creative testimony a driving force behind the will to live, a theme that notably also runs through some of Roth's later work. In a study of Roth's *Sabbath's Theater*, for instance, Jay Halio argues that protagonist Mickey Sabbath, who has been considering suicide, finds it impossible to take his own life once he "has made himself custodian" of his late brother's belongings (203). In much the same way, Chick finds himself unable to surrender to his illness, having also made himself "custodian" of Ravelstein's life through the promise to write his memoir.

In addition to the testaments they feel compelled to make about their own lives, both Chick and Ravelstein also feel bound to direct their testimony outward as well. Specifically, the men feel an increasing responsibility to bear witness to their Jewish history and identity, and the testimony that they (and Bellow) turn into a narrative art is one that remembers and honors the victims of the Holocaust. As Chick and Ravelstein become increasingly focused on the brevity of life and the nearness of death, they struggle to position their own individual mortalities within a century that saw millions of Jews die in the Holocaust. Their ongoing conversations on this point provide material for Chick's biography of Ravelstein, while also serving as a reflective exercise for both men, with the result that they are able to fashion a spoken and written narrative that bears witness to the victims of the Holocaust and also reflects on the meaning of that tragedy in their own lives. What both men discover in this endeavor is that "it is impossible to get rid of one's origins, it is impossible not to remain a Jew," for as Jews they "were historically witnesses to the absence of redemption" (179). This realization becomes particularly significant in light of the fact that throughout his life Ravelstein has continually instructed his students to forget their origins: He himself "had hated and shaken off his own family" and encouraged his protégés to do the same (26). Nevertheless, as Chick says, "in his last days it was the Jews he wanted to talk about" (173). Ravelstein's desire to acknowledge his place among his Jewish people, of which he and Chick are, as he says, "the remainder," is indicative of a personal change that occurs not in spite of but because of the combination of illness and aging, which brings with it this new sense of responsibility (174).

Finally, Chick's act of writing Ravelstein's biography also becomes an artistic legacy for both men, delivering to its subject and its author some form of immortality. The biography provides a means for remembering Ravelstein while also ensuring that he will continue to live through the text and its readers; it affirms Chick's assertion that "the flesh would shrink and go, the blood would dry, but no one believes in his mind of minds or heart of hearts that the pictures *do* stop" (223). The pictures of which Chick speaks are, in one sense, memories of Ravelstein replayed over and over in his mind, but, translated more permanently onto the page, they become a testimony to the life of his friend, a comment on the struggles and strivings of aging, and an affirmation of narrative as a means for coming to terms with the past, present, and future.

Like *Ravelstein*, Roth's *Exit Ghost* depicts a creative act as playing a central role in the ongoing self-discovery in the midst of aging and its attendant struggles. *Exit Ghost* is the final installment in Roth's series of novels featuring Nathan Zuckerman, who, after being briefly introduced in a slightly different guise in *My Life as a Man* (1974), appeared as a central character in *The Ghost Writer*, *The Anatomy Lesson*, and *Zuckerman Unbound*, and then as a narrator of the novels now grouped together as Roth's American Trilogy. All of these works have, in some way or another, dealt with the themes of aging and the impulse to tell a story. *Exit Ghost*, however, functions as a unique capstone to Zuckerman's literary life, largely because we discover in the end that it is meant to be his "swan song"—his final performance before taking leave of Roth's canon. Zuckerman himself knows this, and tells the reader as much: "I'm working here as rapidly as I can while I can," he says, noting that his own fictional work in *Exit Ghost* "will likely be my last attempt to persist in groping for words to combine into the sentences and paragraphs of a book" (159). By infusing its protagonist with this awareness, *Exit Ghost* emphasizes both the deliberateness with which Zuckerman looks back over his life as well as the urgency he feels to move forward with his "last attempt" at a creative testimony.

Though it addresses some of the positive results of this late-life creative impulse, *Exit Ghost* does not evade the realities of aging. Zuckerman has long defined himself by the physical and sexual aspects of his masculinity, and by his abilities as a writer; now well into his seventies and facing the declining health of old age, all of these aspects of his personality seem to him to have been compromised by his advancing years. He is particularly concerned about his deteriorating memory, which he views as integral to his ability to write. "If one morning I should pick up the page I'd written the day before and find myself unable to remember having written it, what would I do?" he asks himself. "If I lost touch with my pages, if I could neither write a book nor read one, what would become of me? Without my work, what would be left of me?" (106). He envisions "something diabolical" residing in his brain, slowly accomplishing its "gleeful goal to turn someone whose acuity as a writer was sustained by memory and verbal precision into a pointless man" (159). Yet rather than abandoning his craft altogether for this loss, Zuckerman turns this fear into an impetus for a creative act. In doing so, Zuckerman essentially writes himself and his anxieties onto the page, further merging himself with his work in a way that defies his own fear of losing touch with his pages.

Zuckerman's creative journey begins with an impulsive decision to move from his remote home in the Berkshires back to New York City. Though he has kept up with his writing in his country home, a trip to the city for a doctor's appointment shakes him out of the calm but somewhat restless routine his life had assumed. On one hand, returning to the city makes Zuckerman feel his age more than ever, forcing him to question a talent he feels to be waning. Yet instead of submitting to his insecurity, Zuckerman channels this into a budding act of narrative creativity:

> All the city would add was everything I'd determined I no longer had use for: Here and Now. Here and Now. Then and Now. The Beginning and the End of Now. These were the lines that I jotted onto the scrap of paper. . . . Titles for something. Perhaps this. . . . A book about knowing where to go for your agony and then going there for it. (41)

Essentially, Zuckerman is able to move forward by looking backward, his return to the city and the ensuing encounters with his past (described in more detail below) prompting him to lament the loss of his youth, but also work to weave the reality of his age and experience into his present identity. Zuckerman's decision to move back to New York City is solidified by two discoveries that also fuse the past and present in this way: He meets a young writer who plans to pen a scandalous biography of E. I. Lonoff, one of his literary influences, and he unexpectedly crosses paths with Lonoff's former protégé and lover Amy Bellette, who is now as old as Zuckerman and dying of a brain tumor. Both Amy and Lonoff played central roles in *The Ghost Writer*, and in reconnecting with them both in different ways, Zuckerman finds himself "precipitously stepping into a new future" that requires a looking back to the past—a phenomenon that Zuckerman deems a "retrograde trajectory" (52).

This trajectory not only defines Zuckerman's final work, but also defines *Exit Ghost* itself, as Roth looks ahead to a future of writing without Zuckerman, though not before he looks back to Zuckerman's past. In other words, the creative endeavors represented in and by *Exit Ghost* operate on two levels. On the narrative level, Zuckerman is the author of his own creative testimony, channeling his nostalgia for youth and his preoccupation with his mortality into a brand new work of fiction. This narrative, a play that is revealed in bits and pieces throughout the novel, is based on Zuckerman's encounters with Jamie Logan, from whom he has chosen to sublet an apartment in New York and with whom he has become smitten. Entitled *He and She*, the play is in part a lament for the lost sexual and physical abilities of his younger self, as his desire for Jamie calls attention to their age difference, and his present impotence in particular. While in this sense *He and She* is an expression of frustration over the physical decline of age, it also allows Zuckerman to unearth aspects of his identity that he had not previously been able to articulate. These insights themselves are not always cheering, but as new realizations they highlight the ways that a creative endeavor can increase one's understanding of the process of aging. Zuckerman himself comments on this fact, acknowledging that penning this play allows him to discover new aspects of himself:

I was learning at seventy-one what it is to be deranged. Proving that self-discovery wasn't over after all. Proving that the drama that is associated usually with the young as they fully begin to enter life . . . can also startle and lay siege to the aged (including the aged resolutely armed against *all* drama), even as circumstance readies them for departure. (123)

Though darkly humorous, this reflection is also what Roth might call "deadly serious."[4] That is, though Zuckerman exaggeratedly points to himself as "deranged," he is only half joking: In pointing to himself as such, he is acknowledging a sudden feeling that he no longer knows himself—that new discoveries about life and his desires are, in fact, still possible. It is only through the act of writing this play, for instance, that Zuckerman can admit that he had holed himself up in the Berkshires largely "to escape the pain of being present," a revelation that highlights the ongoing potential and accomplishment of his creative resurgence (137). As Zuckerman himself muses, "Maybe the most potent discoveries are reserved for last" (123).

On another level, in which Zuckerman is not an author in his own right but an imagined part of Roth's creative endeavor, both author and protagonist look to the past together, simultaneously referencing Zuckerman's fictional past and Roth's previously published novel, *The Ghost Writer*. A particularly notable facet of this self-referential style is that it allows Roth to allude to Zuckerman's past struggles with his Jewish American identity and to imbue Zuckerman with the ability to reflect on the role this plays in his current life. Just as Bellow depicts Chick and Ravelstein searching for a way to acknowledge the tragedy of the Holocaust as an integral part of their Jewish identities, Roth invokes the Holocaust in *Exit Ghost* by reintroducing the character of Amy Bellette. In *The Ghost Writer*, Roth had Zuckerman craft an extended fantasy in which Amy was actually Anne Frank, alive, grown up, and in disguise. In this invention, Zuckerman also envisioned himself marrying Amy/Anne, and thus his reimagining of Anne Frank (perhaps the most recognizable victim of the Holocaust) becomes his way of both bearing witness to those whose suffering he has inherited and of enacting a responsibility to his Jewish history. To meet Amy again in *Exit Ghost*, then, is to call up the memories of this fantasy and all of the conflicted attitudes towards his Jewish family and identity he bore at the time.[5] This in turn prompts him to reflect on his Jewish identity in the present, at which point, as he says, "the moral imperatives pressed upon me then by eminent elders of the Jewish community" had "long since disappeared" (170). Yet at the same time, the years of experience that separate him from his younger self also allow Zuckerman to fashion a more poignant and meaningful testimony not only to his own life but to Amy's history as well, which as it turns out is not all that different from Anne Frank's. As Amy reveals in *Exit Ghost*, she too was forced into hiding during Nazi raids in Norway, and while she eventually escaped, her parents did not. "Now, I understand," he says to Amy after she finishes recounting this history, a statement that refers to his better grasp of her life and her suffering, as well as to his own role in her life, namely his imperative to bear witness to her suffering by documenting her story—which he does, immediately writing it down after their meeting (193).

Aimee Pozorski has called Zuckerman a "character perpetually in mourning," one who is constantly "looking back to that which is lost in the past" while he also "looks forward to anticipate . . . a loss that is yet to come" (155–56). While *Exit Ghost* is most certainly and explicitly about past and potential loss, I would add that is also about the perpetual opportunity—and the sense of responsibility—to turn that loss into an act of creativity that affirms a life that has been lived. Zuckerman counts himself among the "very, very few" for whom "fictional amplification" of experience can be a positive phenomenon rather than an act that merely augments one's personal pain. For these few, fiction "constitutes their only assurance, and the unlived, the surmise, fully drawn in print on paper, is the life whose meaning comes to matter most" (147).

In *The Humbling*, published just two years after *Exit Ghost*, Roth once again engages an aging male protagonist to represent aging's attendant imperative to fashion a testimony to the past as a way to come to terms with the realities of the present. Like his earlier novel and Bellow's *Ravelstein*, Roth's treatment of aging recognizes physical decline and emotional crises, while it also emphasizes the potential of a creative act to foster ongoing self-discovery in old age. *The Humbling*, however, which narrates Simon Axler's struggle to face a loss of identity that he himself associates with aging, is a much darker tale than those earlier novels. Axler's creative endeavor is more self-serving than that of Ravelstein, Chick, or Zuckerman, lacking the same awareness of and testament to the lives of others found in those earlier narratives. Moreover, it is on the whole more difficult to locate the positive tenor of his artistic endeavor, which ultimately ends in suicide. Nevertheless, Axler's brief foray into a new and controversial kind of performance art does allow him, albeit temporarily, to blend his past life with a briefly hopeful vision of the future.

When we meet Axler, he is in the midst of a late-life crisis and nervous breakdown. A renowned stage actor for most of his life, Axler suddenly finds himself unable to practice the art that has sustained him, and refuses to perform on stage, feeling he has "lost his magic" (1). His agent Jerry, in an attempt to bring his client back into the world of theater, has encouraged Axler to immerse himself in the scripts that had always proven to be "liberating" for the actor, in the hopes that they will provide him with the inspiration and motivation he needs to return. This, however, is done to no avail. Rather than returning to the theater, Axler instead crafts a whole new, far more private, and certainly more problematic theater within his relationship with Pegeen Stapleford, the much younger daughter of an old friend, who allows him to temporarily reclaim some of his "magic."

In this new and different creative avenue, Axler does find a temporary liberation, a respite from what he perceives to be the trappings of old age. Despite the fact that for most of her adult life Pegeen has identified as a lesbian, she decides to embark on a sexual relationship with Axler soon after they reconnect. In doing so, she provides him with an outlet to tap into his past career and his past self, allowing him to act out his desire for youthfulness, renewed purpose, and success, while also making her into the character that is necessary for such an act. In the first bit of collaborative performance between both Pegeen and Axler, for instance, Pegeen permits Axler to dress her up to "be a woman he would want instead of a woman another woman would want," in order to foster his visions of embarking on a new life with Pegeen, getting married and starting a family, and then returning triumphantly to the stage (65). During the course of their relationship, Axler fashions Pegeen into a canvas onto which he can paint his deepest desires—some of which are sexual, but many of which are both nostalgic and ambitious; Axler is thrilled and reinvigorated, for example, at the prospect of being able to return to his acting while also developing his art by being the director of this private play.[6]

Yet Axler's shaping of Pegeen into a figure that best suits his own needs, even as it occurs with her permission, is problematic and in large part superficial. Axler cuts Pegeen's hair and buys her new clothes, but each phase of Pegeen's transformation seems only to point more directly to their relationship as an artful fiction. Indeed, Axler himself recognizes as much, noting that his actions have served largely to "dig himself deeper into an unreal world" (126) and wonders whether he isn't "distorting [Pegeen] while telling himself a lie—and a lie that in the end might be anything but harmless" (66). In the end, even Pegeen finally refuses to be a "substitute" for Axler's acting, and leaves him— a loss that he has, in fact, been anticipating throughout the novel (128). Feeling as though he is left with nothing, and recognizing the inherent faults of this performed relationship, Axler finally commits suicide, blaming not Pegeen but rather "the bewildering biography on which he was impaled" (138).

In its depiction of Axler's disturbing suicide, *The Humbling* (unlike *Ravelstein* and *Exit Ghost*) explores the more extreme repercussions of a creative endeavor that, while temporarily recuperative, eventually goes awry. At the same time, the tragedy and hopelessness suggested by this conclusion prompts us to question what purpose Axler's performances with and through Pegeen have served. After all, it would seem that Axler's project has failed, as he cannot reconcile his performance with his lived reality. Yet Roth's point in *The Humbling* has never been that a creative act must be exuberant; rather, as he suggested in *Exit Ghost* and as Bellow made explicit in *Ravelstein*, any creative act that forces one to come to terms with age and mortality is necessarily difficult. Moreover, what further ties this novel to *Ravelstein* and *Exit Ghost* is Roth's ongoing investment in the idea that with aging comes an increased urgency to use art as a way to form a testament life and to come to terms with death. Significantly, Axler is finally able to follow through on his plan to commit suicide only by envisioning this act as his final performance, one that "would constitute his return to acting." In order to "succeed one last time to make the imagined real," he must envision that he is the stage, playing the lead in Chekhov's *The Seagull*—the role that made him famous (139). Thus, his performance art becomes a vehicle for mourning and remembering the past, a tool for attempting to alter the trajectory of his present life, and a revelation that allows him to finally face death—however controversial that confrontation might be.

Though the manifestations and outcomes of the artistic endeavors across these novels vary, they each represent both Roth and Bellow's mutual investment in the idea that creative testimony plays an integral role in the way individuals experience aging and attempt to come to grips with mortality. Indeed, considering the fact that *Ravelstein* was published when Bellow was eighty-five, and that *Exit Ghost* and *The Humbling* were published when Roth was seventy-four and seventy-six respectively, the very novels themselves stand as further evidence of this investment, with the authors' own creative endeavors seemingly reflected in and by their protagonists. In fact, on the subject of his long career and the act of writing into old age, Roth said in a recent interview that writing fiction "fosters endurance," as it "requires the sort of fortitude that keeps one going" ("Age Makes a Difference"). On the whole, the fictional lives of Roth and Bellow's characters invoke a similar message, as each protagonist finds in his art a "sort of fortitude" that allows him to fashion testimonies out of the past, contemplate the realities of the present, and face the future, each in his own way.

Notes

1. In an exception to this trend, Norman Podhortetz has placed the late works of Roth and Bellow in conversation, but has done so by focusing on Bellow's *Ravelstein* and Roth's *The Human Stain*. Otherwise, studies of age in these later works, while insightful, have focused on one author or one work: Elaine Safer examines aging as isolation through a focus on the black humor in *Exit Ghost* and *The Humbling*, Matthew Shipe has read *Exit Ghost* as "an extended meditation" on Edward Said's theory of late style (193), and Sarah Blacher Cohen has focused on the humor in Ravelstein, particularly the novel's "laughter about death" (48).

2. Margaret Morganroth Gullette (one of the pioneers of age studies) argues that in twentieth century literature, "a host of characters in their forties or fifties or in some vague middle age began to appear and simultaneously decay" (27). Henneberg, along with fellow feminist and age studies scholars Kathleen Woodward, Ann Wyatt-Brown, and Barbara Frey Waxman, has emphasized that positive representations of aging women in particular are most absent in culture. In a separate study, however, Toni Calasanti and Neal King have also observed a noticeable absence of the studies of the ways in which aging affects representations of masculinity as well. "Few studies," they claim, "examine old men as men" (4).

3. It may also be read as a possible testimony to the life of Allan Bloom, a philosopher and close friend of Bellow's, on whom many believe the character of Ravelstein to be based.

4. In a 1974 interview with Joyce Carol Oates, Roth somewhat famously remarked, "Sheer Playfulness and Deadly Seriousness are my closest friends" ("A Conversation" 98).

5. In *The Ghost Writer*, Zuckerman fights against having his Jewishness understood or identified through the tragedy of the Holocaust; at the same time, however, he notes that Lonoff's work "had done more to make me realize how much I was still my family's Jewish offspring than anything," observing that "the pride inspired in my parents by the establishment in 1948 of a homeland in Palestine that would gather in the unmurdered remnant of European Jewry was, in fact, not so unlike what welled up in me when I first came upon Lonoff's thwarted, secretive, imprisoned souls" (12).

6. Axler himself refers to his life with Pegeen as a performance. For example, in chapter 3, entitled fittingly "The Last Act," Axler engages in a ménage a trois with Pegeen and another woman, described as follows: "'Three children got together', he said, 'and decided to put on a play,' whereupon his performance began" (114).

Works Cited

Bellow, Saul. *Mr. Sammler's Planet*. New York: Viking, 1970. Print.

___. *Ravelstein*. New York: Viking, 2000. Print.

Calasanti, Toni, and Neal King. "Firming the Floppy Penis: Age, Gender, and Class Relations in the Lives of Old Men." *Men and Masculinities* 8.3 (2005): 3–23. Print.

Cohen, Sarah Blacher. "Saul Bellow's *Ravelstein* and the Graying of American Humor." *Saul Bellow Journal* 18.2 (Fall 2002): 40–49. Print.

Gullette, Margaret Morganroth. "Creativity, Aging, and Gender: A Study of Their Intersections, 1910–1935." *Aging and Gender in Literature: Studies in Creativity*. Ed. Anne M. Wyatt-Brown and Janice Rossen. Charlottesville: UP of Virginia, 1993. 19–48. Print.

Halio, Jay L. "Eros and Death in Roth's Later Fiction." *Turning Up the Flame: Philip Roth's Later Novels*. Ed. Halio and Ben Siegel. Newark: U of Delaware P, 2005. 200–206. Print.

Henneberg Sylvia. "Of Creative Crones and Poetry: Developing Age Studies through Literature." *NWSA Journal* 18 (Spring 2006): 106–25. Print.

Pozorski, Aimee L. "Mourning Zuckerman: An Introduction." *Philip Roth Studies* 5.2 (Fall 2009): 155–62. Print.

Roth, Philip. "Age Makes a Difference." Interview by Hermione Lee. *New Yorker*. Condé Nast, 1 Oct. 2007. Web. 4 Jan. 2012.

___. "A Conversation with Philip Roth." Interview by Joyce Carol Oates. 1974. *Conversations with Philip Roth*. Ed. George J. Searles. Jackson: UP of Mississippi, 1992. 89–99. Print.

___. *Exit Ghost*. Boston: Houghton, 2007. Print.

___. *Everyman*. Boston: Houghton, 2006. Print.

___. *The Ghost Writer*. New York: Farrar, 1979. Print.

___. *The Humbling*. Boston: Houghton, 2009. Print.

Safer, Elaine. "Alienation and Black Humor in Philip Roth's *Exit Ghost*." *Studies in American Jewish Literature* 29 (2010): 139–47. Print.

___. "Philip Roth's *The Humbling*: Loneliness and Mortality in the Later Work." *Studies in American Jewish Literature* 30 (2011): 40–46. Print.

Shipe, Matthew. "*Exit Ghost* and the Politics of Late Style." *Philip Roth Studies* 5.2 (2009): 189–204. Print.

Waxman, Barbara Frey. "Literary Texts and Literary Critics Team Up against Ageism." *A Guide to Humanistic Studies in Aging*. Ed. Thomas R. Cole, Ruth E. Ray, and Robert Kastenbaum. Baltimore: Johns Hopkins UP, 2010. 83–104. Print.

Woodward, Kathleen. "Performing Age, Performing Gender." *NWSA Journal* 18 (Spring 2006): 162–89. Print.

Wyatt-Brown, Anne M. "Introduction: Aging, Gender, and Creativity." *Aging and Gender in Literature: Studies in Creativity*. Ed. Wyatt-Brown and Janice Rossen. 1–15. Print.

CRITICAL
READINGS

"To Rake Suburban Life over the Barbecue Coals": Cultural Criticism in Philip Roth's Early Fiction and Journalism_____

Patrick Hayes

Philip Roth started to emerge as a distinctive new voice in the late 1950s, and like any ambitious young writer of that time, he was keen to assert his intellectual credentials. Among the barrage of short pieces he was submitting for publication was a short autobiographical skit entitled simply (and audaciously—Roth only had three short stories in print) "The Kind of Person I Am," sent to the *New Yorker*, playfully describing his life as doctoral student at the University of Chicago. Roth's graduate thesis was on the fiction of Henry James, and in the opening scene of the article we are given a Jamesian description of a disturbing encounter at a party in which Roth finds himself in conversation with "a lean, intelligent-looking young woman" who seems to see right through him:

> "Do you teach at the University?" she asked.
> "Yes." I sipped off the top of my drink.
> "English," she said.
> "Yes."
> "Do you write?" she asked.
> "Yes, I do."
> "But unpublished," she said.
> I smiled. "For the most part."
> "A story in a little magazine here and there."
> "That's right, as a matter of fact," I said.

None of this seemed to me particularly uncanny. Almost everyone at the party was on the English staff of the University, and as for writing, I suppose I look as much like a writer with little-magazine affiliations as anything else.

She was staring at my clothes. "Read the *Partisan Review*, don't you?" she said.

"Why, yes, I do." Had she gleaned that from my black trousers? My brown sports jacket?

"I don't subscribe," I added.

"Of course not." ("Kind" 175)

The chilling thought that there "must be dozens and dozens of young men just like myself" riles him, so much so that back in his room later that night he can't concentrate on his undergraduate marking. He starts flipping through an anthology with the rather austere name of *Essays Today 3*, and he stops at a piece by Herbert Gold entitled "This Age of Happy Problems"—his "attention caught by the paradoxical phrase."[1] The phrase refers to an America greatly enriched by the postwar economic boom, in which the unhappy problems of mass unemployment and poverty are increasingly distant memories from the 1930s, so much so that "even the cultural élite," Gold is quoted as saying, "labors among the latest in hi-fi equipment, trips to Acapulco and Paris, the right books in the sewn paper editions (Elizabeth Bowen, Arnold Toynbee, Jacques Barzun—these are the cultivated ones, remember) *Fortune* and the *Reporter*, art movies and the barbeque pit" ("Kind" 174). As he reads this, Roth realizes that not only has he been to Paris twice (though never to Acapulco) but that in his room is a hi-fi, many of the "right books," and a copy of the *Reporter*. In a moment of panic, he gathers up all his old copies of the *Reporter* and the *Partisan Review* and puts them outside the door for the janitor to take away. "Let him be a member of the cultural élite," Roth exclaims. But the tone of the article is decidedly light-hearted, and through a series of well-executed comic turns, Roth concludes by explaining that, after all, it is simply impossible to avoid being a type: "There simply was no escape from being some kind of person, damn it!" And if this is so, the conclusion runs, you might as well be the best type of all. So in the end, Roth rather smugly reconciles himself to being the kind of person he already is: He goes to the bookstore and buys the *Times Literary Supplement* and defiantly carries it home "with the cover out."

The young Philip Roth was clearly very self-conscious about "The Kind of Person I Am," and these references to periodicals such as *Partisan Review* identify him in very particular ways with a cultural formation known as the New Liberalism, a term that was used to encompass a diverse range of intellectuals, including historians such as Arthur M. Schlesinger Jr., theologians such as Reinhold Niebuhr, and a variety of figures who spanned different roles as public intellectuals and literary critics, such as Philip Rahv, Irving Howe, Lionel Trilling, and Alfred Kazin, among many others. United more by a common enemy than by any shared definition of a common cause, this group of intellectuals shared disenchantment with the Marxist Left (the "Old Liberalism") and a resolve that there should be new styles of cultural analysis and new concepts of literary value more appropriate to affluent postwar America. The crystallizing moment was the "Our Country, Our Culture" symposium held by (and published within) *Partisan Review* itself in 1952 to explore why the aims of intellectuals in this period had changed. Philip Rahv, editor of the journal at the time, spoke for many in identifying the principle factor as the "exposure of the Soviet myth and the consequent resolve (shared by nearly all but the few remaining fellow travelers) to be done with Utopian illusions and heady expectations" (Phillips 304).

Richard Pells has summarized the broad change of agenda among American intellectuals as follows:

No longer awaiting the inevitable collapse of capitalism or the revolutionary fury of the working class, they began to assess the moral impact of mass consumption and material success. Less haunted than the prewar generation by the specters of unemployment and economic disintegration, they evaluated the uses of leisure time, the manipulative effects of advertising and popular culture, the quality of human relationships in an age of affluence. (186)

Instead of a focus on class struggle and political transformation informed by "Utopian illusions and heady expectations," New Liberalism privileged the discourse of ethics over politics and the achievement of a resistant maturity over social upheaval.

At the outset of his career, Philip Roth was this kind of person: a liberal intellectual in an age of happy problems. He was also keenly interested in scrutinizing the "moral impact of mass consumption and material success" and in cultivating a resistant form of subjectivity. Later in his life, the light-hearted tone of his self-deprecating analysis of what it means to be a member of this particular "cultural élite" began to turn into a truly self-lacerating mockery directed at what the nineteenth-century German philosopher Friedrich Nietzsche described as the "culture-philistine" (22)—the intellectual who uses art as a means for fake spiritual elevation and moral accreditation. But this essay will explore the ways in which his earliest work was deeply influenced by the ethical concern characteristic of New Liberalism across several experiences specific to postwar American life: the spiritual quality of suburbia, the character styles promoted by a postindustrial consumer culture, the manipulations of the culture industry, and, above all, the ways in which literature can help to cultivate a sense of resistant value in such a society.

Between June and December 1957, when he was teaching at the University of Chicago and starting to write the stories that would be compiled in *Goodbye, Columbus*, Roth published eight short review articles in the *New Republic* and the *Chicago Review* on subjects ranging from Hollywood films and television programs to the Miss America Pageant and President Dwight D. Eisenhower at prayer. They feature him sharpening his considerable wit while trying to make a name for himself as a young intellectual to be reckoned with. All this is on display in "Positive Thinking on Pennsylvania Avenue," which begins by quoting Eisenhower's bedtime prayer, as told to the national press by his wife Mamie:

Lord, I want to thank You for helping me today. You really stuck by me. I know, Lord, that I muffed a few and I'm sorry about that. But both the ones we did all right and the ones we muffed I am turning them all over to You. You take over from here. Good night, Lord, I'm going to sleep. (21)

Roth has been a lifelong Democrat and canvassed door to door for Adlai Stevenson. Yet what engages him here is not politics but ethics—the quality of self that the Eisenhower regime promotes and that the President embodies. The shallowness of Eisenhower's prayer is contrasted to the "man of deep religious conscience and conviction" who "traditionally speaks to his God with words of awe, love, fear, and wonder." And with the spiritual stakes raised so high, Eisenhower's chummy American faith is naturally found wanting: "The President's tone is clear," Roth suggests, "if one were to substitute the word 'James' for 'Lord' one might hear the voice of a man calling not to his God, but to his valet. 'I have polished my left shoe, James. As for the right, well—you take over from here'" (21–22).

Compare "Positive Thinking on Pennsylvania Avenue" to another essay of the same year, "The Hurdles of Satire." While ostensibly a review of the popular 1950s weekly television comedy show called *Caesar's Hour*, Roth continues to attack the low quality of experience in America, but on much broader terrain. By the mid-1950s, television had entrenched itself as the dominant national medium, but its colonization of the American home had for Roth only created a new kind of problem: Television, he argues here, has essentially the same kind of soporific effect on American culture as does the religion of positive thinking evident in Eisenhower's bedtime prayer. It is unable to offer any kind of enlivening critical provocation to a "mass audience," for that audience is likely to have become so "committed—or addicted" to the subject of the satire that they will either ignore it or take offence: "Woe unto the satirist, then, who passes judgment, for he is apt to find the bulk of his viewers divided into two groups: the unamused, who recognize the subject but don't get the point of it; and, what is more expensive to the comic's sponsor, the people who get offended" (22).

The "true subjects of satire for a mass audience," Roth claims, must therefore be "the things that contribute to its massness," which include "advertising, the movie and TV heroes, the newspapers," alongside other emblems of the new affluence, such as the split-level homes the masses live in, their work routines, and the products they consume (22). To be effective, though, satire must be intellectually sharp, and this is where Roth's criticism of the Sid Caesar and Janet Blair double act comes in. Their skit on the subject of commuting has been a failure, he believes, not only because they have been cowed by the commercial pressures inherent to the medium itself, but because they haven't read the right books:

> Rarely, if ever, did the Caesar-Blair home resemble the suburbia that David Riesman, William H. Whyte, *et al*. tell us is there. It would in fact be what Sullivan calls "a television first" if Miss Coca and Caesar retained "The Commuter" idea and then when ahead to rake suburban life over the barbecue coals. This, of course, would be satire, and though Miss Coca and Caesar are, I think, at their best as satirists, I wonder if they would risk it. (22)

Sid Caesar's attempt to "rake suburban life over the barbeque coals" falls short because he is uninformed by the latest and most penetrating sociological critiques of the moral and spiritual condition of suburbia—namely "David Riesman, William H. Whyte, *et al.*"

David Riesman was a sociologist best known for *The Lonely Crowd: A Study of the Changing American Character* (1950), and Whyte was an organizational analyst and journalist whose best-selling *The Organization Man* (1956) painted a disturbing picture of the increasingly bureaucratic nature of American corporate life. In his volume of memoirs about the changing intellectual life of postwar America, Irving Howe recalled that Riesman was "the most influential register of intellectual sentiment" in New York of the 1950s (*Margin* 173), and Howe believed this was because of the part Riesman played in articulating and reinforcing the more general desire among American intellectuals to find new ways of exploring the deficiencies of the "age of happy problems." As Riesman himself put it in his preface to the 1961 edition of his text, it simply seemed archaic "to interpret what was wrong" by way of a "Marxist class-analysis" (vi); instead, his analysis explored the declining quality of self that postwar American culture seemed able to sustain. Riesman's post-Marxist sociology was particularly important for the early Roth, and it is worth considering in some depth.

The argument of *The Lonely Crowd* was based on a recognition that between the 1920s and the 1940s, major segments of the American economy had begun to reach a distinctively postindustrial phase, in which the main architecture of advanced capitalist production (the production plant, the accumulated capital) was well-established, leading to a condition in which "fewer and fewer people work on the land or in the extractive industries or even in manufacturing," and more and more grow up with "material abundance and leisure besides"—in fact, Riesman spoke of the "two thirds of 'overprivileged' Americans" (18) as being the focus of his study. The cultural consequence of this shift from a rapidly expanding industrial economy, or an "age of production," to a postindustrial economy, or "age of consumption," was a correlative shift in what Riesman called the "social character." Riesman borrowed the concept of social character from Frankfurt School social psychologist Erich Fromm: "In order that any society may function well," Fromm had argued, "its members must acquire the kind of character which makes them want to act in the way they have to act as members of the society or of a special class within it. They have to desire what objectively is necessary for them to do" (qtd. in Riesman, *Lonely Crowd* 5).[2]

Applying this to the United States, Riesman argued that the rapidly expanding industrial economy of the age of production, which reached its peak in the nineteenth century, had in the past tended to create an "inner-directed" character type, which he defines as "the typical character of the 'old' middle-class—the banker, the tradesman, the small entrepreneur" (21). This kind of social character is an immediately recognizable feature of Roth's novella *Goodbye, Columbus*, where he portrays the inner-directed type in the form of Mr. Patimkin, the gruff but kindly patriarch. A self-made man, Mr. Patimkin has built up Patimkin Sinks and Kitchens out of nothing, and Roth emphasizes that his pioneering labor has created the very fabric of modern America— not without irony we are told that Patimkin provides merchandise lines for the washrooms of the Lamont Library at Harvard University (103). Quite unlike his daughter Brenda, who embodies the newer and much more ominous "other-directed" social character, Mr. Patimkin came to maturity in urban Newark during the 1920s in a poor family (unlike his wife, he still carries around the coarse manners acquired in the inner city), and along with others like him would have experienced childhood as, to use Riesman's words, "a period of deprivation and hardship which leads to compensatory dreams of a life of ease and leisure" (79). He would also have been required, especially by the strong authority of his mother and father, to internalize certain core values important for success in an "age of production," and in an emotional moment at his warehouse, with both his son Ron and what he imagines to be his future son-in-law Neil beside him, Mr. Patimkin gives voice to his inner light:

> Mr. Patimkin looked at his cigar. "A man works hard he's got something. You don't get anywhere sitting on your behind, you know. . . The biggest men in the country worked hard, believe me. Even Rockefeller. Success don't come easy . . ." He did not say this so much as he mused it out while he surveyed his dominion. (74)

In *Goodbye, Columbus* there is a semi-satirical, but nonetheless nostalgic, remembrance of this increasingly outdated character type in the very title of the novella. According to Riesman, American schoolchildren in Mr. Patimkin's day would have been required to memorize poems like Joaquin Miller's "Columbus" (1912), which celebrates the great explorer's pursuit of his inner gleam even when his crew begs him to turn back. "Sail on! sail on! and on!" Columbus is urged, and the poem portrays the cautious crew's reluctance to follow Columbus's inspired leadership as cowardly. Roth's first novella satirizes a society in the process of waving goodbye to the metaphorical Columbus rather than cheering him on, for it is an America becoming dominated by what Riesman defined as new "other-directed" forms of social character.

Brenda Patimkin is a common example of this new character type, so much so that it is as if Roth took Lionel Trilling's suggestion that Riesman's sociology did "literature a service by suggesting to the novelist that there are new and wonderfully arable social fields for them to till" (Trilling, *Gathering* 86). Unlike her father, Brenda's childhood would not have been "subjected to a period of hardship and deprivation," for she grew up surrounded by "gold dinnerware, sporting-goods trees, nectarines, garbage disposals, bumpless noses, Patimkin sinks, [and clothing store] Bonwit Teller," learning how to be a good consumer. The consumer society, Riesman argued, is driven by new ideological needs: to create an expanding domestic market for consumption rather than to pioneer new industrial technology and for a workforce more attuned to working in concert with other people in large and complex bureaucratic corporations. Such a society instills, in manifold subconscious ways, a different kind of social character:

> What is common to all other-directeds is that their contemporaries are the source of direction for the individual—either those known to him or those with whom he is indirectly acquainted, through friends and through the mass media. This source is of course 'internalized' in the sense that dependence on it for guidance in life is implanted early. The goals towards which the other-directed person strives shift with that guidance; it is only the process of striving itself and the process of paying close attention to the signals from others that remain unaltered throughout life. (Riesman 22)

Quite unlike her value-driven father, Brenda is represented as the product of anxiously other-directed constructions of selfhood, and Roth's story confirms that she is thereby made every bit as inwardly "lonely" as Riesman's analysis suggests.

The very first image in the text is of Brenda handing Neil her glasses before she dives into the pool, and this symbolic opening statement of her myopia is quickly confirmed by the narrator's judgment that she is blinded by "the high walls of ego that rose, buttresses and all, between her and her knowledge of herself" (22). Unlike Neil's cousin Doris, who at least pretends to read *War and Peace*, Brenda's ego is formed by the projections of femininity that Roth had been satirizing in his *New Republic* articles—in fact she particularly resembles the disturbing mix of voluptuous beauty and asinine conformity that he described in "Coronation on Channel Two," his report on the Miss America Pageant. As a true daddy's girl with a big friendly jock for a brother, Brenda Patimkin is just like Miss Oklahoma, who "when asked what her ambition was for her first-born, said she wanted it 'to be normal . . . and exactly like my brothers and my daddy.'" When playing tennis, Brenda is every bit as concerned as the Miss America girls to "maintain . . . her beauty" (16); when looking at herself, she does not really see a self, but a face that needs to be corrected to fit with media presentations of feminine beauty and the beauty products it promotes (she has her Jewish nose "fixed" [18]); when she speaks she does so with a "factual tone" (21) curiously devoid of expressive quality; when he embraces her, Neil wonders whether he will find miniature "wings" (17, 18) sprouting on her back like the glossy American angel she anxiously aspires to be; when Neil jokes with her, she struggles to understand him and worries he is "nasty" (18, 20, 21, 44, 47), for she defines nastiness as anything critical of the identity she has anxiously pieced together in conformity with the culture as it speaks to her through its commodities.

More telling than all these signs of the disturbing new social character Brenda embodies is Roth's grimly ironic portrayal of how her inner loneliness poisons her sexual relationship with Neil. Brenda may seem sexually liberated, but the enticingly libidinous realm she and suburban America together open up to Neil is a false paradise. Neil gradually starts to realize that during their erotic adventures, the "real" Brenda is never really there: She rises to high passion only when confronting her mother over the clothes budget ("every cashmere sweater," Neil observes, "a battle with her mother" [27]); her most inspired erotic intensity comes out of a desire for psychological revenge upon her mother following another of their quarrels (57).[3] And finally Brenda plays the trump card of allowing her diaphragm to be discovered, an act perfectly calculated to manipulate not only her mother's outraged envy, but also her loving father's compensatory promise of a new coat (she also thereby gets rid of the now-redundant Neil).

All in all, Brenda Patimkin represents a humanity deeply wounded by the new and psychologically damaging forms of ideological control that come with America's new "age of consumption." And as *Goodbye, Columbus* unfolds, it becomes ever clearer that Brenda is only one among many of the mass-manipulated "lonely crowd" Neil observes on a drive out of the Short Hills suburb:

> They looked immortal sitting there. Their hair would always stay the color they desired, their clothes the right texture and shade; in their homes they would have simple Swedish modern when that was fashionable, and if huge, ugly baroque ever came back, out would go the long, midget-legged marble coffee table and in would come Louis Quatorze. These were the goddesses, and if I were Paris I could not have been able to choose among them, so microscopic were the differences. Their fates had collapsed them into one. (76)

Unlike the Sid Caesar and Janet Blair double-act on television, Roth's *Goodbye, Columbus* draws on the full arsenal of sociological insight developed by David Riesman to accomplish its ethical purpose of "rak[ing] suburban life over the barbeque coals."

One particularly ominous sign that the life of the Patimkins is a decidedly false paradise is that Neil and Brenda's lovemaking frequently takes place "before the silent screen" of the Patimkins' television set (43). In Roth's rather clunky symbolism, the suggestion is not only that the TV screen acts as a self-regarding mirror for Brenda, but that even during sexual intimacy she is anxiously comparing her experience to the norm. The other major "happy problem" Roth highlighted in "The Hurdles of Satire" was the phenomenon of the mass media itself, and here it will be useful to distinguish Roth's approach (and, more broadly, that of the New Liberalism) from the critique of mass culture available in the 1950s that was put forth by the philosophers and sociologists of the Frankfurt School, who had emigrated to America in the 1930s to escape Nazi Germany. Marxist in orientation and scarred by direct experience of totalitarianism in Europe, Frankfurt School intellectuals tended to think about mass culture in political terms and as part of a more generally repressive state apparatus. For example, in "The Culture Industry: Enlightenment as Mass Deception" (1944), Max Horkheimer and Theodor Adorno theorized Hollywood and the popular arts as institutions that promote "obedience to the social hierarchy" (103–4) and contribute to the "absolute power" of the capitalist system; moreover, they argued, the stereotypes they purvey promote homogenization and docility among the population at large in much the same way as other instrumentalizing technologies in the capitalist economy. "In Germany," they warned, "even the most carefree films of democracy were overhung already by the graveyard stillness of dictatorship" (99).

Some of the these concerns were shared by the New Liberalism, and indeed, art critic Clement Greenberg's "Avant-Garde and Kitsch" repeated the explicitly political fear that "encouragement of kitsch is merely another of the inexpensive ways in which totalitarian regimes seek to ingratiate themselves with their subjects" (39). However, more characteristic was Dwight Macdonald's primarily ethical concern that while the culture industry may, at first, be used by the elite to financially exploit the masses, that same elite ends up "by finding their own culture attacked and even threatened with destruction by the instrument they have thoughtlessly employed" ("A Theory" 61–62). As Thomas Hill Schaub has pointed out, this analysis effectively "reverses the direction of exploitation, suggesting that pandering to the tastes of the lower classes unintentionally empowers them" (18)—and so here the concern becomes less about the possibility of mass culture encouraging a docile slide into totalitarianism than about its bringing about a cultural decline, a banalizing of experience, and a leveling off of value.

It is this general ethical concern, rather than the more specifically political fears informing the Frankfurt School analysis, that defines Roth's first *New Republic* article, "Rescue from Philosophy," a review of the film *Funny Face*, a musical comedy featuring Audrey Hepburn and Fred Astaire. As Roth points out, *Funny Face* is a "Cinderella story" repackaged to appeal to the ideological formation of 1950s Americans. "Miss Hepburn," as Roth refers to her throughout, begins the film living in Greenwich Village where she is, in a naïve and comically endearing way, interested in philosophy; she is spotted by Fred Astaire, who plays a fashion photographer who gives her the chance to go to a fashion shoot in Paris. While in Paris she meets Professor Flostra, the philosopher she most admires, but to her astonishment and disgust Flostra tries to seduce her. Fleeing from the professor, she begins to find success as a fashion model, and "by the end of the film Miss Hepburn has thrown out the jargon of philosophy (sic) as well as philosophy itself. Success . . . has re-educated her; she is saved" (22). What most concerns Roth about the film is the fantasy of sexual innocence that Audrey Hepburn embodies and projects to an other-directed mass America. She is a new kind of heroine, Roth points out, quite unlike Astaire's earlier dancing partner Ginger Rogers, "not only because she speaks of Sartre and Tolstoy but also because her moral stance, in its hyper-innocence, is so novel for musical comedy." Ginger Rogers may also have resisted Professor Flostra's advances, but she would have done so out of full knowledge of the world of desire rather than out of shocked innocence: "Miss Hepburn's moral voyage," Roth suggests, "has never shown her this other world" of sexual desire (23). *Funny Face* is therefore for Roth ultimately a dangerous film, not for political reasons but because of its lack of what he calls "moral intelligence," or what, in another essay of this period, he calls "moral imagination," for not only does Hepburn embody a childlike sexual innocence, but Astaire is required to "be as innocent towards her as a father towards his pretty little daughter. The audience seems asked to believe that men over 45 are either unknowing or impotent, or perhaps victimized by a combination of both." The net effect of films like these, Roth concludes, is the infantilization of the American public. They present what he calls "the old moral—or amoral—universe of Hollywood," which is "in its way as naive as Elvis Presley's. Where Presley associates being 'dirty' with being sexual, Miss Hepburn confuses being 'nice' with being innocent. What is unnerving is that the same audience is willing to be convinced of both perversions at the same time."

The ethical critique of mass culture in the *Funny Face* article connects with an uncollected short story from 1960, entitled "The Good Girl" and published in *Cosmopolitan*, where the text is at times accompanied by advertisements featuring women in the various accoutrements of affluent, other-directed American femininity. Resistant to the ways in which this environment constructs female identity, "The Good Girl" portrays a young Audrey Hepburn in the making and critiques the phony idealism of her cultivated and ambitious "good girl" life. It portrays a decidedly other-directed variation on Brenda Patimkin, this time a sophomore named Laurie Brown, who has developed an over-fastidious rejection of the erotic as part of her general assimilation into the high-minded moral atmosphere of late-1950s Cornell University. She has learned from her contemporaries to cast a cold eye on impulse and desire, and the opening scene features her rebuffing the advances of an eager young man. This is how she thinks about him: "She was—to use a word she found at once vague and childish—attracted to him. He might overdo the long meaningful gazes into the eyes; he was nevertheless quite good-looking. He had his merit—to use another imprecise word—physically" (100). Having seen the young man off, she also gives the cold shoulder to Mrs. Lasser, a warm-hearted, fleshy, tipsy, and insinuating friend of her parents. Mrs. Lasser spies on Laurie in her bedroom, where she is adjusting her bra straps in the mirror—finding, in doing so, that she bears a disconcerting resemblance to the full sexuality of the belly-dancer that she had watched that very evening. This is Mrs. Lasser's advice:

> "Too high?" said Mrs. Lasser. "Apples drop from trees, dear. Sag," the woman said despondently, "is the law of the universe. We're supposed to be thankful for gravity, you know . . . I wouldn't try to force things too high, dear. I wouldn't want to bind myself, I don't think, especially if I was slight in the breast to begin with. . . . " (101)

With Mrs. Lasser's Rabelaisian lesson that gravity is the law of the universe, which she repeats a few moments later by drunkenly falling into the bathtub ("Her legs flew up, her lees flashed for an instant, and there staring at Laurie was a maze of hooks and straps, girdle, flesh, stockings" [101]), and her rejection of the "too high," whose resonance among the push-up bra adverts is hard to miss, the moral wisdom of the story lies in its emphasis on the importance of including the erotic within a mature self.[4]

Indeed, the story suggests that the price of ignoring physical desire is to be condemned to the same ultimately "lonely" subjectivity Roth described in Brenda Patimkin. Laurie is portrayed as disconcertingly immature for a sophomore: She has "no ill words to speak of the childhood her parents had created for her" (101), and she remains an essentially infantile person, still yearning for her father's praise and mortified when she discovers that his erotic life is altogether more intriguing than she had imagined. The story reveals that the kind of "good girl" that *Cosmopolitan* itself had played no small part in producing (this is *Cosmopolitan* prior to the editorship of Helen Gurley

Brown) is someone who is in fact psychologically wounded and inwardly alienated: By ignoring the call of the erotic, she has failed to develop her own mature femininity.[5] It explores the way in which the erotic life might be given a partial but distinctive value within a broader ideal of maturity, and Roth carefully ironizes characters whose approach to the erotic is one-sided: both Mrs. Lasser's embarrassing lasciviousness and—with a sharper critical edge—Laurie Brown's over-sophisticated contempt for the body.

The concept of "maturity" was particularly important within the New Liberalism, as it helped define the way intellectuals in this tradition conceptualized the value of high art in opposition to mass culture. The relationship between serious literature and personal maturity was best captured in an essay by Lionel Trilling entitled "Manners, Morals, and the Novel," collected in *The Liberal Imagination* (1950). "Some paradox of our natures leads us," Trilling claimed, "when once we have made our fellow men the objects of our enlightened interest, to go on to make them the objects of our pity, then of our wisdom, ultimately of our coercion. It is to prevent this corruption, the most ironic and tragic that man knows, that we stand in need of the moral realism which is the product of the free play of the moral imagination" (223). In its emphasis on the hazards of utopian politics (making "our fellow men the objects of our enlightened interest"), this passage nicely captures the turn from politics to ethics. Conceptualized as a practice of moral realism, rather than as a moral injunction, Trilling positioned literature as a form of dialectics in which the aim of reading was not to generate determinate forms of action, but instead to cultivate a discriminating roundedness of character—a more "mature" self—that would be competent to navigate its way through the banalizing pressures of the wider culture.

"The Good Girl" is even a somewhat schematic example of this literary mode, as it delineates the way in which the over-fastidious rejection of desire and the over-eager embrace of sexuality have the capacity to infantilize the self—such that, in undergoing the experience of this conflict, the reader develops a greater "realism" in relation to moral situations. However, another short story from this period, "Epstein," collected in *Goodbye, Columbus*, is an altogether livelier variation on the same theme and style. In this story the conflict between moral duty and the realm of sexuality is captured in a farcical dénouement in which Epstein himself is hospitalized with a heart attack brought on by adulterous sex. What the story emphasizes though, and certainly what helped inspire controversy among some of its Jewish readers, is that it is Epstein in his adulterous rebellion, and not the other characters in their moralizing disapproval, who is portrayed as the more mature and thereby more sympathetic sensibility.

Epstein's wife is a thumbnail sketch of suffocating lower middle-class conformity who has allowed her fascination with the kind of spic-and-span home presented in the *Ladies' Home Journal* to destroy her erotic life: The roots of Epstein's adultery, it is suggested, perhaps lie in "that night fifteen years ago when instead of smelling a woman between his sheets he smelled [the cleanser] Bab-O" (157). But on the other hand, equally disapproving of Epstein are his trendy left-wing daughter and her guitar-strumming boyfriend, who Roth portrays as, to use Norman Podhoretz's phrase for the Beat generation, "know-nothing bohemians" (29). Like Podhoretz, the early Roth had no patience with the Beats. In a March 1961 article he published in *Commentary* shortly after Podhoretz had become editor, Roth castigated the Beats for their insufficiently considered mode of resistance: "The attitude of the Beats (if such a phrase has meaning) is not entirely without appeal. The whole thing is a joke. America, ha-ha. But that doesn't put very much distance between Beatdom and its sworn enemy, best-sellerdom—not much more than what it takes to get from one side of a nickel to the other: for is America, ha-ha, really any more than America, hoo-ray, stood upon its head?" (qtd. in *Reading* 172). Moving between the naïve radicalism of Beatdom and the asinine conformity of the affluent society, Epstein—for all his flaws—is presented as at least attempting to come to a more mature understanding of himself.

This point is important to emphasize, as in both "The Good Girl" and "Epstein," what is at stake in the presentation of sexuality is not primarily self-gratification, but the achievement of a deeper knowledge of human nature as a moral whole, especially as achieved through the suffering and personal upheaval that a response to the erotic provokes: Laurie seems to have chosen not to "grow up," and Epstein has left it too late, but the ethical stance of both stories is that while the erotic is not an end in itself, it is certainly part of the way in which the maturing self resists the inauthenticities of the wider culture.

The way Roth's early fiction and cultural criticism addresses itself to American society is based upon the supposition of an evaluative standpoint that is assumed to be in some way disinterested: Where Hollywood delivers ideologically driven fantasies, art delivers moral wisdom; where TV infantilizes, art makes more mature. The wisdom of art stands above, and helps to redeem, the messy, error-strewn partiality of life. Roth affirms this assumption very explicitly in *Goodbye, Columbus* where we find the heartless and inwardly lonely Brenda Patimkin contrasted with a young African American boy who comes to Newark Public Library looking for what he calls "heart." Roth's phonetization of the way he pronounces the word *art* is of course no accident, for it is through art, the story suggests, that the true heart— and by extension the good society—is to be discovered. *Goodbye, Columbus* optimistically suggests that this wave of Newark immigrants ("they're taking over the city" [33], Neil's colleague complains) will not follow the path taken by the Jews, who are in the process of waving goodbye to Columbus and heading for the false paradise of the affluent society, but will instead stay in touch with the genuine vision offered by art.[6] This is the boy's response to Gauguin: "Where is these pictures? These people, man, they sure does look cool. They ain't no yelling or shouting here, you could just see it" (34). The boy confuses Gauguin's South Pacific with the unmistakably American concept of a "ree-sort," but of course the redemptive blueprint for society offered by art is a world away from the psychologically damaging fool's paradise of the Patimkins' country-club resort. What the Gauguin book suggests is that through the vision that art holds out, we might "Go-again," to use the boy's felicitous pronunciation of the artist's name: Like a renewed Columbus, the reader might rediscover the true paradise in America.

In "The Kind of Person I Am," the experiment in self-satire quoted at the beginning of this essay, Roth expressed some uneasiness at being one of the "cultural élite" on these terms, and among the extraordinary acclaim his early work won, there were some who shared his unease. Irving Howe was one of the range of New York intellectuals who found much to admire in *Goodbye, Columbus*, and his review praised the "deadpan malicious accuracy" of Roth's early fiction, finding it "ferociously exact." But he also expressed concern about the basis upon which Roth was grounding his criticism of the "dreary slackness" of postindustrial American life. Are the values that *Goodbye, Columbus* sets against the consumer society "sufficiently energetic and supple," Howe asked, to make a genuine resistance? It was hard, he pointed out, to answer this question, because the nature of Roth's alternative was unclear: He was not certainly finding the "Jewish tradition" a viable form of resistance; nor was he placing any faith in radical left-wing hopes, as Neil Klugman's brief satirical allusion to his dim-witted Aunt Gladys's involvement in the "Workman's Circle" suggested. In fact these reservations connect with the broader concerns Howe had been raising for several years about the turn from politics to ethics so evident in Trilling's concept of moral realism: This seemed to Howe more of a "character style" than a genuine critical response. As such, Howe wondered, is it not as much of an ideology with its own potential for inauthenticity, as the culture it claims to resist?[7]

Roth shared these concerns, and in the years ahead he would rethink several aspects of his early cultural formation, often in spectacular fashion. In his first novel, *Letting Go* (1962), he started to challenge the poetics of moral realism, in particular its idea that life can be understood in a more deeply rational and ethically wise manner through a process of dialectics; in *My Life as a Man* (1974), the concept of maturity was explored as just one among many limiting and falsifying character styles projected by an infantilizing culture, which the self must in its turn resist. More broadly, in a range of novels from *Portnoy's Complaint* (1969) to *The Counterlife* (1986) and *Sabbath's Theater* (1995), he would develop a quite different way of thinking about the ethos proper to a resistant self that owes more to a Nietzschean aesthetics of affective intensity than it does to any capacity for moral dialectics.

But while all these upheavals in the style of his response to the "age of happy problems" are crucially important and even might be said to define his significance as a writer, it is also important to note that in other ways Roth has remained within the parameters of his early cultural formation. In a *New Yorker* interview in May 2000, he spoke about his fears for the future of literature in a way that resonated with the turn from politics to ethics that was so defining of the New Liberalism: Concerned about the narrow and instrumentalizing ways in which literature was being used for political purposes in the university—a concern that he would explore in the contemporaneous novel *The Human Stain*—Roth continued to position literature as a way for the self to resist the narrowing and banalizing pressures of a wealthy consumerist democracy. "One gets the sense," he told David Remnick, "and not just on the basis of the death of reading—that the American branch of the species is being retooled. I see the death of reading as just an aspect of this" (87). While Roth is rightly best known for his later work, which very profoundly revised many of the key ideas of his intellectual formation, the core idea established in "Our Country and Our Culture," that the intellectual should have a settled relationship with liberal democracy, and that the work of art should promote a care for the self rather than politically instrumental forms of action, would remain guiding principles for Roth throughout his career.

Notes

1. Herbert Gold is a novelist and author of *The Prospect before Us* (1954) and *The Man Who Was Not with It* (1956).

2. Riesman draws on Fromm's analysis of the relationship between social character types and power in *Man for Himself: An Inquiry into the Psychology of Ethics* (1947).

3. As Riesman has argued, one of the most significant features of the other-directed community is a shift in the child-parent relationship from authority to manipulation. See *The Lonely Crowd* 52.

4. The text includes specific references to Rabelais, most notably the "gargantuan" embrace Laurie's suitor gives her at the front door of her parents' apartment (100).

5. Helen Gurley Brown took over the editorship of *Cosmopolitan* in 1965, bringing its editorial policy in line with the hedonistic spirit of her bestselling book *Sex and the Single Girl* (1962).

6. Compare Ralph Ellison's slightly later statement on the special powers of high culture in "The World and the Jug" (1963) collected in *The Collected Essays of Ralph Ellison*, Ed. John F. Callahan. New York: Modern Library, 1995. Print.

7. See Irving Howe's essay, "Culture and Radicalism," collected in *Celebrations and Attacks: Thirty Years of Literary and Cultural Commentary.* New York: Horizon, 1979. 63–64. Print.

Works Cited

Greenberg, Clement. "Avant-Garde and Kitsch." *Partisan Review* 6.5 (1939): 34–49. Print.

Horkheimer, Max, and Theodor W. Adorno. *Dialectic of Enlightenment: Philosophical Fragments*. Ed. Gunzelin Schmid Noerr. Trans. Edmund Jephcott. Stanford: Stanford UP, 2002. Print.

Howe, Irving. *A Margin of Hope: An Intellectual Autobiography*. San Diego: Harcourt, 1982. Print.

___. "The Suburbs of Babylon." *New Republic* 15 June 1959: 17–18. Print.

Macdonald, Dwight. *Against the American Grain*. New York: Random, 1962. Print.

___. "A Theory of Mass Culture." *Mass Culture: The Popular Arts in America.* Ed. Bernard Rosenberg and David Manning White. New York: Free, 1957. 59–73. Print.

Nietzsche, Friedrich. *Untimely Meditations*. Trans. R. J. Hollingdale. Cambridge: Cambridge UP, 1983. Print.

Pells, Richard H. *The Liberal Mind in a Conservative Age: American Intellectuals in the 1940s and 1950s*. New York: Harper, 1985. Print.

Phillips, William, and Philip Rahv, eds. "Our Country and Our Culture: A Symposium." *Partisan Review* 19.3 (1952): 282–326. Print.

Podhoretz, Norman. *The Norman Podhoretz Reader: A Selection of His Writings from the 1950s through the 1990s.* Ed. Thomas L. Jeffers. New York: Simon, 2004. Print.

Remnick, David. "Into the Clear: Philip Roth Puts Turbulence in its Place." *New Yorker* 8 May 2000: 76–89. Print.

Riesman, David. *The Lonely Crowd: A Study of the Changing American Character.* New Haven: Yale UP, 1950. Print.

Roth, Philip. "Coronation on Channel Two." *New Republic* 23 Sept. 1957: 21. Print.

___. *Goodbye, Columbus.* London: Deutsch, 1959. Print.

___. "The Good Girl." *Cosmopolitan* May 1960: 98–103. Print.

___. "The Hurdles of Satire." *New Republic* 9 Sept. 1957: 22. Print.

___. "The Kind of Person I Am." *New Yorker* 29 Nov. 1958: 173–78. Print.

___. "Positive Thinking on Pennsylvania Avenue." *Chicago Review* 11.1 (1957): 21–24. Print.

___. *Reading Myself and Others.* New York: Random, 1985. Print.

___. "Rescue from Philosophy," *New Republic* 10 June 1957: 22–23. Print.

Schaub, Thomas Hill. *American Fiction in the Cold War.* Madison: U of Wisconsin P, 1991. Print.

Trilling, Lionel. *A Gathering of Fugitives.* London: Secker, 1956. Print.

___. *The Liberal Imagination: Essays on Literature and Society.* New York: Viking, 1950. Print.

Beautiful, Obscure Strangers: Women in *The Professor of Desire*

Velichka Ivanova

This essay examines Roth's reputation as a self-centered writer unable to depict women as complex characters, specifically with respect to his 1977 novel *The Professor of Desire*.[1] In this narrative, the author himself introduces the issue of misogyny as he makes his character Deborah Schonbrunn blame young academic David Kepesh for his "acting out fantasies of aggression against women" (126). Indeed, the accusation may be right: Recounted by a male character narrator, the narrative is not gender-neutral; rather, it forges a bond of solidarity between the male protagonist and male audience. The preference for such a character takes its origin in the writer's desire to treat themes and material with which he feels most familiar. In Roth's preceding novel, *My Life as a Man* (1974), the young instructor Nathan Zuckerman taught his English composition class exactly this lesson: "Ground your stories in what you know. Stick to that" (66).[2] *The Professor of Desire* follows the same strategy of representation. The character narrator, David Kepesh, makes the immediately observable reality the subject matter of his narrative. Since his own masculine self is the closest and most difficult problem at hand, it becomes the only focus of the story. As a result, the character narrator cannot inhabit the lives of other characters, nor can he imagine women. He can only depict them from the outside. Through an analysis of the structure of the narrative, this essay demonstrates that Roth's allegedly misogynistic representations result entirely from his fictional method and the formal decisions it implies.

Objectification and Dismemberment

"I have from the start been overcome by physical beauty in women," Kepesh admits (57). Unfortunately, the admirer of beauty perceives only the surface of the female body. For example, while still in college, he is irresistibly attracted to his fellow students. He picks them up in the reading room of the library, "a place comparable to the runway of a burlesque house in its power to stimulate and focus [his] desire" (22). In the reading room, he watches transfixed "the girl who plays with the ends of her hair while ostensibly she is studying her History" (22). Then another girl begins to swing her leg and catches his lascivious eye. In this instant, his craving knows no bounds. A third girl leans forward over her notebook, and "with a muffled groan . . . , [he] observe[s] the breasts beneath her blouse push softly into her folded arms" (22).

The way in which Kepesh portrays the girls in the library illustrates the objectification and the dismemberment women are submitted to. His eye registers only parts of their bodies—hair, legs, breasts. Throughout the novel, the character narrator sees the female body as a set of individual pieces rather than a whole. For instance, during his fellowship year in London, he meets Birgitta Svanström, a young Swedish girl whose character is conveyed again through a catalogue of body parts: she "confronts the world with a narrow foxy face, a nose delicately pointed and an upper lip ever so slightly protruding, a mouth ready, if need be, to answer a charge or utter a challenge" (43). Later on, in his thirties, Kepesh falls in love with and later marries the beautiful Helen Baird. Her personality is a mystery to him, but her body is transparent. He enumerates her physical assets from head to toe—"her eyes, her nose, her throat, her breasts, her hips, her legs" (56)—as if to pronounce her, Debra Shostak observes, "as ultimately a grab bag of physical objects" (Shostak 26).

Comfortably reduced to a list of body parts, women are apparently subjected to Kepesh's domination. His loquacity, however, represents his only expression of power. Misled by his boasting, the reader might take him for the "sexual prodigy" he claims he is in his twenties (119). Ironically, Kepesh's verbal exuberance and aggressive candor contradict his real experience: "Given the reputation, you would think that I had already reduced a hundred coeds to whoredom, when in fact in four years' time I actually succeed in achieving full penetration on but two occasions, and something resembling penetration on two more" (23). This retrospective observation points to a crucial feature of the text—the narrator's self-irony. The interpretation of the novel depends on the reader's awareness of Kepesh's self-mocking voice.

Passages where the character narrator expresses self-irony in retrospect are rare. The present tense of the narrative and the coincidence between Kepesh as narrated character and Kepesh as narrator almost entirely eliminate the possibilities of cognitive distance between these two instances.[3] Only the typographical style silently signals to the reader an ironic meaning behind the character's back.

Self-Irony

The periodic use of italics is particularly important in the passages where the first-person narrator describes his sexual exploits during his fellowship year in London. Fascinated with the "mythology of the Swedish girl and her sexual freedom," Kepesh sets out to find his own "sex-crazed young Scandinavian" goddess (29). He meets Elisabeth Elverskog, a shy Swedish student who, out of love for him, agrees to take part in his erotic experiments with her roommate Birgitta. Gentle and compliant, Elisabeth follows Kepesh's every whim against her nature. This leads her to a suicide attempt.

The narrator recounts how Elisabeth "seems often to be *enjoying* herself so much," an excitement he misinterprets as pleasurable and that only the character style suggests is suspect (31). The fact that the events are recounted in the present tense contributes to the impression of simultaneity and identity of narrator and character. Indeed, during his first months in London, the character narrator is "in such an egoistical frenzy over this improbable thing that is happening to me, not just with one but with two Swedish (or if you will, *European* girls), that I do not see Elisabeth slowly going to pieces" (31). Paradoxically, in this sentence, the character narrator tells us what he does "not see" during his two-month ménage à trois. He thus transgresses the knowledge-frame of the character who experiences the events, which means that the information cannot possibly be narrated by the character narrator as one and the same persona. The man who narrates knows already the disastrous outcome of the situation, and, in retrospect, reinterprets the signs he failed to notice earlier. Clearly, the account of Kepesh's adventure in London represents one of the rare occurrences of a cognitive difference between the two instances that support the point of view in first-person narratives: the narrating I and the experiencing I.

The perceptual gap between the knowing self who narrates and the naïve self whose experiences are being narrated suggests a temporal distance. Time has passed since the orgies have taken place and the distance confers on the narrator a lucidity and wisdom that his former self does not possess. Exploitation of this distance allows the narrator to comment on his development, from his naïve and arrogant self at the time of the diegesis till the bruised and undeluded self that tells the story. Only the italics and the rare infraction of perception signal that there may be an ironic distance between them.

Further, the use of italics emphasizes ironically Kepesh's narcissistic choice to place himself not only at the center of the erotic trio but also, and more importantly, at the center of perception in the narrative. His central position is both asserted and mocked. For instance, in her desire to please him, Elisabeth learns to use slang while playing cards with Kepesh. Her newly acquired language skill is evaluated in relation primarily with the satisfaction Kepesh draws from it, for "it pleases her no end—it pleases *me* no end," he declares (32). It is not an accident that later Kepesh cries out in utter awe: "How on earth can she be going to pieces? *I'm* not!" (32). If the character is oblivious to his own selfishness, the italics ironically expose it to the reader.

The italics enhance the reader's awareness that the account is personal and biased. The narrative makes no attempt to disguise its partiality. On the contrary, the narrator takes an obvious pleasure in recounting how his younger self fails to understand Elisabeth. Kepesh thinks she is excited by the sex games of the trio. In fact, she is deeply confused and hurt. The rhetorical question Kepesh asks underlines not only his ignorance, but also his violence: "Isn't it Elisabeth who is in fact more vehement (and innocently simple-minded) than Birgitta, who insists, even when I practically threaten to *slap* some sense into her, that the war was 'everybody's fault'?" (32). The italics show that at the time of the recounted events, Kepesh was ignorant of the mental and physical pressure he put on the young girl but presently he sees the events in a different light.

After the "accident"—so the young people describe Elisabeth's broken arm when she walks in front of a truck sixteen days after Kepesh moved into the girls' basement and started his sexual experiments, his self-serving behavior continues unchanged. Only the occasional italics and the juxtaposition of acts and words reveal the narrator's self-ironic attitude. For instance, despite his self-disgust and guilt, Kepesh continues to sleep in Elisabeth's bed after her departure from London. "And I actually believe that I am staying on there because in my state of shock I am simply *unable* to move out as yet," he explains (33). If the hero prefers to ignore his own selfishness, the narrator ironically underlines it by italicizing the false excuse.

Overcome "with the most unruly and contradictory emotions—a sense of unworthiness, of loathsomeness, of genuine shame and remorse," and at the same time, ironically, with as strong a sense of not being guilty, Kepesh types "earnest apologias and petitions for pardon" to Elisabeth, but intentionally leaves his private correspondence for Birgitta to read because it "surely will impress her with just how *deep* a sultan I am" (34, 38). On the one hand, Kepesh wonders how "this unfathomable Birgitta" could be so deprived of any sense of remorse, shame, and loyalty. On the other hand, ironically, his actions show that he is equally shameless. In all these examples, the italicized words show the regrets of the retrospective narrator for the actions of the arrogant protagonist. The temporal and cognitive difference between them creates the ironic bite. This is why, in retrospect, the narrator concludes: "What an idiot I have been, how callous, how blind!" (33).

Clearly, at the time of narration, the retrospective first-person narrator does not identify with his mindless younger self.

Two perspectives coexist, then, in the account of Kepesh's adventures in London: that of the inexperienced individual and that of his ulterior self. The narrative thus creates what Dorrit Cohn calls "dissonance" as opposed to the "consonance" of stories dominated exclusively by the perspective of the character.[4] *The Professor of Desire* is a first-person narrative in which the point of view of the narrator overlaps with that of the narrated I, but in some instances it diverges from it. Opening up and making explicit the distance between the I who narrates and the I who is narrated, making the former supply contextual information of which the latter was ignorant or unheeding, has an ironic effect.[5]

In her study *Irony's Edge: The Theory and Politics of Irony*, Linda Hutcheon insists on the difficulty of determining an ironic reading for a given passage in a text. She emphasizes the active role of the receiver for the perception of irony and theorizes irony as "a discursive practice or strategy" (3). The scene of irony, Hutcheon argues, is a social scene, and irony is a communicative process (4). Ironic meaning "happens in discourse, in usage, in the dynamic space of the interaction of text, context, and interpreter (and, sometimes, though not always, intending ironist)" (58). Consequently, it depends on the reader whether he or she would be sensitive to the irony encoded in the italicized words. The accent Hutcheon places on the role of the reader invites us to consider the narrative as an interactive and dialogic process. The activation of this process, which is essential for the functioning of irony, depends entirely on the reader's ability to perceive the narrator's self-ironic voice, on attention to character style (italics), and, finally, on genre knowledge, that is, on the reader's awareness of how novels conventionally develop, and in this particular case, how first-person narratives function.

Simultaneous Narration and Consonance

The incipit of David Kepesh's narration—"Temptation comes to me first in the conspicuous personage of Herbie Bratasky" (3)—informs us from the outset about the narrative situation. Kepesh's account of his life takes the form of a monologue addressed to an anonymous audience. The narration is simultaneous, for the narrator tells a story that unfolds as he tells it. He does not know how the story ends. The consistent use of present tense renders the novel's structure transparent and consonant, because the possibility for narrative distance hardly exists. As Robert Greenberg puts it, *The Professor of Desire* is "an unproblematic and uncomplicated first-person narrative in which a reliable, intelligent narrator both suffers and intelligently illuminates his suffering" (492). Kepesh's account of his life lacks past-tense tags like "I thought," "I realized," which would assign the judgments to an earlier consciousness. Only the use of perfect tense marks pastness and retrospection. As a result, the possibility for ironic dissonance seems completely eliminated.

Because the unawareness of the first-person narrator matches that of the character when these two instances merge, Kepesh never fully articulates his understanding of women, and neither does he comprehend his own life. The final events of the story remain unexplained too, and we are left to make our own inferences. On the novel's last page, Kepesh, in the middle of passionate lovemaking, fears dreadful "transformations yet to come" (263). Readers already familiar with the metamorphosis recounted in *The Breast* (1972), to which *The Professor of Desire* is a prequel, will doubtless interpret the ambiguous reference without difficulty. Ironically, metamorphosed into a breast, Kepesh himself will become a passive object and a female body part.

The Effects of Internal Focalization

One of the frequent critiques leveled at Philip Roth is that he "does not sufficiently get inside his female characters' heads and hearts," observes David Gooblar (9). Indeed, throughout *The Professor of Desire*, women are specular as well as sexual objects. The character narrator remains ignorant of their inner world. The effect, however, is intentional. It is produced by the narrative mode.

Roth's selection of first-person narration implies the consistent use of internal focalization. Despite the debates that this notion continues to inspire, we will agree upon the following definition: focalization refers to the mode of regulation of narrative information by adopting (or not) a restrictive point of view (Genette 185–86). The linguistic concept of "deictic center" helps to explain the notions of narrative mode and focalization introduced by Gérard Genette (186). Deictic center designates the point of reference that orients the various spatial, temporal, and character information in discourse. From a narratological perspective, the deictic center not only acts as a mental model of reference for the deictics, but also helps to construct character subjectivity and the point of view from which it is perceived. The place of the deictic center determines the system of focalizations in a narrative. Focalization, therefore, defines the spatial, temporal, and axiological position from which the fictional world is perceived and represented. The center of perception can be embodied in a character. In this case, the perspective from which the elements of the fictional universe are perceived and recounted belongs to him. In *The Professor of Desire*, the information is filtered through, and restricted by, the consciousness of the protagonist narrator David Kepesh. His perceptions cannot go beyond the limits of his subjectivity. This explains why Kepesh cannot understand the women he lives with. He does not have the freedom of a third-person narrator who can adopt internal focalization through other characters in order to explore their consciousness.

Genette notes that internal focalization is rarely applied in a totally rigorous way. "Indeed," he argues, "the very principle of this narrative mode implies in all strictness that the focal character never be described or even referred to from the outside, and that his thoughts or perceptions never be analyzed objectively by the narrator." (192)

An unexpected change in focalization, especially if it is isolated within a coherent context, can be analyzed not simply as a momentary infraction of the code, but as a site of significance. The third-person passage in the otherwise consistently first-person narrative has been pointed to by Shostak (29). The dinner that reunites Kepesh with his father, Mr. Barbatnik, and Claire Ovington, is recounted in the first person, but the narrative suddenly slips into the third person: "The two elders have been seated to either side of her, the lover directly across: with all the love he can muster, he looks upon the fullness of her saucy body" (254). The two-page infraction against internal focalization presents Kepesh as the anonymous object of the narrative—"the lover"—thus underlining the fact that the male self is the object of scrutiny and fictional representation rather than his female partners.

From the outset, the reader is invited to read mimetically, in tune with the male character narrator. The events are represented in chronological order as they affect him, which creates the impression of immediacy and prompts sympathy. The reader follows the events and judges the other characters through the eyes and value system of the focal character. The reader witnesses his thoughts, his feelings, his emotions, and is immersed in his world. The story, personal and biased, calls for an equally subjective response. The reader, especially the male reader, will tend to identify with the protagonist and embrace his masculine values. This explains the impression that the tone of the author Philip Roth merges with the arrogant voice of his protagonist Kepesh, the "visiting fellow in erotic daredevilry" (44). The reason is simple: the narrator communicates his subjective vision as focal character. The value judgments demonstrate Kepesh's way of seeing the events. Internal focalization imprints upon the text the protagonist's gender ideology and may thus strongly influence the reader's judgments.

The reader's awareness of gender as a lens through which to see the world, however, may prompt a reflection on the objectivity of the representations of women. Indeed, all the female characters in *The Professor of Desire* are seen through a male lens. This is how Kepesh presents one of the girls in the cheerleading squad: "Only in the slowly upturning belly of Marcella Walsh is there the smoldering suggestion (inescapable to me) of an offering, of an invitation, of a lust that is eager and unconscious and so clearly (to my eyes) begging to be satisfied. Yes, she alone seems (to me, to me) to sense" (25). The series of parentheses in this passage puts an emphasis on the masculine gaze. Roth does not even attempt to conceal the effects of the narrative device. Rather, he draws the reader's attention to his decision to adopt first-person narration and internal focalization. The parentheses also prompt an interrogation of the protagonist's cognitive limits. Kepesh is incapable of donning other lenses—different from his own—the lenses of the female gender. For instance, he only sees women's physical beauty, which renders him "intrigued and aroused," but also "alarmed, and made deeply, deeply uncertain" (57). Shostak has pointed out that Kepesh does not consider the body as a site of subjectivity. For instance, he wonders how Helen's "conception of self and experience" could only be based on her body. At the same time, Helen's awareness of herself as a beautiful woman, "banalized" as it seems to Kepesh, remains "enthralling and full of fascination." Perplexed, he admits *For all I know, maybe she is right*" (57). The italicized sentence highlights his uncertainty.

Internal focalization invites the reader to identify with the focal character. As a result, if the focal character is perceived as a misogynist from the outset, all the subsequent descriptions of women will be in line with this interpretation. The impression that the narrative is "anti-woman" is reinforced by the fact that, filtered through the consciousness of David Kepesh, the female characters' voices are heard partially only if they enter a conversation with him. The result is, as we have seen, the objectification of women. The representation of women's voices through direct speech, however, restores them the position of independent subjects.

Subjectivity through Voice Representation

The moment of introduction of women's direct speech is carefully chosen. It does not precede; it follows the first phase of Kepesh's perception of them, and then mocks it. For instance, in tune with Kepesh's strategy of objectification, Claire is represented as a ripe fruit, "tender within as without" (151). The noun-adjective compounds that abound in Kepesh's description are particularly meaningful: "Claire's face seems, more than ever, so apple-smooth, apple-small, apple-shiny, apple-plain, apple-fresh ... never more artless and untainted" (251). The repetition of the noun "apple" underlines Claire's orderly and coolheaded personality. This "voluptuous young woman" orders her life with "executive dispatch" and brings patience to their lovemaking (152). David admires "that canniness of hers that seems to sense exactly how much raw carnality and how much tender solicitude" are needed to reassure him and cure his temporary impotence (152). Claire's only pursuit in life and role in the story seems to be the well-being of her lover. She is associated with wholesome meals and with a regular and predictable life. Saturated with her integrity, craving for drama, Kepesh wonders, "How much longer before I've had a bellyful of wholesome innocence—how long before the lovely blandness of a life with Claire begins to cloy, to pall" (251). Certainly, this is the way in which Kepesh prefers to perceive his girlfriend. He weaves a web of plainness around her until, in his eyes, she appears almost entirely devoid of introspection and as simple and unadorned as an apple: "She never speaks of what she does not have, never lingers for so much as a moment upon loss, misfortune, or disappointment. You'd have to torture her to get her to complain. She is the most extraordinary ordinary person I have ever known" (220–21).

However, Claire is anything but ordinary when finally she gives her point of view. Her voice, transcribed in direct speech, proves that she is neither innocent nor simple. The reader learns immediately that she is torn between her feelings for Kepesh and her growing awareness that he is afraid of commitment. Kepesh is astonished to find out that she has had an abortion: "Claire has been pregnant, by me, and I've known nothing." Even if he finally senses "something very sad . . . at the bottom of [that] day's confidences and secrets," he still is "too weak" to fathom what it is (222). Kepesh remains completely unaware of women's inner lives. Indeed, the preference for the "apple" in his description of Claire's face highlights not her extraordinary innocence and ordinariness, but rather her lover's extraordinary ignorance and lack of empathy.

Helen, too, expresses her point of view in direct speech when she pays Kepesh a visit with her new husband (209–19). She confesses that she lives a boring life. She is pregnant, but is hesitating to have an abortion. She does not love her husband, but feels she cannot leave him, because she cannot face again her loneliness and depression: "Each night I toss in my bed with the nightmare of how much I don't love *anybody*," she admits (218). Helen articulates precisely the loneliness and pain Kepesh felt after his divorce with her: "Fastened to no one and to nothing, drifting, drifting, sometimes, frighteningly, sinking" (103). Like Kepesh, Helen is dissatisfied and estranged. More like an alter ego than a foe, she thinks she shares the same predicament with Kepesh and addresses him as "my dear old comrade" (216). These two examples demonstrate that women are not entirely silenced by the first-person narrator. On the contrary, Roth ensures that women's voices are heard, but always a little late, so that they contradict ironically Kepesh's opinions. For Kepesh, however, women are unknowable. They remain beautiful, obscure strangers throughout the novel.

In his review of *The Professor of Desire*, Vance Bourjaily suggests that toward the end of the narrative, like a delayed preface, there occurs a passage that explains its structure. Seated in a café in Prague, Kepesh composes a lecture that might be delivered to his students. Modeled after Kafka's story "Report to an Academy," his address begins with "Honored members of Literature 341" (181). He concludes after four pages in the following way:

> Indiscreet, professional and unsavory as portions of these disclosures will seem to some of you, I nonetheless would like, with your permission, to go ahead now and make an open account to you of the life I formerly led as a human being. I am devoted to fiction, and I assure you that in time I will tell you whatever I may know about it, but in truth nothing lives in me like my life. (185)

Nothing lives in him like his life—taking this as confirmation of the manner in which the book is to be read, the reader should not formulate unrealistic expectations about Kepesh's story. The flatness of the female characters is consistent with its subject matter: the instability of the male self and the fluctuations of male desire.

In conclusion, the reader should not blame Philip Roth for his inability to portray women as complex characters in *The Professor of Desire*. Rather, the representations of women result from his choice to present them through the lens of the male character narrator David Kepesh. His selection of the first-person narrative mode determines the consonant effects of the book. An attentive reader, however, will doubtless notice the silent installation of dissonance. Attention to character style indicates a discretely self-mocking tonality of Kepesh's voice. The numerous question marks sprinkled in the novel's pages highlight his anxiety and uncertainty. Far from portraying a powerful male tyrant, the novel presents a self-ironic artist whose masculine identity is unstable and who feels vulnerable in the presence of his female Other.

Limited by the use of internal focalization, the narrative cannot access the complex personalities of other characters, among them women. As a result, the female characters remain impenetrable both by the male protagonist and through him, by the reader. A different narrative mode and a different protagonist would certainly represent women in a different way, but as the novelist narrator Nathan Zuckerman says in *American Pastoral* (1997), a novel published exactly twenty years after *The Professor of Desire*, this would be "another story—another book" (215).

Notes

1. Critic Hermione Lee, for example, classifies Roth's women characters in four groups: "overprotective mothers," "monstrously unmanning wives," "consoling, tender, sensible girlfriends," and "recklessly libidinous sexual objects" (77).

2. Zuckerman's recommendation is not to be taken uncritically, however. In his article "Why American Novelists Don't Deserve the Nobel Prize," Alexander Nazaryan blames this very precept for the failure of contemporary American authors, including Philip Roth, to win the most prestigious literary award. He

explains that these writers, whom he names the "Great Male Narcissists," are unable to transcend the limitations of solipsism and write inventive fiction. Even worse, he contends, "they have inculcated younger generations of American novelists with the write-what-you-know mantra through their direct and indirect influence on creative programs."

3. In the first-person narration, the two possible supports of perception are two separate instances related to the same individual who is simultaneously a character in the story and the narrator who recounts it. Leo Spitzer, Eberhard Lämmert, and Franz Stanzel distinguish between "erzählendes Ich" and "erlebendes Ich," notions that Bertil Romberg adapts as "narrating I" and "narrated I" (96). The narrated I is the experiencing I, the object of the narrative constructed by the subject, the narrating I.

4. In consonant narration, the homodiegetic narrator identifies with the character, whereas in dissonant narration the narrator takes a critical distance from the character's views and ideology. See Cohn.

5. Narrative distance, or the temporal and psychological distance between the narrating I and the experiencing I, defines one of the main aspects of first-person narration. See Jahn.

Works Cited

Bourjaily, Vance. "A Cool Book on a Warm Topic." Rev. of *The Professor of Desire*. *New York Times*. New York Times, 18 Sept. 1977. Web. 7 Jan. 2013.

Cohn, Dorrit. *Transparent Minds: Narrative Methods for Presenting Consciousness in Fiction*. Princeton: Princeton UP, 1978. Print.

Genette, Gérard. *Narrative Discourse: An Essay in Method*. Trans. Jane E. Lewin. Ithaca: Cornell UP, 1980. Print.

Gooblar, David. "Introduction: Roth and Women." *Philip Roth Studies* 8.1 (Spring 2012): 7–15. Print.

Greenberg, Robert. "Transgression in the Fiction of Philip Roth." *Twentieth Century Literature* 43.4 (1997): 487–506. Print.

Hutcheon, Linda. *Irony's Edge: The Theory and Politics of Irony*. London, New York: Routledge, 1994. Print.

Jahn, Manfred. *Narratology: A Guide to the Theory of Narrative*. University of Cologne, 28 May 2005. Web. 7 Jan. 2013.

Lee, Hermione. *Philip Roth*. New York: Methuen, 1982. Print.

Nazaryan, Alexander. "Why American Novelists Don't Deserve the Nobel Prize." *Salon*. Salon Media Group, 3 Oct. 2011. Web. 7 Jan. 2012.

Romberg, Bertil. *Studies in the Narrative Technique of the First-Person Novel*, Stockholm: Almqvist & Wiksell, 1962. Print.

Roth, Philip. *American Pastoral*. Boston: Houghton, 1997. Print.

——. *My Life as a Man*. 1974. New York: Vintage, 1993. Print.

——. *The Professor of Desire*. New York: Farrar, 1977. Print.

Shostak, Debra. *Philip Roth: Countertexts, Counterlives*. Columbia: U of South Carolina P, 2004. Print.

Philip Roth's Autobiographical Gestures_____

Miriam Jaffe-Foger

With what initially appears as unusual candor, Philip Roth submitted a swift correction to the *Atlantic* regarding a "biographical error" in Joseph O'Neill's April 2012 piece "Roth v. Roth v. Roth," which claims that Roth experienced a "crack-up" in his mid-fifties. Roth's tone impersonates resentment at the term "crack-up," as it describes his mental health during his bout with the psychological effects of Halcion, a now blacklisted sedative that Roth's doctor prescribed to ease the pain of an orthopedic surgery. Indeed, if anything that Roth has written or said publically could be trusted—could be considered a "time out," if you will, in the game Roth has made of his authorial persona—then Roth's sensitivity in the framing of illness could be commended. However, it was Roth himself who coined the term "crack-up" in *The Facts: A Novelist's Autobiography* (1988), with a quasi-fictional reference to the Halcion experience in his opening letter to the fictional Nathan Zuckerman about his very impetus for writing the book (5, 195). Perhaps this is why O'Neill couches his use of the term in quotation marks.

Between the lines of Roth's counterpoint to the *Atlantic*, one sees that the editing of O'Neill is a move that pretends to disentangle the author from his fiction—even the fictions that are purposely dubbed facts; Roth manipulatively complicates the subheading of O'Neill's article: "The Complexities and Conundrums of Reading Philip Roth's Work as Autobiography." O'Neill could have anticipated Roth's response; he opens by saying that "any idea that might occur to us about the author has already occurred to him, only more intelligently," and Roth's one-upmanship in this case proves O'Neill right. To set about finding some lens that would clarify Roth's blur of fact and fiction is futile; yet, as O'Neill concedes, Roth readers feel a compulsion to crack the case: "We must plod on. A crime has been committed and someone has to do the paperwork."

Roth readers began producing the paperwork trail almost as soon as Roth began publishing, starting with his autobiographical gestures as they related to Jewish identity and community, moving on to the ethics of writing about others, questioning the construction of his authorial persona, and psychoanalyzing his control and trustworthiness as a writer of fictions and facts. Roth encouraged his readers' plodding on, especially in *Reading Myself and Others* (1985), where he responds to Hermione Lee's investigation about *The Anatomy Lesson* (1983) for the *Paris Review*; she asks, "Is Zuckerman's rage at Milton Appel the expression of a kind of guilt on your part?"—her question revealing her opinion that Roth's fiction is based on fact. But Roth's response about the fictional portrayal of his detractor Milton Appel follows: "There was the real autobiographical scene, and it had no life to it at all. I had to absorb the rage into the main character. . . . I wasn't going to get anywhere with a Zuckerman as eminently reasonable as myself" (*Reading* 141). Though the mention of Milton Appel in *The Anatomy Lesson* evokes the actual events of Roth's life, Roth's autobiographical gesture is not simply to recall those events through Zuckerman, but to write an emotional response to those events that tests the possibilities of his own psyche. Perhaps Roth puts it best when he explains this kind of gesture as "how [a writer] feeds what's hypothetical or imagined into what's inspired and controlled by recollection, and how what's recollected spawns the overall fantasy" (*Reading* 127).

While I propose that the autobiographical gesture is often a fantasy based on the events and emotions recollected in one's experiences, I understand all too well the urge to locate the truth behind the fantasy. Roth, as Ben Jeffery cites, promotes "the happy tease," positively as "a dare to his audience," so that he should be obsessed over; as Jeffery continues, it all has to do with a fame that confounds fans into a state of needing to prove that what they think they feel as truth between the lines goes hand in hand with "how convincing [Roth] makes himself seem even while he assures us that what he's telling us isn't true." This "relative realism," these "postmodern" stylistics, these "metafictions," as de la Durantaye cites them (313, n15), have been authorial strategies ages before postmodernism—think of slave narratives or local color fiction for recent examples. These forms of fiction, and straighter forms of fiction, aim to expose some angle of truth relating to humanity at large, and when we read Roth without the madness of trying to figure out what is real and what is not, we see that Roth as a fiction writer certainly attends to universal truths. But Philip Roth is the master of the fact/fiction blur, and that is why Roth readers and scholars cannot quit their antics and why he will never quit his. For all we know (and we know he has handpicked an authorized biographer), Roth has plans in place to keep the ruse going posthumously.

Yet no one can pinpoint what to call Roth's versions of the fact/fiction blur, especially when it comes to understanding Rothian narrators and characters. Indeed, there are many versions of the trick. Jeffery calls them "likenesses," "counterparts, aliases, self-portraits and doppelgangers." Jeffrey Berman calls Roth a "ventriloquist" (94), while Roth, in *The Facts*, employs words like "masks," "disguises," and "distortions" (6). When the stand-out Roth scholar Deborah Shostak offers her reading of *Operation Shylock: A Confession* (1993), she must make a rather lengthy note regarding the naming of characters "since the marker 'Philip Roth' indicates simultaneously the writer of the novel, and the doppelganger." Shostak decides that the "socially and legally" Philip Roth (who "receives [the novel's] royalties" is "Roth," while "Philip" or "the narrator" make reference to the writer/character in the text, and that "the other Roth" shall be called "Pipik (as Philip names him) . . . 'the double' denotes the counterself-in-the-flesh" (Shostak 727, n3). I quote Shostak's clarification in the shadow of what it meant for Roth for himself to figure out what to call the character he finally determines to be a "double," after toying with terms like "the imposturing other," "the usurping self," and "the counterself" (*Operation Shylock* 29); moreover, as Shostak notes, Roth toiled over what to title the very book itself. An early draft was called *Schizo: The Autobiography of an Antithesis* (Shostak 728).

In the fact/fiction blur, the term "autobiography" is and should be hotly interrogated, especially given *The Facts* or even, in some draft, *Schizo*, as a version of autobiography. "Autobiography," as James Olney asserts, is a misnomer, because the central term, "life," could refer to one's history, one's present, the "mythic history and psychological character of a whole group of people" or a person's "psychic development." Olney continues that the only truth in autobiographical writing is that "it cannot fail to reflect and reveal the autobiographer as he is and understands himself to be and wishes himself to be as he sets pen to paper" (213–14). Too many theorists to name here question the accuracy of testimony, memoir, life-writing, and autobiography as pure truth, even if truths appear recognizable or the nature of writing points to larger truths—truths that may be in contest with themselves and in contest with history.

While Aimee Pozorski does not focus upon the autobiographical gesture in *Roth and Trauma: The Problem of History in the Later Works* (*1995–2010*), in her chapter on *The Plot against America* (2004), in which Roth imagines a young Philip Roth living through a "counterhistory" of American anti-Semitism during the Nazi era in Germany, the subject of autobiography-in-contest-with-history falls directly in line with what Olivier Asselin calls "autofictions . . . works through which authors create new personalities and identities for themselves, while at the same time maintaining . . . (their real name) . . . as a hybrid practice, situated between autobiography and the novel" (Asselin 10). Asselin, like Pozorski, goes on to expose the problem that autofictions as alternate versions of autobiography play on history: "The decline of traditions [as related to traditional renderings of history] renders identities, and communities, fragile" (Asselin 16). Asselin and Pozorki suggest that the blur between what readers take to be historical reality set against the reimagining of that reality triggers new versions of trauma as readers contend with divergent, and thus uncomfortable, truths. An engagement with the idea of multiple truths destabilizes readers in ways that compel their searches for consolation in the realm of a truth that might be hidden beneath the guise of fictions that jolt them. Certainly, Roth's versions of Jewish history, in autofictions ranging from *The Plot*, back through *The Ghost Writer* (1979) with its recasting of Anne Frank, to the genesis of what Norman Podhoretz categorized as memoir in Roth's early short stories, and which ran "under the rubric of 'From the American Scene'" in *Commentary* in 1957 (Podhoretz 35), rendered Jewish identity fragile, which caused half of the outcry over the blur between fact and fiction in Roth's autobiographical gestures.

As Roth came to be termed a "Jewish American writer"—much to his chagrin, however much it initially propelled his career—his autobiographical gestures became forms of autoethnography. The term *autoethnography* carries with it a history of critical debate that is well-rehearsed in James Buzard's essay "On Auto-Ethnographic Authority." As Buzard backtracks through the evolution of autoethnography, he pauses to find that the concept maintains the kind of essentialist theory that scholars since the 1960s and 1970s had hoped to eliminate, that it falsely assumes a peoples' shared mentality "overriding all (epiphenomenal) internal differences" (63). Buzard contends that some definitions of autoethnography allow a collective only a static voice, which in turn produces a very limited understanding of a peoples' diversity and potential, which Roth, of course, rallies against. When individuals tell their own stories in a blur of fact and fiction, readers cannot trust them as representatives, but readers want to, searching for some simple truth that would be easier to swallow than the presence of multiple truths. Buzard's problem with autoethnography, besides the essentialism it promotes, as Roth would agree, is the contention that there are "insiders": "We need to know more about why we should trust this particular insider's angle of vision on his own culture. We need to look at the rhetoric by means of which autoethnographers indicate their fitness for their task, and even at the degree to which *they* take for granted their right to perform that task" (71). Until that score is settled, the idea of truth in an autoethnographer, or, in this case, an American Jewish representative, is drivel.

To compare Roth as an autoethnographer, however, with Zora Neale Hurston's role as autoethnographer for some clarification of the term, Buzard turns to Françoise Lionnet's writing on Hurston: "[The] author 'opens up a space of resistance between the individual (*auto-*) and the collective (*-ethno-*) where the writing (*-graphy*) of singularity cannot be foreclosed,' in which that author 'simultaneously appeals to and debunks cultural traditions' she helps to redefine" (Buzard 79). Hence, Hurston's rendering of autoethnography negotiates boundaries of self versus group, much like Roth's, resulting in a *discussion* that seeks to elicit a conformity that is unresolved and unrealistic. If Hurston's autoethnography "negotiates," then the *discussion* serves the ideology that group status must be internally challenged through a rather personal dissent. Even if Roth rejects his function as an autoethnographer as part of his autobiographical gesture, his fiction continues or at least evolves a literary tradition in the vein of Hurston's fiction.

Of course, the nature of American Jewishness in fiction, which shares some kinship with but is not the same as the nature of African Americaness in fiction, is an important aspect of Roth's autobiographical gestures. Whether they are considered definitively autoethnographic in frame or not, Roth's early works, especially, caused uproar among many American Jews, who accused Roth of anti-Semitism toward himself and others in his depiction of Jews. Hana Wirth-Nesher describes his confrontation with "the role of Jewish self-definition and allegiance in the dialogue between art and society, aesthetics and morality, the facts and their literary representation" during the 1962 Yeshiva University conference where middle-class Jews, some influential Rabbis included, claimed Roth as a Jewish writer in an attempt to control the way he portrayed Jewish people (162); as *The Facts* purports, Roth did not want to be considered part of the Jewish Writer's Circle, but his Jewish audience attempted to force him into ethnic categorization through tortuous insult and pressure. Wirth-Nesher's use of the word "allegiance" works best to invoke how Roth's personal narrative (the "auto") as a Jewish person plays into his writing: Roth never denies his Jewish roots, so to speak. And for what it is worth, Roth's ex-wife, Claire Bloom, claims that Roth was practically disgusted by her assimilationist qualities. But more important is that, as Shostak notes, Roth's "contradictory desires at once to refute the essentialist self and to find some way to recognize Jewishness" are implicit in the "fundamental indeterminacy of the Jew" (745). As Roth progresses through to his later works, this autoethnographic theme persists; in *Operation Shylock* and *The Counterlife*, Roth explores "self-dividedness" as a Jewish condition (743). Thus, Roth cannot escape the relationship between autobiographical gestures and the genre of autoethnography.

In *The Human Stain* (2000), Roth experiments with the notion of using a double to contemplate a way out of this fate, or at least to explore it further, by producing a black double named Coleman Silk. Silk, who was born into an African American family, chooses to pass as Jewish because he feels that his possibilities to create an individual identity are limited by racial categorization. This plotline, which reflects Roth's quest to evade the static representation of Jewish community, invokes Josh Cohen's essay on "Roth's doubles." Cohen employs the Freudian concept that the double serves to face up to the "impulses which disturb [one's] sense of who he is" and suggests that Roth uses doubles as part of his autobiographical gesture in order to deal with the problems in his psyche (84). If Roth can create a double who can overcome "the we's overbearing solidity" (*Human Stain* 108), then perhaps he might himself personify the tactics of his fictional character.

Some readings have suggested that Roth created Silk with Anatole Broyard, the famous *New York Times* book critic, in mind. Elaine B. Safer notes that "John Leonard, who had been Broyard's colleague at the *New York Times*, guesses that 'the idea of Coleman Silk was inspired by the case history of . . . Anatole Broyard . . . I am told that he and Roth were almost neighbors in Connecticut.'" Broyard was "resolved to pass so that he could be a writer, rather than a Negro writer" (Gates 184), and the salient connection between Broyard, Silk, and Roth is the ideal of living unfettered by societal expectations about what it means to belong to or represent a racial or ethnic community. Indeed, there are many small parallels between Silk's fictional experiences and the biographical details that Henry Louis Gates describes in his essay "The Passing of Anatole Broyard." Silk's sister, Ernestine, for example, is respectfully "baffled" but willing to accept passing, as was Broyard's sister, Shirley (Gates 213). In *Thirteen Ways of Looking at a Black Man*, Gates repeatedly mentions Broyard's legs, thus Roth emulates this trope—"the girls, in turn, liked his legs," anatomy that Steena turns into poetry (*Human Stain* 109–10). And the depiction of neighbors in New England mimics the geographical closeness of Broyard and Roth, but fictionally, Zuckerman, instead of Silk, suffers the cancer from which Broyard eventually died. Most importantly in readers' minds are Silk's lustful encounters involving Steena in his Greenwich Village apartment, which evoke Broyard's passing plot in *Kafka Was the Rage* (1993). Other similarities between Broyard and Silk include their military experience, unsuccessful endeavors in composing autobiographical narratives, and blatant withholding of genetic information from offspring whose features never turned out to air family secrets.

Though Broyard had essentially passed to counter the problem of racial representation due to his white appearance, Roth's Jewish name, autobiographical gestures, and Jewish themes caused him to experience the fate that Broyard may have been afraid of. The irony of Broyard's racial escape in the face of Roth's entrapment, brings to mind the notion that weak American Jewish and African American ties are the result of accurate accounts that Jews pass more easily as white and/ or mainstream. In *The Human Stain*, Broyard's mantra that literature operates "on more than one level" (Gates 183) is omnipresent. Still, the ethics of Roth's writing on the autobiographical level—especially if he involves aliases or likenesses to Broyard, or the names of actual people, like Anne Frank and members of his family, or even when he blurs the fact/fiction line in descriptions of himself—are a major concern.

Recently, Roth openly challenged a Wikipedia entry that linked Silk to Broyard, only to be scolded in print by Broyard's daughter, Bliss:

"There was a legitimate reason that many reviewers of the book and movie drew the comparison to my dad's life. Not only are there many similarities between Silk and my father's basic biographies, but many of these details Roth could have known (despite his protests otherwise) by glancing through my father's two memoirs" (Bloomgarden-Smoke). Bliss Broyard goes on to say that Roth's objection to the information on Wikipedia is counterfactual to her personal memories, particularly her description of herself and her father being in Roth's company. These events exemplify ethical concerns related to autobiographical gesturing, because Roth's dismissal of what Bliss Broyard remembers as fact is painful to her. Still, Roth tried to clarify in a post on a *New Yorker* blog that the true inspiration for Silk was Mel Tumin. So then how is Tumin's family to respond to the germination of a fictional character? It seems that Roth's publicity stunts, such as his public announcement of retirement, are self-serving; therefore, his letter to Wikipedia and his citation of Tumin are to be taken with his self-invention of a public persona in mind rather than as a true defense of his fiction as fiction. The artfulness of the public persona is thus mixed with Roth's fiction in ways that cannot be divorced, though one might claim they should be.

Here, it is appropriate to turn to *Patrimony* (1991), which, in Simon and Schuster's first edition by several interesting turns of the publication frame, is advertised as "A True Story." While the book is known and most often referred to quite simply as *Patrimony*, the words "A True Story" appear beneath the title as if after a colon, the same setup as *The Facts*. The colon as a mark of punctuation signifies the Aristotelian logic of "equal to"; the colon suggests content formal or even academic, and it is not carried in the titles of his other "fiction" books. Interestingly, Amazon advertizes both titles with colons after the main title, to capture the cover matter—and perhaps entice the reader—but while *The Facts* does carry a colon in its Library of Congress categorization, the 1991 Simon and Schuster version of *Patrimony* does not cite "A True Story" as part of the title at all. In fact, the first lines of the inner jacket copy make it clear that "a true story" is not part of the title: "*Patrimony*, a true story," note the publisher's italic casing of the title in relation to the standard font, purports the book will "touch the emotions as strongly as anything Philip Roth has ever written." The wording is manipulative. It appears that Roth has not entitled his piece as a "true story," but his publishers did, and thus, one must wonder who okayed that decision and why. If we take the publisher's act at face value, it seems that at last, readers are to expect facts of Roth's experience—as if he could cite the intricacy of dialogue found in *Patrimony* with such lucid memory and without the writerly impulses and strategies of word choice. Simon and Schuster (and maybe Roth himself in his "mastermind behind the scenes" role) invite the notion that *Patrimony* will expose a truth differently from "anything Philip Roth has ever written," as if to say, "don't worry, his truth is as emotionally touching as his fiction." Yet there is no clear distinction, especially given the ending lines of the jacket copy, as to whether or not *Patrimony* is just another "of the trilogy of recent books in which Philip Roth writes as Philip Roth" even though, the jacket copy argues, "*Patrimony* is the most nakedly direct and most emotionally powerful." Hence, the blur of fact and fiction is not only present in the publication history, it serves to raise the question of what exists as a more powerful truth when fact is set against fiction this way: If writing as Philip Roth is, in either memoir or fiction, the most "naked" (read: self-exposing) and "emotionally powerful," then what is the real aesthetic difference or purpose in serving humanity's emotional needs when using either kind of autobiographical gesture? In other words, does it matter if something is framed as fact or fiction if the objective is to relate a deeply emotional truth for a reader to thrive upon? Roth's rationale for the autobiographical gesture seems driven by the idea that there is no perfect truth in rendering historical events, and that his version of truth is, indeed, more powerful in its reach to capture through imperfections, or creativity, the truth of feelings over and above what Hayden White refers to as "the Burden of History"—that the transmission of history is inherently artful, a type of propaganda tool that justifies the representation of a more broad understanding.

De la Durantaye offers that "if, as Roth writes, 'the governing motive' in an autobiography 'is primarily ethical as against aesthetic,' then the author who cedes to the temptation of telling the best story, as opposed to the most scrupulously exact or truthful one, betrays it" (328); but the other side of the ethical dilemma concerning the autobiographical gesture is a betrayal of a different kind: the representation of real people. When Roth reveals the "nakedness" of his father in *Patrimony*—which is forbidden by Jewish law and is thus connected to Roth's autobiographical gesture as it relates to his Jewish identity—Roth's father is without control when it comes to how he is portrayed. David Gooblar's essay, "The Truth Hurts: The Ethics of Philip Roth's 'Autobiographical' Books," zooms in on a textual example from *Patrimony* that bears and bares much of the complication involved in the ethics of Roth's autobiographical writing. When Philip's father (whom we see practically naked in a family photo that is literally picture-framed on the cover of the Simon and Schuster edition), "beshat" himself (an undoubtedly biblical word play on Roth's part that refers to the Jewish law aforementioned), a rather common yet perhaps embarrassing side effect of illness at any age, Roth practically bathes himself in the telling of the story: "The shit was everywhere, smeared underfoot on the bathmat, running over the toilet bowl edge and, at the foot of the bowl, in a pile on the floor. It was splattered across the glass of the shower stall from which he'd just emerged, and the clothes discarded in the hallway were clotted with it" (172). After Roth dutifully cleans up and gets his father into bed, Herman says to his son:

> "Don't tell the children," he said, looking up at me from the bed with his one sighted eye.
>
> "I won't tell anyone," I said. "I'll say you're taking a rest."
>
> "Don't tell Claire."
>
> "Nobody," I said. (173)

As Gooblar writes, "Herman . . . is absolutely clear in telling his son that this is an event he wishes no one to ever know about. And yet, even as he portrays his father's shame, as well as his own promise not to tell, Roth includes it in his book, making of it, in fact, a central scene" (Gooblar 37). Gooblar goes on to cite Roth's vague awareness of "the necessary 'unseemliness' that goes into the making of a book," especially one about a beloved father's illness and suffering (38). Some might say this kind of book requires a mix of ethicality and empathy, but even in Gooblar's word choice in describing the novelistic construction, the words "in fact" jump out, maybe in Gooblar's confusion over whether or not this scene is fact or fiction; conceivably it is the solicitation of empathy from Roth for himself, or it is just the "making of a book." When it is unclear why there must be a divide between those two out of many possibilities, the ethics of the autobiographical gesture fall to, as author James Frey might term it, a million little pieces.

Of course, one of those pieces is the use of other people's real names. Roth's ex-wife, the actress Claire Bloom, referred to as "Claire" in the excerpt above, retaliated against Roth's portrayals of her with her own memoir of their marriage—a piece of writing that outraged Roth to the point that he made an explicit decision not to discuss her or the book in the documentary *Philip Roth, Sans Complex*. In her *New York Times* review of Livia Manera's interview footage, Celestine Bohlen reports that Manera told her there was to be "no mention . . . of his toxic marriage to the British actress." Roth attempts to call the shots when it comes to the way those he has portrayed characterize him; he considers his employment of real names as aesthetic, but, with some acknowledgement that "he wouldn't want to be living with a loudmouthed novelist" who might invade his privacy, he insists that "privacy is the domain of the novelist," that the intimacies provided are the reader's demand (Rothstein 200). What readers demand and what writers supply involve a special set of responsibilities for the writer, who must juggle the need to please with ethical and aesthetic considerations. Roth's magic show juggles these responsibilities before his readers' eyes, he performs the act as the writer and his readers examine it and its consequences.

Along the lines of this amusement, Roth makes the issue of his right to write whatever he wants one of his right to personal privacy and the public control of his image. In his seminal essay "To Invent as Presumptuously as Real Life: Parody and the Cultural Memory of Anne Frank in Roth's *The Ghost Writer*," R. Clifton Spargo makes the case that Roth tactically invites the public to make the writer-reader relationship personal. Alluding to the controversy surrounding Roth's reimagining of Anne Frank, Spargo writes, "From what we know of his controversial career, we can safely say that Philip Roth would not only have anticipated much of the negative reaction to *The Ghost Writer*, he would have counted on it" (89). This taunt and provocation of public interest in the celebrity author is part of the autobiographical gesture in his novels; for example, Zuckerman, as a Rothian double, must face the consequences of his offensive and "autobiographical" *Carnovsky* straight through the novel of his death, *Exit Ghost* (2007), where he worries, full circle, via E. I. Lonoff from *The Ghost Writer*, about celebrity image and the issues of fact versus fiction. In *Exit Ghost*, Amy Bellette, whom Zuckerman had once momentarily imagined as Anne Frank, rather ironically argues against the "biographical reductivism" of literature, calling it "the invasion of privacy" (182). Yet it is exactly this scandal that Roth lives and writes that might be called a house of mirrors (it is located up in the Berkshires—take a tour on YouTube). And while Roth scorns scholars in his 2005 interview with Martin Krasnik in the *Guardian*—Roth says: "I would be wonderful with a 100-year moratorium on literature talk," implying that he rejects scholarly interest in his life and works—Spargo is ultimately right: He counts on it.

Nevertheless, Spargo's realization presents an ethical dilemma for those who write and publish on Roth. While parsing out Roth's autobiographical gestures, we must be careful about the "facts" we present. In

"Revisiting Roth's Psychoanalysis," the scholar Jeffrey Berman made a discovery his was not sure he had the right to disclose about Roth. As he researched a biographical connection between Peter Tarnopol (from the 1970 novel *My Life as a Man*[1]) and Philip Roth's own participation in psychoanalysis, he found that Roth had used his own therapist's case study on Philip Roth as patient to describe Tarnopol. What was more jarring than the fact that Roth used what his therapist wrote about him to describe his narrator, however, was that the therapist had published, with a few calculatedly changed details for anonymity, a thirty-page essay on his sessions with Roth at all. Berman writes:

> I realized instantly that the discovery thrust me into an ethical dilemma: the publication of my finding would reinvade Roth's privacy . . . After much soul-searching, I decided in favor of publication, believing then, as I believe now, that I was justified because Roth had left enough fictional clues in *My Life as a Man* for a psychoanalytically oriented literary sleuth to piece together the story.
>
> I don't mean to dismiss the possibility that critics, especially psycho-analytic ones, can harm living authors, not only by invading their privacy but also by "diagnosing" their characters. (97, 100)

What happened when Berman confronted Roth's psychoanalyst about the case study is that he was threatened with a lawsuit from the doctor! We might take from this example that the human desire for facts is constantly and in ways unbelievably met by the power of imagination. Imagination, even as a form of diagnostic case study—the scientific nuance is so misleading—still produces, as Wirth-Nesher writes, "a truth of a certain kind." We try to "determine what happened, to ascertain the facts, and then to write a story that is the result of interpreting and evaluating those facts" (166–67). Scholars, clinicians, historians, novelists, poets, and readers alike all participate in the autobiography, unless, one might argue, the whole game is madness.

This reference to madness is not an attempt to dismiss the topic, but quite the opposite. Discussions of Roth's autobiographical gestures are maddening and may be, in some way, the stuff of madness. As de la Durantaye close reads Roth's authorial state in the introduction to *The Facts*, he diagnoses that the novelist is not always so artful. He cites the words "exhaustion," "confused helplessness," and "breakdown" to agree with Roth that he suffers from "fiction fatigue." De la Durantaye continues, "Roth's letter to Zuckerman demonstrates the extent of this 'fiction fatigue' and the attendant 'confused helplessness.' Roth [may be using] his fictional character to convey a deeply personal truth, writing more searchingly and authentically about himself with Zuckerman's fictional aid than he could do without," as if to align Roth with symptoms of schizophrenia (306). It is possible that as the personal experience of madness is examined in his fiction through autobiographical gestures, Roth explores his psyche through writing as healing, or maybe Roth's writing sends him more deeply into the experience of madness—or maybe healing and madness happen simultaneously, thus causing his writing, his gestures, his creative products, to be absolutely brilliant. After all, as Shostak implies, the novel *Operation Shylock*, so thoroughly infused with doubles in their various disturbing forms, is born directly from "the deformations of self experienced by the narrator during his 'Halcion madness'" (728–29). It should be noted, here, that from writing about the narrator's Halcion madness came Roth's PEN/Faulkner prize for *Operation Shylock*.

With so many literary awards under his belt, one might be tempted to dismiss the fact that Roth's writing about multiple selves—whether one calls it madness or not—is not just praised because of its use of a narrative device or novelistic edginess, but also because so many people can relate to the topic of multiple selves, conflicting urges, and the kind of creative introspection necessary to the processing of an event or an experience. Moreover, the relationship between mental illness and artistic creativity is well-documented.[2] I do not propose any clinical diagnosis of Roth as "cracked up"; suffice it to say that his autobiographical gestures express the imaginative possibilities unique to his production of characters that embody the self-reflexivity found in people searching for wholeness through the introspective discovery of the doubles, disguises, and distortions within.

Notes

1. My 1993 First Vintage International Edition of *My Life as a Man* is suspiciously titled *A Life as a Man* on the binding, even though the cover reflects the true title. I wonder whether this was a publication error or an overt attempt to confuse the personal nature of the word "my," indicating the autobiographical gesture, with the most unspecific grammatical article "a" to describe the life of an everyman.
2. See, for example, James.

Works Cited

Asselin, Olivier. "Autofictions, or Elective Identities." *Parachute: Contemporary Art Magazine* 105.1–3 (2002): 10–19. Print.

Berman, Jeffrey. "Revisiting Roth's Psychoanalysis." *The Cambridge Companion to Philip Roth*. Ed. Timothy Parrish. Cambridge: Cambridge UP, 2007. Print.

Bloomgarden-Smoke, Kara. "Broyard's Daughter Responds to Philip Roth." *Observer.* Guardian News and Media. 20 Sept. 2012. Web. 11 Jan. 2013.

Bohlen, Celestine. "Rare Unfurling of the Reluctant Philip Roth." *New York Times*. New York Times, 16 Sept. 2011. Web. 8 Jan. 2013.

Buzard, James. "On Auto-Ethnographic Authority." *Yale Journal of Criticism* 16.1 (2003): 61–91. Print.

Cohen, Josh. "Roth's Doubles." *The Cambridge Companion to Philip Roth*. Ed. Timothy Parrish. Cambridge: Cambridge UP, 2007. Print.

De la Durantaye, Leland. "How to Read Philip Roth, or the Ethics of Fiction and the Aesthetics of Fact." *Cambridge Quarterly* 39.4 (2010): 303–30. Print.

Gates, Henry Louis, Jr. *Thirteen Ways of Looking at a Black Man*. New York: Random, 1997. Print.

Glaser, Jennifer. "The Jew in the Canon: Reading Race and Literary History in Philip Roth's *The Human Stain*." *PMLA* 123.5 (2008): 1465–78. Print.

Gooblar, Josh. "The Truth Hurts: The Ethics of Philip Roth's 'Autobiographical' Books." *Journal of Modern Literature* 32.1 (2008): 32–53. Print.

James, Kay Redfield. *Touched with Fire: Manic Depressive Illness and the Artistic Temperament*. New York: Free, 1996. Print.

Jeffery, Ben. "What's Next Isn't the Point: Philip Roth in Age." *Quarterly Conversation*. Scott Esposito, 6 Sept. 2011. Web. 8 Jan. 2013.

Krasnik, Martin. "It No Longer Feels a Great Injustice That I Have to Die." *Guardian.* Guardian News and Media, 13 Dec. 2005. Web. 8 Jan. 2013.

Olney, James. "The Value of Autobiography for Comparative Studies: African vs. Western Autobiography." *African American Autobiography: A Collection of Critical Essays.* Ed. William Andrews. Englewood Cliffs: Prentice, 1993. Print.

O'Neill, Joseph. "Roth v. Roth v. Roth." *Atlantic.* Atlantic Media, Apr. 2012. Web. 8 Jan. 2013.

Podhoretz, Norman. "The Adventures of Philip Roth." *Commentary* 106.4 (1998): 35–43. Print.

Pozorski, Aimee. *Roth and Trauma: The Problem of History in the Later Works (1995–2010).* New York: Continuum, 2011. Print.

Roth, Philip. *Exit Ghost.* Boston: Houghton, 2007. Print.

___. *The Facts: A Novelist's Autobiography.* New York: Vintage, 1988. Print.

___. *The Human Stain.* New York: Vintage, 2000. Print.

___. *Operation Shylock: A Confession.* New York: Simon, 1993. Print.

___. *Patrimony.* New York: Simon, 1991. Print.

___. *Reading Myself and Others.* New York: Vintage, 1985. Print.

Rothstein, Mervyn. "Philip Roth and the World of 'What If?'" *Conversations with Philip Roth.* Ed. George Searles. Jackson: U of Mississippi P, 1992. 198–201. Print.

Safer, Elaine. "Tragedy and Farce in Roth's *The Human Stain.*" *Critique* 43.3 (2002): n.pag. *Academic Search Premier.* Web. 8 Jan. 2013.

Shostak, Deborah. "The Diaspora Jew and the 'Instinct for Impersonation': Philip Roth's *Operation Shylock.*" *Contemporary Literature* 38.4 (1997): 726–54. Print.

Spargo, R. Clifton. "To Invent as Presumptuously as Real Life: Parody and the Cultural Memory of Anne Frank in Roth's *The Ghost Writer.*" *Representations* 76 (2001): 88–119. Print.

White, Hayden. *Tropics of Discourse.* Baltimore: Johns Hopkins UP, 1986. Print.

Wirth-Nesher, Hana. "Roth's Autobiographical Writings." *The Cambridge Companion to Philip Roth.* Ed. Timothy Parish. Cambridge: Cambridge UP, 2007. Print.

The Mechanics of History in Philip Roth's American Trilogy_____

Michael Kimmage

Art is a comfortable part of historical inquiry. It is the stuff of intellectual history, supplying primary sources of incomparable depth, plasticity, and beauty. Familiar as art's service to history is, the relationship between art and history is not a relationship of equals. Mostly the historian employs art—painting, music, film, literature—to interpret the historical record. Art is raw material, there to be used; its significance is for others to establish. Art matters for what it might contribute to a particular historical argument.[1] The historian reading *War and Peace* would more likely use this book, first published in 1869, to describe Russia in the 1860s or to discuss Leo Tolstoy than to interpret the Napoleonic invasion chronicled and analyzed in the novel itself. Yet the artist has freedoms that are less available to the historian, and art is more than raw material. It can generate historical understanding. Literature, for example, offers pertinent and possibly unique insight into two historical issues. One is the construction of narrative, and the other is the sensation of history, the way in which people feel historical change. The authority of the professional historian, with a few recent and nineteenth-century exceptions, follows from a promise not to write fiction. There is a degree of loss implicit in this promise.[2]

The twentieth century abounds in historically minded literature. The novels of Thomas Mann diagram German history, from *Buddenbrooks* (1901) to *The Magic Mountain* (1924) to *Doctor Faustus* (1947), from Wilhelmine Germany through to the Third Reich. Vasily Grossman's epic *Life and Fate* (1959) rewrites *War and Peace*, with World War II substituted for the War of 1812. John Dos Passos crams centuries of American history into his *USA* trilogy (1930–38), melding literary and cinematic techniques. William Faulkner's novels are entirely inseparable from history—not just the history of the Civil War but the more mundane history of those living after that war, persevering in their haunted modernity.[3] In its plot and its unnamed protagonist, Ralph Ellison's *Invisible Man* (1952) traces the history of the black migration, among other historical phenomena. A more recent instance of the genre is, like Dos Passos's *USA*, a trilogy. Often referred to as Philip Roth's American trilogy, it comprises *American Pastoral* (1997), *I Married a Communist* (1998), and *The Human Stain* (2000). This trilogy was completed in the fifth decade of Roth's literary career, and it has much to teach the historian (and the reader) about the construction of narrative and the sensation of history.

I

History did not preoccupy the young Roth. Born in 1933, he was first celebrated as a practitioner of the Jewish American mode in American fiction, writing stories and novels typically set in Newark, New Jersey. Roth dramatized the lives of Newark's Jewish residents, capturing their milieu, their families, their foibles, their appetites, and their speech.[4] The apogee of Roth's fame as a Jewish American writer was his scandalous and scandalously successful novel *Portnoy's Complaint*, published in 1969. If Roth's terrain was the psychosexual hang-ups of American Jews losing and discovering themselves amid the postwar newness, every limit was reached in *Portnoy's Complaint*.

After *Portnoy*, Roth turned the temperature down, seemingly turning inward. In the early 1980s, he completed a series of novellas that amounted to a long novel. It was released in 1985 as *Zuckerman Bound*, and its protagonist is Nathan Zuckerman, a writer whose biography mimics that of his creator. *Zuckerman Bound* is a portrait of the artist as an aging American. The layering of text within text, of story within story, of authorial sensibility within authorial sensibility, culminates in *The Counterlife* (1986), in which Zuckerman is yet again a character. Stories and characters break into countless fragments in this novel. Validating the postmodern mood of the 1980s, *The Counterlife* is an essay on literature and stories, on the perplexities of writing and reading. Roth appears well informed about American, European, and Israeli history without exhibiting a sustained interest in history per se.

In the 1990s, history invaded the Rothian landscape, shadowing both *Operation Shylock* (1993) and *Sabbath's Theater* (1995). *Operation Shylock* invokes history by surveying the will to evade it. One of its characters fantasizes about reversing Zionism and leading the Jews back from Israel to Europe. Other characters, taken from actual history, are on trial for historical reasons: John Demjanjuk because of alleged crimes committed during the Holocaust; Leon Klinghoffer for the simple reason that he is a Jew. A man on a cruise, an American Jew on holiday from history, Klinghoffer is caught in the clutches of political zeal and ultimately killed in the name of this zeal. The hero of *Sabbath's Theater* is a broken and ridiculous man. At first, Mickey Sabbath seems broken by the ruthlessness of his inner appetites: Having broken others, his appetites finally break him. By the novel's end, though, Mickey Sabbath's fractured psyche is revealed to have a historical origin. Sabbath's brother fought and died in World War II, and his mother was driven mad by the news of her son's death. To escape from his mother's grief, Sabbath threw himself into heedless eroticism. Whether or not the personal is political, in *Sabbath's Theater*, the personal is emphatically historical, and such is the guiding principle of Roth's American trilogy.

The master story of the American trilogy reprises Roth's earlier work. Much of the trilogy is set in Newark's Jewish neighborhoods. Roth's immersion in the intricacies of literary life—the Zuckerman phase, one could call it—shapes the American trilogy as well, since its narrator is none other than Zuckerman himself. Zuckerman hears about his characters, learning pieces of their story. These pieces enter his imagination before he knows they will be fashioned into stories. The postmodern notion of narrative as something manufactured by the imagination, contingent rather than set in stone, flows into the American trilogy from *The Counterlife* and from *Operation Shylock*. The trilogy's leitmotif, which may be Roth's or may be Zuckerman's, is that people are at history's mercy. They think they control their destiny, when in fact their destiny, in the form of history, is controlling them. Of the trilogy's three protagonists, two are Jewish and one is black. All three are born in Newark, and each leaves Newark in a disguise of some kind. The Jews transform themselves into successful Americans in no need of an ethnic past; the black man changes himself to white. Camouflaged as radiant American citizens, they gain wealth and status. Then some unanticipated shift occurs and success turns to failure, failure to persecution. All three protagonists find themselves squeezed by circumstance and degraded by an unwanted destiny. Their problem, finally, is the durability of the disguises they constructed while fleeing Newark. This is a problem they cannot solve. They take it with them to their graves, after which it solves Zuckerman's problem (of not being able to write) by giving him fabulous stories to tell.

History does not resolve into harmony, the American trilogy contends, but into narrative. Crisis yields ultimately to the narrative of crisis, and only in this yielding do history's crises relax their hold. Nathan Zuckerman, the trilogy's historian, is a personified narrator. His well-documented career makes him a known entity for regular Roth readers.[5] Though Nathan's presence in the American trilogy is modest, it exposes the mechanics of history in these novels, pointing to one concern about which historians have written extensively and indicating another about which they rarely speak. The known concern is that of narrative and evidence; the less well-known concern involves the narrator's psyche.

There are gaps in the record, an everyday dilemma for historians. Much like a classicist or an anthropologist, Zuckerman has only small fragments to work with, shattered pieces of the past. These fragments and pieces are not documents, with the solidity of documents, but words articulated in a human voice. In *American Pastoral*, Zuckerman goes to his high-school reunion, where he meets Jerry Levov, the brother of a star athlete whom he revered as a child and met a few times as an adult. From Jerry he hears a story of family tragedy. After assimilating the story, Nathan goes home to write. What we read in *American Pastoral* is a novel written by Nathan Zuckerman, or such is the novel's conceit. Similarly, in *The Human Stain*, Zuckerman hears the story of his friend Coleman Silk from Coleman's sister, Ernestine. This he turns into a novel called *The Human Stain*. In *I Married a Communist*, it is Ira Ringold's brother, Murray, who speaks with Nathan night after night in rural Massachusetts, narrating the story long before Nathan can get to it. The ubiquity of siblings here is telling. Siblings know more than cousins and more than outsiders to the family circle, but their statements and stories are ruthlessly subjective. The words Nathan hears from his team of siblings are true, as far as the reader knows, but their truth is not to be detached from their tone, from the voices of those who pronounce them or from the bonds of kinship in which these words and stories originate. The narrator's tone proceeds from the innuendo latent in his "primary sources." Nathan is trapped within the preconceptions of those with firsthand knowledge, following the dictation of others. He thereby demonstrates an ancient problem of historical narrative. Consciously and at times unconsciously, Nathan tells the stories that his sources tell him to tell.

This is literally the case in *The Human Stain*. When Nathan attends the funeral of his friend Coleman Silk, he discovers, from Coleman's sister Ernestine, who Coleman was. Nathan never knew that his friend was black. The writer is seen listening: "It was from Ernestine . . . that I learned most of what I know about Coleman's growing up in East Orange" (317). The writer's source speaks until "the torrent of disclosure [is] over. Ernestine had said all there was to say" (333). Ernestine tells the basic story, shaping the narrative and naming the facts within which the writer must operate. In this novel, literary narrative can be reduced to a formula. Narrative is fact plus mystery, or it is fact expressed as mystery, as Nathan observes when distinguishing between Ernestine's facts and the exigencies of his own writerly imagination: "I couldn't imagine anything that could have made Coleman more of mystery to me than this unmasking. Now that I knew everything, it was as though

I knew nothing, and instead of what I'd learned from Ernestine unifying my idea of him, he became not just an unknown but an uncohesive person" (333). Literary narrative draws its inspiration from Ernestine's unmasking, honoring the true story of Coleman Silk, born to a black family in East Orange, New Jersey. Literary narrative simultaneously acknowledges the coherence of masks and the terrible obscurity of an unmasked man. Hard questions materialize the moment somebody's secret is revealed. In *The Human Stain*, Nathan contemplates Coleman's mystery while telling Ernestine's story.

In *American Pastoral*, Nathan tells Jerry's story. Nathan is highly self-conscious about his vocation, a writer fascinated by writing and by the prospect of gaining an accurate image of another person. Nathan knows that he has only "traces" of the Swede; that these traces come from a fallible source, the Swede's brother; and that his "portrait" is an arrangement of the available evidence:

> Of course I was working with traces; of course essentials of what he was to Jerry were gone, expunged from my portrait, things I was ignorant of or I didn't want; of course the Swede was concentrated differently in my pages from how he'd been concentrated in the flesh. But whether this meant I'd imagined an outright fantastical creature, lacking entirely the unique substantiality of the real thing; whether that meant my conception of the Swede was any more fallacious than the conception held by Jerry (which he wasn't likely to see as in any way fallacious); whether the Swede and his family came to life in me any less truthfully than in his brother—well, who knows? Who *can* know? When it comes to illuminating someone with the Swede's opacity, to understanding those regular guys everybody likes and who go about more or less incognito, it's up for grabs, it seems to me, as to whose guess is more rigorous than whose. (76–77)

All the concessions to subjectivity take one unexpectedly to a defense of the writer's craft. If nobody has the real version of events or an objective grasp of another person's character, then error is inevitable. Yet it is not definitive. Error is the price paid for trying to know the real version and for approaching an objective understanding. The result is up for grabs. The writer's guess, tainted by the opacity of others, may well be the most rigorous of all.

If siblings, like Ernestine and Jerry, provide the primary sources, it is Nathan who gives the reader a finished narrative. In this labor he is a professional. He lets the reader know what is known—within a fictional world, of course—and what is invented, and a great deal is invented. The trilogy's lack of polish is a spur to reflection. One conclusion drawn from such reflection is that narrative respects the dictates of genre. This is Hayden White's thesis in *Metahistory*, an avant-garde book published in 1973.[6] The literary genres of tragedy, comedy, satire, and epic shaped the grand narratives of nineteenth-century historiography, White claims, as they did the philosophies of history devised by Georg Hegel, Karl Marx, and Friedrich Nietzsche. Historical narrative matches the shape of literary genre. For Nathan, narrative stands between evidence—the opinionated evidence given him by opinionated individuals—and genre. (The genre of the American trilogy is tragedy.) The medium, the place where evidence and genre meet, is narrative, and narrative heightens the mystery of Nathan's stories. The sequence is chronological: the tragic hero is born, takes action, suffers, and then dies. All the while, the hero lives in historical time, suffering for reasons decreed by history. When change comes, for the trilogy's three heroes, it is historical change: 1960s turbulence in *American Pastoral*, McCarthyism in *I Married a Communist*, and the rise of political correctness in *The Human Stain*. Once a narrative is complete, it is not verifiably true or false; rather, it succeeds or fails. It succeeds by making emotional sense of historical sequence and of an individual whose suffering is reflected in historical patterns. Narrative is an emotional process. The literary feel of this point should not invalidate it for historians wrestling, as they constantly are, with the intangibles of narrative.

The other connection between history and narrative foregrounded in the American trilogy is psychological. When historians speak about the powers that orient their work, they usually speak about politics. One writes in a certain way about the New Deal if one is a Democrat. One writes a certain way about Ronald Reagan if one is a Republican. In the American trilogy, Nathan is probably a Democrat, as Roth has described himself in interviews. If so, this position has little discernible impact on Nathan's storytelling; the impetus behind his narrative is not political but psychological. Nathan has a psychological need to tell the stories he chooses to tell. He left Newark as a young man, has lived in several American cities, and is living in rural New England at the time of the American trilogy. After Newark's collapse into urban ruin, he ceased to be a writer. He knows what has become of himself since leaving Newark, and he is not much interested. It is the story of others who have left his hometown that consumes him. Nathan has a personal relationship with the protagonist in each of the trilogy's three novels. In each novel, he learns some surprising detail about these protagonists from conversation, from the idiosyncratic rhythms of the spoken word; in each, he is seen spinning word and detail into narrative, and each narrative brings him back to the Newark of his youth. The return to Newark via narratives of its native sons stimulates Nathan's Newark-educated psyche. His fascination with leaving Newark echoes his own departure from the city, and its terrible postwar decline correlates with Nathan's personal loss of Newark, the loss of his childhood world, giving the American trilogy its elegiac quality.

Nathan, who was once the enfant terrible of American letters, is now a senior citizen, and his ties to the past, to Newark, are much tighter than his ties to the present. His life in real time seems frighteningly bare: no spouse, no children, no friends, no parents, no siblings. In *I Married a Communist*, Nathan spends several evenings with his old high-school English teacher, Murray. When they part, Murray asks him about the strange solitude to which he has retired:

"Why do you live up there, alone like that? Why don't you have a heart for the world?"

"I prefer it this way," [Nathan] said.

"No, I watched you listening. I don't think you do. I don't think for a moment the exuberance is gone. You were like that as a kid. That's why I got such a kick out of you—you paid attention. You still do. But what is up here to pay attention to? You should get out from under whatever's the problem." (315)

Nathan has listened, intoxicated, to Murray's stories. In such listening, the exuberance is still there, and it is, for psychological reasons, an exuberance for the past, the same exuberance Marcel Proust slipped into the title of his masterpiece *Remembrance of Things Past*, which has also been translated as *In Search of Lost Time* (1913–27). To Murray, however, literature is literature and life is life, which is why Nathan's Proustian isolation is a problem, one that art alone cannot solve.

Among academics, a psychological tie between author and narrative can be intuited at times from the acknowledgments to books, but in formal discussions, vastly less attention is paid to psychology than to politics. Historians are reluctant to disclose their psychological motivations for writing particular books and for fashioning particular narratives. They do not necessarily know what their psychological motivations are. They might profit nevertheless from charting the link between the historian's psyche and his or her narrative. The very will to speculate about the past, as opposed to the future or the present, must have psychological causes behind it. If the trend of psychohistory ended in embarrassment, perhaps it was because the historian was so strenuously excluded from its field of vision. Napoleon and Hitler were put on the couch, while the historian stayed seated in the analyst's chair.

II

The construction of narrative revolves around timing. Change has a speed, and those who experience change do so in time and according to time's contingencies. "The moral world had changed," the historian Samuel Moyn writes in his book *The Last Utopia* (2010). "'People think of history in the long term,' Philip Roth says in one of his novels, 'but history, in fact, is a very sudden thing.' Never has this been truer than when it comes to the history of human rights" (4). Here the novelist's bon mot, extracted from the American trilogy, confirms the argument of an academic historian. A sudden impact registers in the senses, and sensory description is second nature to novelists. Perhaps this is why Moyn quoted a writer of fiction, rather than a fellow historian, when making his point. Conventional historical writing has trouble with the sensory dimension, with the quick and immediate aspects of experience (Moyn 4). As if to compensate for this difficulty, historians overdo descriptions of weather, especially in the first paragraphs of narrative history. Though mention of rain or sun or heat or cold may be thematically irrelevant, it helps the reader to enter, with senses alert, into the domain of the past. Other sensory experiences beyond weather lend themselves less well to historical description. In addition, professional historians are taught to excel at the scrutiny of long-term structural change, while novelists, unburdened by causal demonstration and liberated from the long term, can, if they wish, jump headlong into the feel of things.

The American trilogy does this incessantly. Its protagonists are made to feel history, and it helps here that they are neither venerable historical actors nor the authors of historical change. Nathan's heroes do not resemble the Napoleon of *War and Peace*. The great man may be less great than he thinks he is, if we believe Tolstoy, but he is still Napoleon. Nathan's characters must learn the historical recipes for destruction and self-destruction. In *American Pastoral*, the Swede is an affluent American businessman. His beloved daughter is undone by her political radicalism, and before his eyes she reverses the heroic saga of immigration and assimilation. The Swede visits this daughter in a devastated Newark neighborhood, his thoughts a treatise on the terrors to which history can amount. "Of old," he thinks. "Stories of old. There were no longer stories of old. There was nothing. There was a mattress, discolored and waterlogged, like a cartoon-strip drunk slumped against a pole. The pole still held up a sign telling you what corner you were on. And that's all there was" (236). America is redefined for him because of his ruptured family, its history inverted from ascent to descent: "His daughter lived even worse than her greenhorn great-grandparents had, fresh from steerage, in their Prince Street tenement." The Old World is preferable to the new, the past to the present. The immigrants have emigrated from good fortune: "Three generations. All of them growing. The working. The saving. The success. Three generations in raptures over America. Three generations of becoming one with a people. And now with the fourth it had all come to nothing. The total vandalization of their world" (237). The word *vandalization* here suggests the fall of the Roman Empire, its loss of agency and autonomy at the hands of conquering Vandals.

Such passages reveal in the negative historians' enormous bias toward actors and agency. For centuries, this bias drew historians to great men like Napoleon. In the second half of the twentieth century, history from the bottom up, grassroots history, increased the number of historical subjects by declaring agency a wider phenomenon than "great man" historians had allowed. Great men were actors, it is true, but so too were those outside the perimeter of greatness. Factory workers were actors. The Victorian-era Chartists were historical actors, women were historical actors, minorities were historical actors, the subaltern was a historical actor, and so on. At the Stonewall Inn in Greenwich Village, gay men fought their way into historical agency, their struggle tantamount to fighting their way into history. But what of those who were acted upon, who left no mark, and whose lives were shaped, deformed, or crushed by historical change? When historians look past the domineering question of agency, they can open their eyes to sensation. To history from the bottom up can be added history from the sidelines, which invites the literary devices of irony, tragedy, and comedy: the irony of thwarted intentions, the tragedy of defeat and victimhood, and the comedy of agency as hoped for, as opposed to the small slivers of agency that people usually possess. The history of the passive is the history of consciousness, and it can be traced in many primary sources, including letters, diaries, telephone conversations, oral interviews, and memoirs. At the same time, consciousness is punishingly elusive for historians. It may, by rhetorical sleight of hand, be said to embody an age: the age of the Enlightenment, of romanticism, the era contained within the word *modernity*. Yet consciousness is an abstraction owned by the individual. If it spills over at times into primary sources, it is just as often secret, hidden, not noticed and therefore lost. Often the best one can do, as a historian, is to imagine someone's consciousness, working off the available fragments, doing what Nathan Zuckerman does with the fragments he is given. Nathan's imaginative method is the historian's imaginative method, at least when it comes to envisioning the alien consciousness of others. Where Zuckerman fails in getting the story right, the historian may well fail, and where he succeeds in this same endeavor, the historian may also succeed.

Notes

1. A beautiful book that makes precisely this point is Frances Haskell's *History and Its Images* (1993), which traces the incorporation of images into the writing of history.

2. Isaiah Berlin begins his great essay on Tolstoy and history, "The Hedgehog and the Fox," by noting that history has been overlooked in Tolstoy's writing. "Tolstoy's philosophy of history has, on the whole, not obtained the attention which it deserves, whether as an intrinsically interesting view or as an occurrence in the history of ideas, or even as an element in the development of Tolstoy himself," Berlin writes, describing his own essay as "an attempt to take Tolstoy's attitude to history as seriously as he himself meant his readers to take it" (24).

3. An excellent study of Faulkner and history is *Faulkner's County* (2001) by Don Doyle.

4. The young Roth did not write only about Newark. In fact, his first two novels, *Letting Go* (1962) and *When She Was Good* (1967), were set mostly in the Midwest and very much in an American, as opposed to an exclusively Jewish American, milieu. Nevertheless, Roth was an American writer whose reputation had Jewish American connotations in the 1960s and 1970s.

5. A brilliant book on Roth, narrative, and the character of Nathan Zuckerman is *Philip Roth and the Zuckerman Books* (2011) by Pia Masiero. For recent scholarship on Roth's American trilogy, see also *The Major Phases of Philip Roth*

(2011), by David Gooblar; *Fiction, utopie, histoire: Essai sur Philip Roth et Milan Kundera* (2010), by Velichka Ivanova; and David Brauner's *Philip Roth* (2007).

6. In, *Metahistory*, White argues that the structure of historical argument is derived from literary, dramatic, and poetic forms:

> In every case, dialectical tension evolves within the context of a coherent vision or presiding image of the form of the whole historical field. This gives to the individual thinker's conception of that field the aspect of a self-consistent totality. And this coherence and consistency give to his work its distinctive stylistic attributes. The problem here is to determine the grounds of this coherence and consistency. In my view, these grounds are poetic, and specifically linguistic, in nature. (30)

Works Cited

Berlin, Isaiah. "The Hedgehog and the Fox." *Russian Thinkers*. Ed. Aileen Kelly. New York: Viking, 1979. 22–82. Print.

Brauner, David. *Philip Roth*. Manchester, England: Manchester UP, 2007. Print.

Dos Passos, John. *USA*. New York: Lib. of Amer., 1996. Print.

Doyle, Don. *Faulkner's County: The Historical Roots of Yoknapatawpha, 1540–1962*. Chapel Hill: U of North Carolina P, 2001. Print.

Ellison, Ralph. *Invisible Man*. New York: Mod. Lib., 1994. Print.

Gooblar, David. *The Major Phases of Philip Roth*. New York: Continuum, 2011. Print.

Grossman, Vasily. *Life and Fate*. Trans. Robert Chandler. New York: Harper, 1985. Print.

Haskell, Francis. *History and Its Images: Art and the Interpretation of the Past*. New Haven: Yale UP, 1993. Print.

Ivanova, Velichka. *Fiction, utopie, histoire: Essai sur Philip Roth et Milan Kundera*. Paris: L'Harmattan, 2010. Print.

Mann, Thomas. *Buddenbrooks*. Trans. H. T. Lowe-Parker. New York: Knopf, 1976. Print.

___. *Doctor Faustus*. Trans. John Woods. New York: Knopf, 1997. Print.

___. *The Magic Mountain*. Trans. John Woods. New York: Knopf, 2005. Print.

Masiero, Pia. *Philip Roth and the Zuckerman Books*. Amherst, NY: Cambria, 2011. Print.

Moyn, Samuel. *The Last Utopia: Human Rights in History*. Cambridge: Harvard UP, 2010. Print.

Proust, Marcel. *Remembrance of Things Past*. Trans. C. K. Scott Moncrieff and Terence Kilmartin. New York: Vintage, 1982.

Roth, Philip. *American Pastoral*. Boston: Houghton, 1997. Print.

___. *The Counterlife*. New York: Farrar, 1986. Print.

___. *Goodbye, Columbus*. New York: Mod. Lib., 1995. Print.

___. *The Human Stain*. Boston: Houghton, 2000. Print.

___. *I Married a Communist*. Boston: Houghton, 1998. Print.

___. *Letting Go*. New York: Random, 1962. Print.

___. *Operation Shylock: A Confession.* New York: Simon, 1993. Print.

___. *Portnoy's Complaint*. New York: Vintage, 1994. Print.

___. *Sabbath's Theater*. Boston: Houghton, 1995. Print.

___. *When She Was Good*. New York: Random, 1967. Print.

___. *Zuckerman Bound: A Trilogy and an Epilogue, 1979–1985*. New York: Lib. of Amer., 2007. Print.

White, Hayden. *Metahistory: The Historical Imagination in Nineteenth-Century Europe*. Baltimore: Johns Hopkins UP, 1975. Print.

Late Style in the Later Novels_____

Debra Shostak

> What might have been and what has been
> Point to one end, which is always present
> (T. S. Eliot, "Burnt Norton")

In *Exit Ghost* (2007), Philip Roth's aging protagonist Nathan Zuckerman composes stage directions for a dialogue he writes, movingly describing German composer Richard Strauss's exquisite *Four Last Songs* as the soundtrack to the scene. Zuckerman chooses the music "for the profundity that is achieved not by complexity but by clarity and simplicity. For the purity of the sentiment about death and parting and loss. . . . The composer drops all masks and, at the age of eighty-two, stands before you naked" (124). Later, the elderly Amy Bellette reports the last words of the writer E. I. Lonoff, who appears centrally in the first novel about Zuckerman, *The Ghost Writer* (1979): "The end is so immense, it is its own poetry. It requires little rhetoric. Just state it plainly" (*Exit Ghost* 152). Both passages describe the condition of lateness for an artist. Does Zuckerman himself achieve simplicity, purity, or plainness—to stand before us naked? Even more important, does Roth?

Born in 1933, Roth has published more than thirty books in five decades. During his late middle age, he produced an astonishing run of energetic, large-canvassed novels: *Operation Shylock* (1993), *Sabbath's Theater* (1995), *American Pastoral* (1997), *I Married a Communist* (1998), *The Human Stain* (2000), and *The Plot against America* (2004). But beginning with *The Dying Animal* in 2001, Roth has also produced some slimmer, more concentrated and austere novels, also including *Exit Ghost* and the Nemeses tetralogy, which comprises *Everyman* (2006), *Indignation* (2008), *The Humbling* (2009), and *Nemesis* (2010). Following David Gooblar's division of Roth's work into "major phases," these books constitute Roth's late major phase, offering unique challenges to the reader, in part because they signal Roth's own lateness.

These six novels do not wholly depart from Roth's previous work, not even in their brevity, anticipated as early as Roth's first book, *Goodbye, Columbus* (1959). All return to Roth's enduring preoccupations: the stresses of bodily existence, especially for a desiring, sex-obsessed, and socially transgressive male, and the life of the American Jew, notably the second-generation Jew in New Jersey. Likewise, Roth's distinctive tone of voice remains intact, alternately assaultive and lyrical, ruthless and sentimental. Roth even resurrects two protagonists: David Kepesh of *The Breast* (1972) and *The Professor of Desire* (1977) and his frequent companion, the narrator Nathan Zuckerman, to whom he bids farewell in *Exit Ghost*.

Then what is different here? Roth regularly tests his protagonists by giving them the avid desire to refashion a self—a "counterlife," as he titled one of his finest novels—according to the great American myth of self-reinvention. Although the psychological and social conditions in which his characters find themselves frequently thwart their desires, the invigorating force of desire has driven his narratives, including their shape and their voices, from Portnoy's comic cry that he wants to put the "id back in Yid" (*Portnoy's Complaint* 139) to David Kepesh, transformed into a six-foot mammary gland in *The Breast*, quoting the poet Rainer Maria Rilke, "You must / change your life" (89). Yet Roth kicks this prop away in these recent novels, which are haunted by disease, decay, and death. Characters' desires seem self-defeating rather than renewing, their ironies overshadowing their energies and possibilities. In *Everyman*, for example, Roth openly rejects the illusion that one can construct a counterlife: "There's no remaking reality. . . . Just take it as it comes," says his "stoical" protagonist (4–5). What happened to the irresistible desire propelling Roth's fiction? The narratives have become translucent, membranes rather than whole cloth, static; desire has become a permanently ironic, because unsatisfiable, condition. Roth has always unsettled the reader, but the novels of the late major phase find new formal means for dissonance, whether in the narrative structure; the perspective, at times surprisingly distant from its objects of scrutiny; or the prose style, stripped down to the point of un-Rothian silences.

The concept of late style, introduced by Edward Said in his posthumously published book *On Late Style* (2006), illuminates Roth's recent work.[1] Said draws on the German philosopher and social critic Theodor Adorno's essay "Late Style in Beethoven" to distinguish between the serene, transcendent late works of some artists, such as Shakespeare, Bach, and Matisse, and the "artistic lateness [expressed] not as harmony and resolution but as intransigence, difficulty, and unresolved contradiction" (Said 7) that Adorno finds in Beethoven. Adorno's remarks about Beethoven's late works are metaphorically evocative when translated from musical to narrative form: "The conventions find expression as the naked representation of themselves. This is the function of the often-remarked-upon abbreviation of his style. . . . The caesuras, the sudden discontinuities . . . are those moments of breaking away; the work is silent . . . and turns its emptiness outward" (Adorno 566–67). In late style, Said uncovers a modern "moment when the artist who is fully in command of his medium nevertheless abandons communication with the established social order . . . and achieves a contradictory, alienated relationship with it" (Said 7–8). Late style is premised on the artist's consciousness of mortality but need not represent it explicitly. Instead, it insists on irascibility, irresolution, and a sense of exile: "The power of Beethoven's late style is negative, or rather *it is negativity*: where one would expect serenity and maturity, one instead finds a bristling, difficult, and unyielding—perhaps even inhuman—challenge" (12). *Lateness* connotes "the idea of surviving beyond what is acceptable and normal. . . . There is no transcendence or unity" (13). Lateness opposes the poetic form typically associated with the end of things, the elegy, which makes death timely. If in the traditional elegy, "emotion, originally expressed as a lament, finds consolation in the contemplation of some permanent principle" (Preminger 215), neither consolation nor permanent principles inhabit the forms of late style.[2]

Late style is an imprecise concept, deeply metaphorical, but still useful in relation to Roth's late phase. My thesis is this: In these severe, abbreviated novels, steeped in the ravages of the flesh, Roth remains preoccupied with masculinity, bodily existence, desire, and identity; the books are as aggressive and unapologetic as ever but find new modes of intransigence and irresolution. In fresh forms that complement the diminishments of aging, Roth insists thematically on narcissism, objectification of others, impotence, exile, and the failure of self-reinvention, and formally on restrained prose and monological (single-voiced) rather than dialogical (plural-voiced) narrative discourse as the conditions of mortality and late style. Roth's themes and forms represent the inevitable solitude of the declining human and define his own intentionally "alienated relationship" with "the established social order."

The Dying Animal marks the transition to Roth's late phase and addresses lateness centrally. Roth depicts unfettered heterosexual masculine desire traumatized by time and loss when his narrator, David Kepesh, sexually obsessed in his sixties with a young woman, "violate[s] the law of aesthetic distance" (99) that he previously upheld in objectifying sexual relationships with young women. Kepesh strives to maintain his "ferocity of objectivity" (35), pursuing erotic pleasure without commitment as a means to face down his fear of death and of his indecorous desires.

Roth's late style can be detected in his choice of a narrative voice. The unseemliness of Kepesh's narration challenges the reader to maintain ethical balance; his solipsism drives the reader away from the confiding premise of the first-person pronoun. The novel takes the form of Kepesh's monologue to an anonymous, unseen interlocutor, to whom he occasionally refers as "you." The reader meets the interlocutor only on the book's final page, when he or she speaks just four short lines. *The Dying Animal* is thus dominated by a monological or single-voiced narration as Kepesh cynically explains how he exploits his position as a professor and public intellectual to seduce female students.

Kepesh summarizes the physical attractions of the object of his obsession, Consuela Castillo, by alluding to art objects by Constantin Brancusi and Pablo Picasso, exalting her "good heart, . . . lovely face, . . . [and] gorgeous breasts" (5). His "aesthetic distance" from his lust appears in his reflexive references to art and his focus on Consuela's body. Roth does what he has always done well, risking the reader's sympathies by luring us into the consciousness of a character who offends our sensibilities. On one hand, Roth mercilessly topples Kepesh through his astonished experience of jealousy, exacerbated by his awareness of how much older he is than Consuela. Cherishing the maxim that "sex is . . . the revenge on death" (69), Kepesh fears that, in losing sexual power with Consuela, he will lose his self. On the other hand, Kepesh still presumes a position of masculine power: "I am the author of her mastery of me" (32). Roth tempts the reader to loathe Kepesh; still, we may find ourselves uncomfortably infiltrated with Kepesh's point of view. What is the matter with sexual desire, even at a (moderately) advanced age? Are we not fooling ourselves to think that desire is not stimulated by physical beauty?

The key to the novel, and to Roth's effect of late style, appears in Kepesh's control over the narration, the driving single voice that Roth maintains until the last page, when he reminds the reader that the whole of the narrative has been "oral" and retrospective. In the closing section, Kepesh says that, after years of silence, Consuela visits him to confess her impending mastectomy. Roth counterbalances the tender moment when Kepesh kisses Consuela's head, balding from chemotherapy, with the cruelty in Kepesh's voice when he reports that "I couldn't have slept with her" and with the final narrated event (134). Returning readers abruptly to the present of the storytelling, a panicked Consuela telephones to request that Kepesh visit her before her surgery. To Kepesh's plea that "I have to go. She wants me there," the interlocutor replies, "Don't go. . . . Think. Because if you go, you're finished" (156). Articulating Kepesh's own narcissism, the novel's final words—the only moment when the novel becomes a dialogue—demand that Kepesh return to objectivity.

The Dying Animal thus exemplifies what might be called late closure. Roth violates both narrative and social conventions. First, he refuses to resolve the incompatibility between love and freedom. Kepesh may choose against the social contract with no consequences except his own solitude. Were he to remake himself through a compassionate response to Consuela, however, the novel would trace a socially redemptive narrative arc. But Roth does not disclose Kepesh's answer to her. Does he resume his aesthetic distance? If so, he rejects the chance to invent a counterlife, and a reader may feel disgust at his narcissism. Roth refuses the closure of reconciliation, between Kepesh and Consuela and of Kepesh with himself. In Said's terms, Roth shapes the narrative to "abandon communication with the established social order." Second, just as Kepesh is poised to transgress against humane values, Roth transgresses against the regularity of fictional form: The jarring second voice intrudes to flout consistent narrative perspective. In a novel structured around death and the anxieties of aging flesh, Roth maintains a form that is resolutely non-elegiac. No mourning that is not solipsistic, no higher principles, no transcendence.

In stark contrast to *The Dying Animal*, *Everyman*, the first novel of the Nemeses tetralogy, makes numerous gestures toward elegy but still defeats them in the end. Material for grief abounds: the book chronicles one man's bodily failures and medical treatments from childhood through late middle age. The "menace of oblivion" (30) is never very far from view. *Everyman* mourns the abject body, juxtaposing the reminders of mortal decay with flickering moments of erotic desire. In such novels of the 1980s and 1990s as *The Counterlife* (1986), *Operation Shylock*, and *Sabbath's Theater*, Roth keeps Eros and Thanatos, the Freudian life and death drives, in dynamic tension. In *Everyman*, however, the erotic is fitful and humiliating; the balance is all on the side of death. The novel reaches few consolatory peaks. Instead, it is anti-elegiac, existential, consumed with the concrete.

Roth frames *Everyman* with scenes set in the cemetery, beginning with the protagonist's burial. Roth's characters have visited the grave-yard before, notably in the climactic scenes of *The Anatomy Lesson* (1983) and *Sabbath's Theater*, where the graveyard offered a pathway back into life. Roth offers no such transformation here. When the un-named protagonist attends his father's funeral, Roth stunningly depicts the sensory particulars of the son's grief at graveside. He perceives only the weight of the earth: "he saw his father's mouth as if there were no coffin, as if the dirt they were throwing into the grave was being deposited straight down on him, filling up his mouth, blinding his eyes, clogging his nostrils, and closing off his ears" (59–60). In an intense moment of sympathy and identification, the protagonist "taste[s] the dirt coating the inside of his mouth well after they had left the ceme-tery" (62). Death is no more than dirt and suffocation. The novel's pen-ultimate scene, however, strikes a contrary tone. Visiting the cemetery where his parents lie, the protagonist converses with a gravedigger, asking about the business of burial, its technologies and logistics. The gravedigger matter-of-factly conveys the meaning of the scene in the words of his mate: "What it comes down to for Thelma is just diggin' a hole," he tells the protagonist. "You gotta do what you gotta do. That's her philosophy" (179). The body is just a body, an object in a hole, and that is the end of it.

"You gotta do what you gotta do." "There's no remaking reality. Just take it as it comes." "This is how it works out, he thought, this is what you could not know" (161). These quotations are the home truths, the clichés that anchor the novel, no more artful or profound than the commercial art that has served as the protagonist's profes-sion. The beauty of Roth's writing in this novel lies just in its flatness and tautologies. The style is pared down to its single syllables and its naming of things. The unimpassioned third-person voice distances the reader while thrusting the unvarnished facts of illness and dying to the surface. There is no escape, not even in flights of language, and the structure of the narrative, too, seems tautological, circling back on itself, getting nowhere beyond the fact that Everyman, like the rest of us, can only sicken and die.

The language and narrative of *Everyman* all revolve around negation: the blank identity of the anonymous protagonist; the repetitive descriptions of illness; the "utter otherness" of pain (91); and the visits to the burial ground, where Everyman's parents are "just bones, bones in a box" (170). "Death is just death," he thinks, "it's nothing more" (119). The knell of "nothing" echoes through the novel, coming to a crescendo when Everyman thinks, "It had all come to nothing . . . he was lost in nothing, in the sound of the two syllables 'nothing' no less than in the nothingness, lost and drifting, and the dread began to seep in" (103). Everyman's "nothing" echoes *King Lear*, perhaps, or *Hamlet*, or even Samuel Beckett. And his negativity reverses the medieval morality play from which Roth takes his title, *The Summoning of Everyman*, in which the unknown playwright confronts his Everyman with allegorical figures from his life—for example, Fellowship, Kindred, and Good Deeds—as preparation for death, a means of spiritual reckoning. Roth strips away the sense of both preparation and reckoning, or, in Hamlet's terms, readiness. Instead, despite the manifold clues given to him, Roth's Everyman doggedly, without irony, faces the present as the "unforeseen and unpredictable" (160). Of course, nothing is unpredictable, there are no narrative surprises; we know from page 1 that he will die, just as he should have known.

Yet Roth teases both his protagonist and the reader with brief passages of promise, and it is from these fleeting, defeated moments of counter-imagination that his effect of late style most clearly emerges. Consider the extraordinary moment when Everyman remembers bodysurfing as a boy in the Atlantic, the "ecstasy of a whole day of being battered silly by the sea," "intoxicated" by the taste and smell "so that he was driven to the brink of biting down with his teeth to tear out a chunk of himself and savor his fleshly existence" (127). But such transcendent, pastoral moments are sentimental illusions, blissful memories of psychological and physical wholeness, ironic in retrospect. Sinking under anesthesia for a routine operation, Everyman thinks in rhapsodic language of that day on the beach: "Oh, the abandon of it, and the smell of the salt water and the scorching sun! Daylight . . . an optical treasure so vast . . . that he could have been peering . . . at the perfect, priceless planet itself." Then, in truncated sentences, the narrative stops abruptly: "He never woke up. Cardiac arrest. He was no more, freed from being, entering into nowhere without even knowing it. Just as he'd feared from the start" (182). There is no magic transfiguration of the hard facts, no realized fantasy of sensory boundlessness, no accommodation of a reader's desire for timeliness.

Indignation, appearing two years later, complements *Everyman*. *Everyman* is infused with the consciousness of physical infirmity, and its emotional note is resignation; *Indignation*, about a young man, sounds the youthful emotion of the title. While both novels demonstrate how oblivion remains stubbornly unanticipated—how we willfully deflect consciousness of the end—Everyman's body supplies his constant reminders, while for Marcus Messner, it is his father's irksome wisdom. When Mr. Messner, fearful that Marcus will be drafted and killed in Korea—as in fact he will be—warns him, "It's about life, where the tiniest misstep can have tragic consequences," Marcus dismisses him: "Oh, Christ, you sound like a fortune cookie" (12). Both novels echo the hard truth of *Indignation*'s closing insight: "the incomprehensible way one's most banal, incidental, even comical choices achieve the most disproportionate result" (231).

Roth develops Marcus's fatal choices in keeping with his signature subject matter—how a Jewish boy, son of a kosher butcher in Newark, New Jersey, tries to reinvent himself as an American unfettered by his ethnic past. To escape his father's smothering anxiety, Marcus attends a midwestern Protestant college, where he refuses to join the Jewish fraternity, gets mixed up with a suicidally disturbed young gentile woman, and is expelled no more for sex with her than for skipping out on his mandatory chapel attendance and cursing the dean. As with other protagonists of Roth's, such as Swede Levov in *American Pastoral* and Ira Ringold in *I Married a Communist*, Marcus's fatal flaw is his innocence, his belief that he can somehow occupy a position outside history. With comic poignancy, Marcus remakes himself from the outside in, secretly buying "collegiate" clothing to imitate the cover of the Winesburg College catalogue (114–16). But Marcus's experience in Ohio never matches that glossy image; instead, he seems to be punished for attempting to claim a counterlife as an American.

Indignation echoes Roth's earlier fiction more closely than *The Dying Animal* or *Everyman*, because of its focus on Jewish assimilation in the mid-twentieth century and its moments of dark comedy, as when Marcus discovers his dorm room in chaos, covered in the semen of a deranged former roommate, or when, called on the carpet by the dean, he vomits all over the dean's office. Comedy is rare in these late books, however; Roth told an interviewer in 2008, "I don't think I know how to be comic any more" (McCrum). Likewise, while Roth's prose style retains some of the intricate, fluid long sentences that, appearing deceptively simple, mark his mature work, these are framed in *Indignation* by flat, Möbius-strip sentences that, like the prose in *Everyman*, announce the uncompromising truths of late style. "You do what you have to do" (5), Marcus learns from his father. And, from his later state of limbo, he thinks, "I am dead. The unpronounceable sentence pronounced" (211–12).

Roth unprecedentedly kills off his protagonists at the beginning of both *Everyman* and *Indignation*. Yet whereas *Everyman*, whose first scene describes the protagonist's burial, contains no narrative surprises, Marcus's death is merely foreshadowed in *Indignation*'s first chapter title—"Under Morphine"—and suppressed until the stunning announcement that the nineteen-year-old narrator makes a little later: "And even dead, as I am and have been for I don't know how long . . ." (54). The pronouncing of that sentence is one of the novel's bald tricks. A narrator says, "I am dead," not long before he is dead, but the reader knows this for sure only because, in just the last eight pages, chapter 2 begins, and the narration of *Indignation* switches from the first person to the third. Roth flouts conventions of consistent viewpoint and verisimilitude: A dying character in a morphine haze remembers minute details, conversations, cinematic scenes, and lengthy monologues from his entire past, and all two hundred and more pages of memories occur, with great clarity, within the compressed time of his suffering last moments, his young body bayoneted to shreds. Roth here plays another turn on the monological narration of *The Dying Animal*. It is as if he takes the jokey cliché of life passing before one's eyes literally and then neither acknowledges the humor in doing so, as he might once have done, nor feels obliged to resolve any narrative contradictions. As with *Everyman*, the sole resolution is the finality of death, to which *Indignation* adds the ruin of the family. Nothing is timely about this death; there is no fulfillment, no readerly consolation, just senselessness and a plaintive, futile series of "if only" clauses and indignant exclamations echoing on the final pages.

To step back to *Exit Ghost*, the novel of the preceding year, is also to find material that Roth inverted in *Indignation*. However frustrated by the social mores of the early 1950s, young Marcus Messner is at the height of his sexual powers. The aging Nathan Zuckerman, however, suffers in *Exit Ghost* the humiliating results of prostate surgery: impotence and incontinence. Almost all of *Indignation* is retrospective, an extended memory, as Marcus's consciousness travels from his childhood toward the present, fixed moment of his death. Zuckerman's narrative, though related in the past tense, moves from the present toward an uncharted, frightening future. The contrast is poignant: Marcus deserves a future; Zuckerman should be comforted by long memory. Roth therefore makes the capacity for remembering central to *Exit Ghost*. Because Zuckerman discerns that his memory is beginning to fail, he, as a novelist, grasps the end of his life in the most bitterly unforgiving way. If he cannot remember, he cannot tell a story. If he cannot do that, he can no longer be.

In *Exit Ghost*, Roth largely associates being with writing, and this choice constitutes the novel's version of late style. The novel is peopled with writers, dead writers, and would-be writers, and it is layered with allusions to texts, by Roth himself and by others. Formally, it is built around the juxtaposition of different types of discourse: straight narrative, play-like dialogue, letter, and eulogistic essay. *Exit Ghost*'s dense intertextuality supports the central metaphor of the ghost, as its repeated allusions to other texts bring out the devastation of Zuckerman's diminishing capacity to write.

Roth's title arguably derives from either *Hamlet* or *Macbeth*, but most immediately refers to Zuckerman's first full-fledged appearance, in 1979's *The Ghost Writer*. The writer figure Zuckerman has allowed Roth to pursue many questions about writing, serving well through some eleven books: as the protagonist of the *Zuckerman Bound* tetralogy from the 1980s, as the narrator of the so-called American trilogy from the 1990s, and even as the critical voice framing Roth's autobiography. In resurrecting the ghost metaphor in *Exit Ghost*, Roth turns *The Ghost Writer* inside out. In that novel, the young Zuckerman apprentices himself to a master, Lonoff, by "ghosting" an outrageous counterlife story for Lonoff's attractive young assistant: He imagines Amy Bellette as a secretly surviving Anne Frank. In *Exit Ghost*, Zuckerman is now the ghostlike, aging, reclusive writer, his powers—sexual and writerly—failing. Amy reappears as another ghost, a confused survivor of a brain tumor, carrying around the ghosts of her real Holocaust past as opposed to the one Zuckerman had imagined for her. Lonoff is dead, another ghost, and his secrets are about to be publicized by an arrogant biographer who unnervingly seems the ghost of Zuckerman's brash young self. The ghosts of other artists also populate the novel, from John Keats, Nathaniel Hawthorne, Anton Chekhov, and Joseph Conrad to T. S. Eliot, Dylan Thomas, and George Plimpton. As Zuckerman narrates, the voices of the dead seem to constitute him in the present, displacing the past that he has tried to erase by retreating from society to his Berkshire mountain home. His self has been reduced to the texts he has read.

That is, until, visiting Manhattan in a futile attempt to restore the continence he lost in surgery, he rashly decides to trade residences with a young couple. He chooses to live in the present, to replace the "habit . . . of solitude without anguish" that enables him to be "free above all of [him]self" (58) with "the pain of being in the world": "I was back. . . . Back in the drama, back in the moment, back into the turmoil of events" (103). Sexual infatuation with Jamie, the wife of the couple with whom he is to swap houses, stimulates Zuckerman's impulsive choice. Smart, attractive, articulate, at once insecure and self-possessed, she becomes Zuckerman's test of himself back in the world. He fails the test, not because he is physically impotent—he is, but it never comes to that—but because his infatuation exposes his reduced mental powers, his vanishing being as a writer.

When Roth inverts *The Ghost Writer* in *Exit Ghost*, the juxtaposition exposes his narrator's increasing imaginative impotence. Zuckerman's youthful reinvention of Amy as Anne Frank was stunning proof of his growing narrative powers. A metafictional intrusion into the world of the novel, the illusion rang as true as the rest of the fiction's realism. In *Exit Ghost*, however, not only does the feeble Amy deflate that earlier fantasy, but her young double—consider the blatant Amy/Jamie rhyme—overtly resists Zuckerman's inventions as the young Amy did not. Jamie, many years Zuckerman's junior, is embarrassingly inappropriate as an object of desire for him. Roth makes the reader uncomfortable insofar as Zuckerman seems deaf to the incongruity of his fantasy. Because Zuckerman reads Jamie's noncommittal responses to him as flirtatious, he embarks, as in *The Ghost Writer*, on a project of invention. He writes four dialogues between "He" and "She" that fulfill his fantasies of her reciprocal desire. Admitting that "the conversations she and I don't have [are] more affecting even than the conversations we do have," Zuckerman reasserts the superior valuation of fiction over life that has marked his construction of identity across many books: "For some . . . the unlived, the surmise, fully drawn in print on paper, is the life whose meaning comes to matter most" (147).[3]

This is why the aesthetic failure of Zuckerman's little plays is especially painful. Not only do they lie at an increasing distance from reality, but they also fail to compel belief; we have little reason to accept that the young woman feels desire for this older man. The fantasy seems cheap. However "real" the voices momentarily become, they still tend to fall flat, to strain too much. In the third and longest of the He/She dialogues, for instance, Roth includes an unbelievable exchange in which Zuckerman claims not to know who Tom Cruise is (217). Zuckerman cannot escape his obsolescence; rather than being "back," he has simply been "buffeted by the merciless encounter between the no-longers and the not-yets" (279). Fiction fails to replace the satisfactions of life itself: "Oh, to wish what is into what is not, other than on the page!" he laments (273).

And yet he persists. The novel ends with the fourth He/She playlet, perhaps the least believable of all. Although Jamie has just rejected Zuckerman's advances, in the final dialogue, the She voice agrees to come to He's hotel room to be his lover. And He plays the trump; in the stage directions that conclude the novel, Roth has him make a final ambiguous gesture: "She's on her way and he leaves. Gone for good." The moment can be read as Zuckerman's fear and failure, and Roth encourages that view by noting that "he disintegrates" (292). At the same time, it can be read as Zuckerman's last, pale assertion of his masculine power: He has summoned her, set her up for humiliation, and departed before he can suffer any assault to his pride. Either way, Zuckerman has the last word, maintaining monologic control over the apparently dialogic form of the playlet and reasserting the power of fiction making that the rest of the novel has insistently eroded. Still, for the reader, Zuckerman's final, desperate gesture toward a counterlife is as likely to render him a pathetic as a triumphant figure.

Roth's willingness to risk the failed art of the dialogues, comprising some quarter of the novel's pages, intimates the novel's late style. While Zuckerman's insistence on a closing fantasy of potency may hint that a life force survives, it also portends permanent—and rather unseemly—self-delusion, thus falling short of redemption or transcendence. Roth permits the reader to discern aesthetic inadequacy in the dialogues, however deaf Zuckerman is to the clues. Consider the reverence Zuckerman expresses toward Strauss's *Four Last Songs*, quoted in the opening paragraph above. Zuckerman does not, in these fictions, achieve simplicity, or composure, or plainness, so as to stand before us naked. Rather, in the self-deceiving fervor of his misguided desires, he exposes his nakedness despite himself; he is stripped of his masks not by his will to clarity but by his desperate need for fantasy.

If the elderly Zuckerman briefly, if inauthentically, escapes his doom in a fantasy of being other than he is, Simon Axler, the aging actor of *The Humbling*, is doomed because he cannot transform himself into fantasy. *Everyman* construes mortality in terms of the failing body, *Indignation* as the bitter unfairness of a wasted young life, and *Exit Ghost* as the loss of memory and the ability to narrate an identity. *The Humbling* depicts death as the vanished talent to create a counterself, beginning with Axler's mortification on stage and his suicidal despair. At sixty-five, he is paralyzed by self-consciousness and can no longer lose himself in his roles, to be "in the moment." Axler's existential crisis exposes an empty self that he previously would have filled with performances. If, in *The Counterlife*, the middle-aged Zuckerman joyfully claimed that "in the absence of a self, one impersonates selves" (320), Axler finds himself "impaled" on his "bewildering biography" (*Humbling* 138). He cannot act a counterlife so as to be, any more than the aging Zuckerman in *Exit Ghost* can write himself into full being.

Roth frames Axler's narrative in three chapters, according to the three-act structure of the well-made play. The first chapter and the end of the third, punningly titled "The Last Act," convey the "universal nightmare" of Axler's exile from self. Employing the structuring metaphor of Axler's profession, Roth makes him capable of acting—of committing suicide—only by impersonating a suicidal character in Chekhov's *Seagull* (1896). Roth's irony overreaches; when Axler succeeds in his "last act" as he has not done in his recent acts, the hasty closing, accomplished in just over two pages, feels at once inevitable and flat.

The part of the novel that seems most intransigent, however, turning the late subject matter into late style, is its middle chapter. When Roth complicates the conditions of Axler's psychological impotence, he introduces his customary trope, sexual desire. Unlike Zuckerman, Axler remains virile; his impotence instead takes the form of self-deception. Accordingly, Axler recovers when he becomes sexually involved for a time with a younger woman, a forty-year-old lesbian, Pegeen, who has been recently dumped by her lover. The chapter's title, "The Transformation," refers at once to Pegeen's astounding embrace of heterosexuality for Axler and Axler's renewal with her. The erotic interest is implausible, potentially offensive to readers. With echoes of George Bernard Shaw's *Pygmalion* (1912), and perhaps Alfred Hitchcock's *Vertigo* (1958), Axler makes Pegeen over into "a woman he would want instead of a woman another woman would want" (65), with a wardrobe of stylish clothes and jewelry, an expensive haircut, and the pleasure of cooking for him. The makeover is an objectifying exercise of narcissistic masculine power, and the sex scenes underscore the novel's devotion to male fantasy, posing a green dildo against the "living thing" (92) of the male member. The eventual threesome with another woman predictably returns Pegeen to lesbianism, with the unmemorable explanation to Axler that "I made a mistake" (126). Axler is not so much humbled as fully humiliated. Roth has never shied away from provocation, but this novel appears unseemly—not as Roth has always been unseemly for his representations of male lust, or women, or Jews, but because we expect more expressive material from a writer of his stature and skill.

My point is not that the lateness of Roth's style here necessarily redeems these choices for any reader, but rather that it puts in context *The Humbling*'s relentless indignities and spareness of form. The narrative is slight, the voice cool, contained, detached—so unlike Roth's former passionate, curious, noisy narrators. His prose can seem perfunctory, especially in the crucial sex scenes. Pegeen is little more than a function in Axler's descent, designed to confirm his intuition, derived from dramatic structure, of "the likelihood of reversal" (17). But can one really not be a narcissist when faced with the annihilation of the self? Axler is obsessed with Prospero's parting speech, in which "all spirits . . . / Are melted into air, into thin air" (*Tempest* 4.1.149–50). In a beautiful passage that recalls the "nothing" passage in *Everyman*, Roth shows how the "two syllables" of *thin air* "were chaotically repeated while [Axler] lay powerless in his bed in the morning. . . . His whole intricate personality was entirely at the mercy of 'thin air'" (7). These echoing syllables characterize Roth's thin form in *The Humbling*, reinforced by another example when, one cold morning, Axler spots a scruffy, feeble possum, thrust out of its nocturnal rhythms and "nearing its end." At the mouth of its snowy den, Axler spies "a collection of sticks. . . . Six sticks. So that's how it's done, Axler thought. I've got too much. All you need are six" (47). Like the dying Lonoff's dictum—"Just state it plainly"—Roth gives Axler the insight of late style: All you need are six sticks. Roth is uncompromising. Six sticks can construct no shelter for the exiled, dying narcissist.

In his later phase, Roth makes even a figure so apparently far from narcissism, Bucky Cantor in *Nemesis*, suffer the fate of exile. Roth concludes his tetralogy with the story of another young man whose life is effectively over before it begins. *Nemesis* echoes the concerns of the other late novels, including masculinity, bodily failure, and the "tyranny of contingency" natural to the human condition (242–43). Bucky, the "superior athlete" afflicted with symbolic "poor vision" (11), treasures an impossible ideal of manhood as power and the capacity to protect others. He innocently believes that his escape from the fictional 1944 Newark polio epidemic to nature and love—to the "island" (87) of a summer camp and his girlfriend, Marcia—will shield him in "as secure a refuge as you could find from the killer on the rampage at home" (174). When the killer follows him to the camp, Bucky takes up his quarrel with the "fiend" (264), "God, who made the virus" (127). Bucky is ruined both by his blind faith that one can escape contingency and his blind fury requiring that chance suffering have a rational cause. Beset by grief, guilt, and shame because he thinks he silently carried the polio virus, with his own beautiful body crippled by the disease, he withdraws from human companionship. Unlike Marcus Messner's, Bucky's life ends long before his physical death.

Roth strikes much the same tone of voice in *Nemesis* as he did in *Everyman*: matter-of-fact, descriptive, apparently objective, and yet loomingly foreshadowing the suffering to come. The rhetorical omens of austere late style become apparent, from the opening sentence's reference to "the first case of polio" in Newark (1) to such moments as when Bucky visits the father of a boy killed by the disease. The grieving Mr. Michaels laments, "You do only the right thing, the right thing and the right thing and the right thing, . . . and then this happens," and asks where the "fairness" or "sense in life" is. Bucky can reply only, "There is none" (47). The "right thing" is of course what Bucky has honorably, desperately committed himself to doing. As in the tolling sound of "nothing" in *Everyman* or "thin air" in *The Humbling*, "the right thing" repeats in the rhetoric of *Nemesis* only to clash with bitter irony against Bucky's new knowledge of no sense and no fairness. When polio breaks out at the camp, Bucky recalls the earlier scene, but as if it were happening in the present, as Roth uncannily transforms a common noun into a startling metaphor: "All at once he heard a loud shriek. It was the shriek of the woman downstairs from the Michaels family. . . . Only he didn't just hear the shriek—he was the shriek" (225). Roth thus collapses time, much as the experience of trauma does, so that the traumatic moment seems to exist in a perpetual and unmoving present.

This moment occurs in a narrative that mostly seems to obey the rules of chronology and perspective. Unlike its closest model concerning doomed youth, *Indignation*, *Nemesis* offers what appears at first to be a more conventional narrative, complete with an "omniscient" narrator. Still, as in *Indignation*, Roth belatedly and abruptly clues the reader in to the circumstances of the narration, when we learn that among the boys contracting polio is "me, Arnie Mesnikoff" (108). For a hundred pages, Roth has given the reader no hint that the narration is in the first person. We must recalibrate our reading of the remainder of the narrative. This becomes especially important as the novel approaches its close, because we gradually come to understand that we have never left Arnie's perspective.

During the course of *Nemesis*, Roth offers a few brief moments of pleasurable action, like that of Everyman at the beach, retrospectively heartbreaking in their illusory promise of sensuality and good health. Bucky savors a sweet peach, for example, just as he asks Marcia's father if they may become engaged; later, Bucky, freshly arrived at the camp, takes a swan dive, as perfect in its form as its embracing element, as he "plumbed the cold purity of the lake to its depths" (156). The most important such moment, however, appears at the close of the narrative, and this closure seals the impression of late style in *Nemesis*.

In the climactic episode, Arnie, who has made a success of his life after polio, enters the narration to visit his former teacher. When Bucky, with "the aura of ineradicable failure," a "gender blank" "demoralized by persistent shame" (246), tells how he has repudiated his own life, Arnie concludes that "there's nobody less salvageable than a ruined good boy" (273). He recognizes Bucky's refusal of the chance nature of their tragedy and realizes that Bucky has needed "to find a necessity for what happens," making him a "martyr, this maniac of the why," thus finding himself eternally guilty. Arnie illuminates the essential narcissism in Bucky's self-negating pursuit of causality. Arnie's judgment makes explicit what the image of the physically and spiritually depleted Bucky signifies: Given a chance to remake himself, Bucky fails, victim of "stupid hubris" (265). As the narrating intermediary, Arnie's voice detaches the reader from Bucky's norms, however well-intentioned, which have dominated the reader's perceptions. In subjecting Bucky's innocence to Arnie's harsh critique, Roth returns to a monological discourse. It thus seems at first surprising that he concludes with the final flashback, a remembered scene of joy, when the twenty-three-year-old Bucky, before the epidemic, demonstrates a javelin throw to the awed boys. Arnie's description of Bucky as "primordial man" (279) at the height of his physical perfection brings the novel to a close with the blunt, adoring assertion that "he seemed to us invincible" (280). This might seem to leave the novel on just the transcendent point missing from the other later novels, but a closer look undermines the consolatory reading. Arnie's nostalgic memory returns the reader to Bucky's innocent past, but it is a past constrained and erased by the sorrowful contingent events of the narrative. Arnie's ringing last word—"invincible"—therefore bears a heavy weight of irony, since everything leading up to it proves that a man is anything but invincible.

In Roth's refusal to apologize, redeem, or give solace is a terrible beauty of sorts. As he remarked to McCrum, "I don't think anybody's gotten out alive in my last five books," and neither, in a sense, does the reader, forced toward the discomforts of late style. As the writer stands before us naked, he in turn strips us of our cloaks of convention, consolation, even coherence. We confront Said's pure negativity—naked selves, naked art, emptiness turned outward. Six sticks must suffice.

Notes

1. I am indebted to Michael Rothberg for bringing Said's work to my attention during a roundtable discussion at the 2008 American Literature Association conference (Royal 20).

2. For other efforts to grapple with late works of art, see Updike and Arnheim, the latter of whom, like Adorno, identifies the "unorthodox and uncompromising qualities of late styles" (286), focusing on visual art.

3. See Shipe on the "He and She" dialogues as Zuckerman's last works (197, 200–201).

Works Cited

Adorno, Theodor W. "Late Style in Beethoven." *Essays on Music*. Ed. Richard Leppert. Trans. Susan H. Gillespie. Berkeley: U of California P, 2002. 564–68. Print.

Arnheim, Rudolf. "On the Late Style." *New Essays on the Psychology of Art.* Berkeley: U of California P, 1986. 285–93. Print.

Gooblar, David. *The Major Phases of Philip Roth.* New York: Continuum, 2011. Print.

McCrum, Robert. "The Story of My Lives." *Observer*. Guardian News and Media, 20 Sept. 2008. Web. 3 Jan. 2013.

Preminger, Alex, ed. *Princeton Encyclopedia of Poetry and Poetics*. Princeton: Princeton UP, 1974. Print.

Roth, Philip. *The Breast.* New York: Vintage, 1994. Print.

___. *The Dying Animal*. Boston: Houghton, 2001. Print.

___. *Everyman*. Boston: Houghton, 2006. Print.

___. *Exit Ghost*. Boston: Houghton, 2007. Print.

___. *The Ghost Writer*. New York: Farrar, 1979. Rpt. in *Zuckerman Bound.* By Roth. New York: Farrar, 1985. 1–180. Print.

___. *The Humbling*. Boston: Houghton, 2009. Print.

___. *Indignation*. Boston: Houghton, 2008. Print.

___. *Nemesis.* Boston: Houghton, 2010. Print.

___. *Portnoy's Complaint.* New York: Fawcett, 1985. Print.

Royal, Derek Parker, ed. "Zuckerman Unsound? A Roundtable Discussion on Philip Roth's *Exit Ghost*." *Philip Roth Studies* 5.1 (2009): 7–34. Print.

Shipe, Matthew. "*Exit Ghost* and the Politics of 'Late Style.'" *Philip Roth Studies* 5.2 (2009): 189–204. Print.

Updike, John. "A Critic at Large: Late Works." *New Yorker* 7 Aug. 2006: 64. *New Yorker Digital Edition*. Web. 16 Dec. 2009.

Coping through Collecting: Stamps as a Means of Facing Trauma_____

Namoi Desrochers

In his novel *The Plot against America* (2004), Philip Roth portrays a terrifying alternative version of America where civil liberties and social justice disappear in the wake of government oppression and fearmongering. Confronted with the unsettling fractures taking place within both the nation and his family, the author's protagonist, who is given the name "Philip Roth," struggles to maintain a hold on his fleeting sense of normality by finding a stable reference point in his own small world. In one of the novel's introductory paragraphs, the now-adult Philip describes his youthful temperament at the onset of the changes within the country, classifying himself as "an embryonic stamp collector inspired like millions of kids by the country's foremost philatelist, President Roosevelt" (1). Though initially a simple token of the interests of childhood, Philip's stamp collection takes on deeper significance after a nightmare he has and after the aviator and Nazi sympathizer Charles Lindbergh is elected president of the United States: The collection becomes a symbolic representation of the pre-Lindbergh familial and societal stability he once enjoyed—a feeling of normality he desperately hopes to maintain.

Much of the narrative concerns Philip's attempts, both active and passive, to protect his collection, physically and symbolically, from events and people that threaten to destroy his only reference to the secure world he once inhabited—a personal coping mechanism through which he tenuously holds onto the past. Tragically, the collection that serves as a symbol of constancy disappears during a time when stability in both Philip's life and that of the nation fall apart, forcing Philip to face his personal trauma alone. In her book *Unclaimed Experience: Trauma, Narrative, and History* (1996), Cathy Caruth explores the effect a traumatic event wreaks upon an individual—how the mind at first shields the sufferer from consciously acknowledging the trauma, preventing it from coming to light until a later time (4). Just as Philip's collection serves as a means of coping with the changes in his life, allowing him to hold onto the life he once knew, the loss of his stamps is a necessary step if he is ever to confront the truth, that it is impossible to go back to the way things once were.

If he is to come to grips with the reality of the trauma surrounding him, Philip must acknowledge the changes both in his life and in the larger American society. I argue here that Philip's stamp collection serves as the primary vehicle through which he attempts to cope with the traumatic shifts at both of these levels. Though the collection initially serves as his reference to a familiar and secure time, the disappearance of Philip's stamps causes the young protagonist to face his trauma and begin a move toward recognizing and reconciling with those overwhelming changes. Although Philip's eventual assemblage of a new album during a time of relative quiet seemingly indicates a step backward, toward a past point of reference, the new stamps he collects are Canadian, symbolizing that he must focus his sentiments on the reality of the new mode of familial and national life.

At the onset of Lindbergh's presidential candidacy and growing American anti-Semitism, Philip regards his stamp collection with the typical fervor and enthusiasm children reserve for personal pursuits. When small changes begin to occur within the political and ideological thinking of the country, however, Philip starts his own shift from viewing his collection as a simply youthful pleasure, to unconsciously using it as the lens through which he analyzes potential impediments to his family's way of life. Though the danger of Lindbergh's victory looms as a significant threat to Philip's future, he fails to fully comprehend the vast changes that would come with a Lindbergh presidency. Unable to process the unsettling feelings of worry that he and his community share regarding the popular Republican candidate, Philip filters these unfamiliar emotions through his familiar and pleasurable interest in stamps in an attempt to negate his personal sense of unease.

Philip's view of his stamp collection as a representation of normalcy is arguably a truthful representation of the way children seek comfort in familiar things and places when faced with problems they find upsetting or strange. Roth himself discussed the importance of maintaining the realism of childhood in the novel in a 2004 interview, stating, "It's the children in the book who join the trivial to the tragic" ("The Story Behind"). In the novel's narrative, Philip's collection serves as the "trivial," while the changes in his home life and the country supply the "tragic" half of Roth's dichotomy. As such, the connection between Philip's sentiments toward his stamps and his overwhelming desire for life to remain as it is seems obvious. The collection serves as the coping mechanism through which Philip can filter and attempt to negate the trauma surrounding him. Once again, the words of the author himself support such a reading, as he outlines his desire to control the perspectives in the work while touting the significance the collection holds for his young protagonist:

> The storytelling is very direct in this book, and I tried to keep both the boy's perspective and the adult's perspective from overwhelming the events. I had also somehow to make the two one, the mediating intelligence that sees the general, and the child's brain that degeneralizes the general, that cannot see outside the child's own life and that reality never impresses in general terms. Whereas his father struggles with his America falling apart and the terrible invasion of history, the boy is still living in the heroic America of his stamp collection. . . . He is a practical child in a turbulent time, his world made of concrete and immediate fears. ("The Story Behind")

Roth's comments point out an important fact that readers must remember when reading the novel: Although a young Philip Roth serves as the novel's protagonist, it is the adult Philip Roth who narrates the tale. As such, the events discussed within the text are analyzed and discussed by an adult, a grownup who possesses the clarity of mind to identify obviously traumatic events. Young Philip, however, lacks the skills necessary to understand the larger implication of Lindbergh's presidency, Sandy's secret drawings, and other events that signify a fracture in the way of life he has known for so long. Roth acknowledges his attempts to control the disconnect between child and adult, and points to a child's inability to clearly see and experience the things outside his world. Philip's stamp collection, however, serves as the lens through which he views and interprets the world, its changes, and possible threats to his well-being. By aligning the stamps with the heroism of the nation, Roth indicates that Philip needs his collection if he is to maintain his view of America as a place of freedom and justice, especially when so much of his existence points toward the inevitable downfall of such idealism.

At the outset of the novel, the political and social changes that might take place in a country run by Lindbergh are largely unknowable (yet no less worrisome) until they actually occur, and Philip attempts to allay his personal fears by noting the direct and positive effect Lindbergh's success will bring to one particular stamp in his collection. As the owner of a ten-cent airmail stamp commemorating Lindbergh's transatlantic flight, Philip "immediately realized . . . that its worth would only continue increasing (and so rapidly to become my single most valuable possession) if Alvin was right and the worst happened" (27). Lindbergh exists as a potential, rather than a definite, threat at this juncture, one that Philip is free to process at his own pace and through his stamp collection, which stands as his own personal coping mechanism. Philip's reliance on his stamps as a symbol of normalcy and security remains a largely unconscious dependency until Lindbergh's election appears inevitable, at which point the collection's importance moves to the forefront of the young boy's mind. Unable to face the fears underlying his dependence on the stamp collection, Philip enters into a realm in which multiple malicious factors threaten to simultaneously undermine the integrity of his pristine coping mechanism as well as his own personal sense of security and stability. Yael Maurer has proposed that

Roth's fictional rewriting of history becomes a way of revisiting his childhood as a nightmarish scenario. He recasts his childhood as a site where fear takes over the seemingly safe and ordinary existence of a nine-year-old child. . . . Roth creates a world where everything that is familiar and known becomes strange and threatening and, by telling the story through young Philip's eyes, allows us to feel the full extent of this menacing change. (52)

In essence, Roth creates a narrative in which his protagonist toes the line between a world that is both familiar and stable (represented through his stamps) and strange and frightening (represented by both the changes in his world and threats to his symbol of normalcy). As a young child possessing no insight into the looming imbalances in his minute world, Philip possess few coping mechanisms through which he can reassert his sense of balance. As such, he can only cope with the European war and the uncertainty of America's future through childish means such as social play and ascribing symbolism to his stamp collection.

At the beginning of the work, Philip views the changes in Europe with some interest and engages with the unfamiliar European conflict through a game of war he and his friends play, called "I Declare War." Philip's participation in this communal activity marks his first attempts at staving off the fears only beginning to grow in his heart. John J. Stinson has explored the impact of the game on Philip's ability to deal with both the war in Europe and the cultural war occurring within the United States, remarking that "the boys' armor of innocence is by no means impenetrable," and "an ill-boding impingement of the real and brutal outside" seeps into Philip's realm of existence through the war game (42). Though largely unaffected by the changes in the outside world, Philip's engagement with the game and his eventual focus on his stamp collection indicate his awareness of the shifts in both global and American society respectively. Although Philip plays I Declare War without seeing much of its import, Stinson notes that "the violent and ominous street game . . . played incessantly, is revealed as both an accurate predictor and a mirror: the Roth household embodies a microcosm of what is happening in Jewish families across Lindbergh's America" (45). Just as the game reflects the injustices occurring halfway across the world, so too does it indicate the inevitable fracture between the Roth family and their own country, as well as within their own family unit.

Eventually, the reality of the "menacing changes" in the larger world encroach on Philip's sense of stability in a way that he cannot hope to combat through simple social play, necessitating that he shift his attention to a symbol of stability rather than conflict, chiefly his stamp collection (Maurer 52). Although Philip moves from engaging with a symbol of frightening change to one of reassuring familiarity, thoughts of the former remain in his mind, threatening to undercut the importance of the new symbol he has chosen to rely on. I refer again to Stinson's essay and a lengthy passage recounting Philip's nightmare. Here the most important ideas Stinson discusses are "the connection between the game and a Hitler-friendly administration under Lindbergh," which is "made early in the novel when the young Philip has a nightmare" in which he runs from an unseen pursuer and drops his collection at the location where he plays I Declare War (44). Upon picking up the album (still in his dream), Philip is horrified to see the images of his stamps desecrated by the presence of black swastikas. By falling at the place where Philip plays his disturbing game, his stamps take on the attributes of the fascist elements of the larger world. Since Philip's small collection represents both his own small realm of existence and his sense of security, he suddenly feels an overwhelming need to protect it.

Some four pages of the novel chronicle the horrifying dream that overcomes Philip, a nightmare that literally places him back at his most infantile state by causing him to fall to the floor, a once nightly occurrence that hadn't happened since he first switched from a crib to a bed. Philip remains at his most vulnerable in this position, robbed of his sense of agency and control over his own destination as he finds himself in a heap on the floor, having rolled out of bed while in a sound slumber—a time when a person should be most at peace. In a way, Philip's discovery of falling to the floor without his conscious knowledge or choice mirrors the content of his nightmare, a terrifying shift during which "the design on two sets of my stamps had changed in a dreadful way without my knowing when or how" (41). If the images on these stamps and the ideals they stand for can change without the protagonist's knowledge or control, how secure are the current tenets of the society in which he lives?

By transforming the familiar American images on Philip's stamps into the emblems of fascism—Hitler and a swastika, respectively—the dream temporarily removes the collection's ability to symbolize both the best in American culture and politics as well as "everything that was the bluest and the greenest and the whitest and to be preserved forever in these pristine reservations" that Philip's family had enjoyed until the stamps' sudden effacement (43). The change that overtakes the stamps also reflects the greatest fear of Philip's mother and father: the seemingly guaranteed victory of Lindbergh over Roosevelt that assuredly threatens to encourage a shift in the national mindset from democratic and welcoming to fascist and exclusionary. While the sentiments expressed by Philip's parents are largely their own, Philip also feels these emotions and fears to a degree, worrying that the country at large will come to view the greater Jewish community as the biggest danger to the American way of life, rather than "acknowledging us to be a small minority of citizens vastly outnumbered . . . by and large obstructed by religious prejudice from attaining public power and surely no less loyal to the principles of American democracy than an admirer of Adolf Hitler" (15–16). Upon waking from his unnerving dream, Philip dedicates himself to preserving the integrity of both the stamps themselves as well as their symbolic representation of American democracy and his family's right to live in a country free from oppressive regimes and jingoistic threats.

Although the collection successfully acts as a security blanket for the young protagonist, Philip's sense of normalcy can only remain while the stamps are present and untainted, or as Maurer puts it: "Philip's dreams and hallucinations center on the notion of death and dramatize the fear of change . . . in his hitherto secure world" (54). Roused by the fear of change invoked within him through his nightmare, Philip resolves to diligently protect his symbol of stability, holding fast to the comfort provided to him by his collection, his sole means of cementing his sense of place and fixity. As Caruth notes in her discussions of the wound and the voice, the trauma of change is much more than a pathology affecting Philip, it is "a wound that cries out, that addresses us in the attempt to tell us of a reality or truth that is not otherwise available" (4). Essentially, Philip's dream is his mind's attempt to awaken him to the reality that his once stable life has already changed, and will continue to do so radically if Lindbergh attains the presidency. To Maurer, "this iconic dream, which dramatizes the fear of monstrous change . . . encapsulates the whole drama and impetus of Roth's novel" and Philip's attempts to protect his iconic stamps indicate his small and solitary fight against the changes that threaten to undermine both his family's connection to one another, and their place in American society (55). Despite his mind's effort to reveal the truth of trauma to Philip, he remains unable or unwilling to face this realization, focusing instead on preserving the physical and symbolic integrity of his collection.

Philip's desire to maintain the collection's import takes on greater significance when Lindbergh is elected, requiring a more conscious attempt to preserve the collection than he has previously demonstrated. Philip appears aware of the need for this increased effort by acknowledging the important connection between the collection and his own sense of normalcy and stability. Philip notes that practically his first goal upon getting the album was to accumulate all the stamps he knew "FDR had a hand in designing or had personally suggested," constructing a collection in which much of the content aligned with the political climate where he and his family felt safe (56). The most significant of the FDR stamps are the ones emblazoned with the year "1933," the year in which Philip was born, stamps that provide a direct connection between himself, and a man whose presidency signified a period of stability for Philip and his greater community.

In the days leading up to his family's trip to Washington, Philip successfully convinces his mother to allow him to bring his stamp collection along as a direct result of his nightmare:

> I was afraid to leave the album at home . . . either because I'd done nothing about removing the ten-cent Lindbergh airmail stamp . . . because Sandy had lied to our parents and his Lindbergh drawing remained intact . . . or because of the one filial betrayal conspiring with the other—a malignant transformation would occur in my absence, causing my unguarded Washingtons to turn into Hitler, and swastikas to be imprinted on my National Parks. (57)

The ten-cent airmail stamp that Philip once used as coping mechanism to deal with Lindbergh's presidential candidacy by putting a positive spin on the announcement now stands as a symbol of shame for the protagonist, made all the worse when combined with his brother's secret praise of Lindbergh and his own compliance in hiding that sentiment from their parents. Since Philip views himself as personally responsible for compromising the normalcy of life his collection symbolizes, he feels the stringent need to protect the stamps from events and people that threaten to undermine their significance. In an ironic twist, Philip finds himself most concerned with maintaining the integrity of his stamp collection in a place that should do nothing less than bolster their worth: Washington, DC. Though the family vacations in a town that is in itself a symbolic representation of America's democratic nature, the fresh inauguration of Lindbergh has already begun to undermine the purity of the nation's capital. As if in anticipation of the anti-Semitic experience that is to befall his family at their hotel, Philip acknowledges his "one concern from the time we entered Washington until we left—preserving my stamp collection from harm" (61).

As the Roths' trip progresses, Philip's concern over protecting the integrity of his stamps appears justified in light of the insults they suffer at the Lincoln Memorial, derogatory comments that stem from his father's exercise of his right to free speech—an event that foreshadows further injustices to come. As his father continues his tirade against Lindbergh and the crumbling of American values following this incident, Philip finds himself at a loss for how to act in the face the blatant prejudice from which his home life has sheltered him thus far. Left to follow his mother's commands, Philip acknowledges his inability to deal with the situation by identifying himself as "a boy whose stamp collection still represented nine-tenths of his knowledge of the world," a collection he sees as symbolic of everything stable and comforting in his existence (57).

Daniel Grausam notes that just as Philip's stamps symbolize his own sense of stability in a rapidly changing country, so too do they "represent and symbolize a shared (if flawed) national history, and thus play a crucial role" (625). Philip's collection serves as the means through which he can connect to America's political and social past, a time in which freedom and justice served as the cornerstones of democracy to create a country in which both he and his family felt safe (631). Unfortunately, Philip's belief in the familiar and protective America he studied in school for so long undergoes another blow when his family is turned away by the hotel in which they planned to stay, presumably as a result of anti-Semitism. Roth the author has acknowledged the truth of this bigotry and the differing effects such occurrences have on those who suffer them:

> Jews were deliberately and systematically excluded from partaking of certain advantages and making certain affiliations and entering important portals at every level of American society, and exclusion is a primary form of humiliation. . . . In this book it's the humiliation that helps to tear apart and very nearly disable the family, inasmuch as each person in the family responds to it differently. ("The Story Behind")

In the moments that follow his family's dismissal by the hotel staff, Philip's sense of belonging to his country continues to suffer, as the police officer who his father insists will set things right upholds the prejudice exhibited by the hotel management. Through his failure to follow his duty in protect citizens' rights by helping the Roth family, the policeman immediately registers in Philip's mind as a threat to his stamp collection. When the policeman ask Philips about the item he holds in his hands, the young boy quickly responds with the phrase "my stamps" and hurries away, admitting that he "just kept going before he could ask to see my collection and I had to show it to him to avoid arrest" (71). Despite the problems plaguing his family and their rights as Americans during the trip, Philip still clings to the meaning he assigned to his collection, refusing to let go the feelings of stability and familiarity associated with it, a relinquishment he views as a potential byproduct of showing his stamps to a person he views as antithetical to their value.

Philip's interactions with Mr. Taylor, on the other hand, indicate his willingness to display his collection to those individuals he deems worthy, people who pose no threat of jeopardizing its symbolic nature. In fact, the family's tour guide stands as a polar opposite to the police officer, a kindred spirit whose fixed focus on his own romanticized historical vision of America is in keeping with Philip's own idealization of his stamp collection. Grausam complicates the connection between stamps in general and American society, noting: "The culture that stamps represent is, obviously, hugely problematic, given that they tell a sanitized version of American history in which suffering and injustice are easily replaced by commemoration" (631). The interaction between Philip and Mr. Taylor certainly supports this assessment. Despite the negative experiences his family endures in the capital, and despite his own fears for his collection's safety, when Mr. Taylor looks at and comments on his Martha Washington stamp, Philip states, "For me all the complications of our being a Jewish family in Lindbergh's Washington simply vanished and I felt the way I felt in school when, at the start of an assembly program, you rose to your feet and sang the national anthem, giving it everything you had" (74).

In essence, both the stamp collection and Mr. Taylor represent a familiar and safe view of America and the belief that anyone, regardless of race or creed, can enjoy the pleasures that come from living in a democratic society. Mr. Taylor fails to truly acknowledge the prejudices that he sees the Roth family endure, as doing so risks marring his historically aesthetic view of America, and Philip himself suffers a disconnect from reality by placing so much faith in his stamp collection, a symbolic coping mechanism he soon must lose. Upon their initial arrival in Washington, Philip describes the reverence his family felt toward the democratic and historical idealism represented by the capital, stating, "We had driven right to the very heart of American history . . . delineated in its most inspirational form, that we were counting on to protect us against Lindbergh" (58). The injustices Philip and his family suffer in Washington, however, demonstrate that this version of American history can no longer protect his family, and that simple idealization of places and things does little to stop the malicious entities that threaten the ideals they signify. Just as his parents come to realize that the America they thought they knew has changed, Philip must eventually face the folly of his own efforts in his avoidance of facing the changed reality in which he now lives.

Although Philip's stamp collection appears frequently within the first seventy-odd pages of the novel, it drops from the narrative entirely for the next hundred and fifty, emerging in full force again following Philip's decision to run away from home. Though provoked into leaving his home as a result of the now-undeniable changes overtaking both his country and home life, Philip continues to demonstrate his need for the stamp collection, as well as his fervent desire to protect it from harm:

There was only one thing I couldn't leave behind—my stamp album. . . . Perhaps if I could have been sure it would be preserved undisturbed after

I was gone, I wouldn't, at the last moment . . . have stopped to open my dresser drawer and . . . lifted it from where it was stored. . . . But it was intolerable to think of my album ever being broken up or thrown out, or worst of all, given away wholly intact to another boy, and so I took it under my arm. (233)

Philip's use of the terms "preserved," "undisturbed," "broken up," and "thrown out" indicate an intense fear of his stamp collection losing its significance. Since Philip regards the stamps as his main connection to the familiar life he led before Lindbergh's presidency, he regards the possible physical damage to his stamps as ultimately leading to the destruction of their symbolic worth. Up until this point, Philip has done everything in his power to avoid acknowledging the traumatic truth that both America and his family are already permanently changed, a realization he continues to avoid through his desire to run away. Even maintaining the collection and passing it off to another boy remains abhorrent to him, for if the stamps symbolize familiarity and stability, giving them away transfers Philip's connection to the idyllic past from himself to another. Once again, this avenue leaves Philip with no choice but to recognize the shifts in the larger world around him. As such, Philip makes the ultimately disastrous decision to take them along, unaware he will soon lose his one reference to normalcy, causing him to acknowledge "that he will never again possess his 'unfazed sense of security'" (Maurer 53).

Unsuccessful in his attempts to run away, Philip is further devastated when he discovers that his beloved stamp collection, the item which represented so much of himself, which symbolized his stable life before Lindbergh, that which he sought to protect above all else, has disappeared. In the boy's own words:

I was devastated . . . because my stamp album, my greatest treasure, that which I could not live without, was gone. I didn't remember having taken it with me until the day after I got home from the hospital and got up in the morning to get dressed and saw it was missing from beneath my socks and my underwear. The reason I stored it there in the first place was to see it first thing every morning when I dressed for school. And now the first thing I saw on my first morning home was that the biggest thing I had ever owned was gone. Gone and irreplaceable. (235)

The large gap in references to the stamp collection in the middle of the novel seems to indicate a lessening of their importance, perhaps even a willingness in Philip to finally face the changes in his life; this passage reveals, however, that while the text fails to mention the stamps for a lengthy period, Philip's purposeful decision to place them in a location he sees every morning indicates a continued (yet secretive) reliance on their symbolic importance to help him through the day. Upon losing this reference to his pre-Lindbergh life, Philip now lacks the lens through which he can distort the changes around him, a realization that causes him to finally face the trauma affecting both his family and the country. Without those stamps to remind him of the security he once enjoyed, he must come to grips with that fact that life "will never be able to return to the way things were before this cataclysmic event [Lindbergh's presidency]" (Maurer 60). Without his symbolic reference to normalcy, Philip must undergo an "awakening [that] is itself the site of trauma" as he finds himself in direct confrontation with his father's decision to quit his job, the disconnect between Sandy and the rest of the Roth family, and the myriad of other changes he moreover successfully avoided (Caruth 100).

Philip's first stamp collection served as his reassuring reference to the ways things were before the sweeping changes of Lindbergh's presidency upset the balance of both his political and social world. As Philip's life underwent a profound entrenchment in the new American order, the album gained new significance once it went missing: That loss undermines his sense of placement and security, leading him to acknowledge that his life has already been irreparably changed. Philip's later endeavors at composing a new stamp album seem to indicate a renewed desire to connect to his pre-Lindbergh existence, yet the fact that the collection contains Canadian stamps indicates his acceptance that life has in fact changed. Philip's new album symbolizes the young boy's realization that he cannot go back to the way things were, yet does not lessen the significance that the first set of stamps held for him throughout the bulk of the narrative. Although Philip must ultimately lose his American stamp collection if he is to mature, they remain no less important to his development as a person, and to the novel itself.

Works Cited

Caruth, Cathy. *Unclaimed Experience: Trauma, Narrative, and History*. Baltimore: Johns Hopkins UP, 1996. Print.

Grausam, Daniel. "After the Post(al)." *American Literary History* 23.3 (2011): 625–42. Print.

Maurer, Yael. "'If I Didn't See It with My Own Eyes, I'd Think I Was Having a Hallucination': Re-Imagining Jewish History in Philip Roth's *The Plot against America*." *Philip Roth Studies* 7.1 (2011): 51–63. Print.

Roth, Philip. *The Plot against America*. New York: Houghton, 2004. Print.

___. "The Story behind The Plot against America." *New York Times*. New York Times, 19 Sept. 2004. Web. 4 Jan. 2012.

Stinson, John J. "'I Declare War': A New Street Game and New Grim Realities in Roth's *The Plot against America*" *ANQ* 22.1 (2009): 42–48. Print.

Philip Roth's Heroic Ideal in *Indignation* and *Nemesis*_____

Gurumurthy Neelakantan

Philip Roth's *Indignation* (2008) and *Nemesis* (2010) dramatize the fortunes of young men who, in seeking to defend their dignity, attempt to defy fate, despite knowing full well that death and defeat is their inevitable lot. Unlike Roth's earlier protagonists Alexander Portnoy, Nathan Zuckerman, David Kepesh, and Mickey Sabbath, Marcus Messner and Eugene Cantor of *Indignation* and *Nemesis*, callow in the affairs of the world and bereft of self-reflexivity, are far from adept at transgressively engaging the conflicts and dilemmas of being human. More strikingly, these latter-day protagonists of Roth's, in being essentialists who place responsibility and duty above the self, are a clear throwback to Swede Levov, the hero of *American Pastoral* (1997). Characteristically, *Indignation* and *Nemesis* revisit Roth's heroic ideal, steeped in the moral earnestness that is much in the foreground in earlier works such as *Goodbye, Columbus* (1959) and *Letting Go* (1962). However, unlike Neil Klugman and Gabe Wallach, Marcus Messner and Eugene Cantor—youthful protagonists of the 1950s and 1940s, respectively—are blighted, and the only prospects that await them are gruesome death on the Korean battlefield or the maiming of the body and spirit in an epidemic of polio.[1] Paradoxically but appropriately, the young heroes of these late novels share the same reality as the aging protagonists of *Everyman* (2006), *Exit Ghost* (2007), and *The Humbling* (2009), works that treat in significant detail the travails of old age, debilitation, and death. Poignantly enough, *Indignation* and *Nemesis*, in espousing an existential vision of life that underscores the futility of human agency, dramatize the tragic lives of their young heroes, who are cannibalized by the dark forces that beleaguer the Rothian universe. Thus, given the Camusian sensibility that pervades *Indignation* and *Nemesis*, Roth's heroic ideal in these novels acquires significant depth and resonance. This essay seeks to illuminate in broad terms Roth's heroic ideal vis-à-vis the treatment of this enduring trope in Western literature in general and American literature in particular. More important, this analysis will also map the evolution of Roth's fictional vision, which, in obsessively returning to the earlier decades of the postwar era, succeeds in placing the historical and political developments of the American century in a broader sociocultural matrix.

Significantly, *Indignation* and *Nemesis*, besides their obvious etymological correspondences,[2] also explore concerns that underwrite an existential vision of life. Both these works dramatize how their protagonists, overtaken by cataclysmic events, are plunged into unmerited suffering that either kills them or leaves them living dead. Discussing the Nemeses novels, which include *Everyman*, *Indignation*, *The Humbling*, and *Nemesis*, Michael Sayeau notes, "Each is a modern tragedy that locates the causal logic of its plot in its protagonist's tendency towards reluctance and stoical refusal rather than hubristic grandeur" (19). Aptly enough, Sayeau's observation neatly captures the philosophical premise that drives Roth's *Indignation* and *Nemesis*. Structured along the lines of Attic tragedy, these novels endow their central characters with an identifiable hamartia, or character defect, and a strong sense of tragic irony. Reminiscent of "the Rebel-victim" (Gross v) typical of American literature, Roth's protagonists have much in common with the heroes of literary masters such as Ernest Hemingway, F. Scott Fitzgerald, John Updike, Saul Bellow, and Bernard Malamud. If, in modern American literature, "the individual serves a moral ideal which openly opposes a cultural or social authority" (Gross ix), Roth's delineation of his heroes perfectly answers to such a vision by dramatizing how they resist the repressions thrust upon them by religion in their quest for freedom and happiness. In mining the Jewish Newark of the 1940s and 1950s in *Indignation* and *Nemesis*, Roth celebrates the spirit of the common humanity that has endured and survived the vagaries of American history.

Roth clearly privileges a heroic ideal steeped in existential vision in both *Indignation* and *Nemesis*. He is well versed in modernist masters like Fyodor Dostoevsky, Anton Chekhov, Nikolai Gogol, Franz Kafka, and Samuel Beckett, and his predilection for the absurd and the bizarre informing human affairs has been unmistakable from the beginning of his career. His signature style of conceiving literary protagonists bespeaks his existential vision. As Roth himself admits, "I have concerned myself with men and women whose moorings have been cut, and who are swept away from their native shores and out to sea, sometimes on a tide of their own righteousness or resentment" (Searles 55). Not only do Marcus and Eugene allow themselves to be carried away by "righteousness or resentment," they are also too unrestrained to ever engage with life pragmatically.

Mostly told in first person, *Indignation* recounts the story of Marcus Messner, a conventional young man and the son of loving Jewish parents who run a kosher butcher shop in Newark. As irony would have it, he dies dismembered on the Korean battlefield, owing partly to his fierce independence and partly to the machinations of fate. Though Marcus is nauseated by blood and clearly "interested in things that matter" (11), like pursuing knowledge and culture, his seven-month stint working alongside his father in the butcher shop, between his early graduation from school and his enrollment at Robert Treat College in Newark, both provides an idyllic experience and brings him an awareness of a certain way of being in the world. The basic philosophy of Messner Sr. is that "you do what you have to do" (5), a lesson that Marcus, for all his admiration of his father, fails to internalize himself. The loving Messner household becomes a site of conflict when the father, overcome by paranoia about losing his son, begins severely curtailing the latter's independence and perpetually harassing and humiliating him. Ironically enough, Marcus himself is conventional, and his actions are geared to rising in life and becoming a source of delight and pride for his parents. Accordingly, Marcus declares, "I had been a prudent, responsible, diligent, hardworking A student who went out with only the nicest girls, a dedicated debater, and a utility infielder for the varsity baseball team" (3).

It is his father's unrelenting surveillance that drives Marcus to assert his independence and seek a transfer to Winesburg College in north Ohio, which is five hundred miles away from Newark. At Winesburg, he continues to excel in scholarship and even works part time in the campus cafeteria to support his education. Waiting tables, he occasionally becomes the target of anti-Semitic remarks, but he persists with his duties, mindful of his goal to become the valedictorian of his class. He experiences emotional turbulence following his difficulty adjusting to the other residents of the dormitory room allotted to him in Jenkins Hall. Having changed his accommodation twice in less than a few months, he is called in for questioning by the dean of men, Hawes D. Caudwell. Discovering that Marcus has not been attending chapel regularly, the dean questions him to ascertain his religious views, only to provoke the young man to explode in indignation and hurl the expletive "fuck you" at the dean (192). Further, Marcus's emotional involvement with Olivia Hutton, a fellow sophomore transfer student at Winesburg College, draws the attention of the dean when Olivia is precipitously withdrawn from the college by her parents following her pregnancy. But what really wrecks Marcus's college career and consigns him to the draft to die on a Korean battlefield is his intransigence and refusal to apologize when it is exposed that he has bribed a fellow student to substitute for him on chapel days. Incensed by Marcus's nonconformist ways, the dean recommends that he submit an apology letter addressed to the president of the college and promise to make amends for his errant behavior by attending chapel regularly for eighty days. Believing what he did is in no way wrong, Marcus flares up at the dean's verdict and insults him for the second time, using the same expletive as before. Following his expulsion from Winesburg College, he is drafted, serves in the Korean War as a private, and dies severely wounded. Thus Roth traces the trajectory of his protagonist's life from the ambitious through the abject into the absurd.

While critical reception of *Indignation* has been mixed,[3] the novel acquires significance vis-à-vis the novelist's continuing experimentation with narrative[4] and also his riff on characterization. If Roth's ongoing experimentation with narrative styles impacts his depiction of character, as critics have shown, it needs to be remembered that readers often tend to place a higher premium on character portrayals in assessing and appreciating literary works. In this respect, *Indignation*, even as it continues engagement with Roth's signature concerns found in his later fiction—namely, death, debilitation, and mortality—nevertheless evocatively returns to the idealism of his earlier novels. Derek Parker Royal, a noted Roth critic who finds Marcus "more striking as a narrating voice than he is [as] a character," gives the novelist credit for not making "a hackneyed return to the trodden grounds of [his] early career" and instead "participat[ing] in the thematic explorations found in much of his more recent fiction" (132). And there is the diametrically opposed view in an anonymous review in the *New Yorker* to consider: "Roth blend[s] the bawdy exuberance of his early period and the disenchantment of his recent work" ("Books"). While Roth succeeds in narrative experimentation in *Indignation*, as Royal ably shows, the novelist succeeds as much in creating a powerful heroic ideal informed by an existential vision. Therefore, this essay will investigate the depiction of the heroic ideal in Roth's late novels *Indignation* and *Nemesis*.

With the Korean War raging in the background, Messner Sr. is paralyzed by the fear that, like his nephews Dave and Abe, who died fighting in World War II, his son, Marcus, will become a sacrificial victim to the Korean War. Overcome by fear himself, Marcus asserts his independence by transferring to Winesburg College in Ohio. Once there, he works hard at both his courses and ROTC to ensure that he would serve as a lieutenant in the intelligence wing of the army and thereby minimize his chances of getting killed in the war. Reminiscent of Coleman Silk, the tragic protagonist of *The Human Stain* (2000), Marcus is fiercely individualistic and does not consider any sacrifice too big in his pursuit of the freedom to live life on his own terms. Happily conforming to the prevailing sociocultural mores of the American 1950s, he invokes the code of *non serviam* (I will not serve) only when his freedom is under serious threat. According to Tim Parks, "It is [Marcus's] manic oscillation between self-assertion and fearful withdrawal into the safety of convention . . . that gives the book its nervous edge." Much to his consternation, Marcus understands that his need to maintain a distance from his father by transferring to a midwestern campus has been rendered meaningless by his own propensity to continually imagine visions of death, thereby betraying his inability to throw off the patriarch's influence. At Winesburg, he finds his roommates Bertrand Flusser and Elwyn Ayers Jr. either too aggressive and obstructive or too complacent and judgmental. Even when Marcus seeks the help of Sonny Cotler, the nephew of a Jewish acquaintance of his father, to evade weekly chapel attendance, he realizes that Sonny is the kind who would like to take over and run the lives of others. In some way, each of these young men is an authority figure, much like Marcus's own father or the dean of men, who have no qualms about imposing their versions of the real on him.

Commenting on Marcus's character, Christopher Hitchens observes that he "evinces a Holden Caulfield–like disdain for sharing with others at close quarters." Accordingly, Marcus avoids staying with Flusser or Elwyn, either because it scuttles his project of applying himself with single-minded devotion to his scholastic work or because he finds their conduct unacceptable. It is his inability to adjust to his fellow residents in the dormitory that draws the attention of the dean of men. As it happens, Caudwell, an alumnus of Winesburg who prides himself on being a custodian of the college's "tradition" (20), turns out to be "the great exemplar of Winesburg conformity" (Cooper 261). Painful memories of his subjugation to the irrational forces exemplified in the figure of his father still lingering, Marcus is in no mood to let the dean go unchallenged for seeking to impose Christianity on him. As he confides in the reader, "I objected not because I was an observant Jew but because I was an ardent atheist" (80). With the Chinese national anthem that celebrates fiery resistance as his credo and his own intellectual commitment to the vision of life advocated by the analytic philosopher Bertrand Russell ever so strong, Marcus, by stoutly refuting the charges the dean levies against him, oversteps himself continually and jeopardizes his own cause. Examining Marcus's character, William Deresiewicz aptly observes that "he seems to be playing a role that he has written for his own admiration." To be fair to Caudwell, despite his confirmed religious views and snide ways, he strikes the reader as being nonpartisan in ensuring that the values of Winesburg College are not undermined by gross indiscipline. On the contrary, Marcus seems to be "overreacting or misjudging situations and people" (Aldama 207) and is quick to take offense not only with the authority figures like his father and the dean but even with his peers. Like James Joyce in *A Portrait of the Artist as a Young Man* (1916), Roth operates a double vision in *Indignation* that makes readers both admire Marcus's talent and fierce sense of independence and also distance themselves from his overweening pride that makes him cavalierly dismiss others. True, Marcus "never undergoes any sort of development or evolution," as Michiko Kakutani argues, though it would be difficult to agree with the reviewer that Roth's protagonist becomes "a victim not of his own narcissism or foolishness, but of others' folly and the sheer, stupid randomness of fate" ("Dead Man"). If anything, Marcus seems to be half in love with gruesome death, and this death drive, if you will, is what compels him into an absurdist vision of life.

At the core of *Indignation* lies a love story, which is propelled by the death drive that is an integral component of both Marcus's and Olivia's absurd outlooks on life. Olivia, a fellow traveler and romantic companion whom Marcus befriends in his history class, is the daughter of a successful doctor. During her stay at Mount Holyoke College in Massachusetts, she had tried to slit her wrists and bleed to death, perhaps owing to the trauma caused by the divorce of her parents. Marcus is infatuated with her, and Olivia, despite her alleged sexual involvement with other boys, clearly holds him in high esteem. She tells Marcus, "You are not a simple soul and have no business being here. . . . You

should be studying philosophy at the Sorbonne and living in a gar-
ret in Montparnasse" (70). If Olivia recognizes him for his intellectual
leadership, Marcus simply finds her to be made of the stuff of heroines.
Recounting Olivia's traumatic life, he expresses his admiration for her
heroic power of endurance thus: "The history of drinking, the scar, the
sanitarium, the frailty, the fortitude—I was in bondage to it all. To the
heroism of it all" (77). Refusing to brook Elwyn's dismissal of Olivia
as "a cunt" (73), he acts peremptorily by moving into another room.
Entertaining the desire to "have intercourse before [he] die[s]" (52),
Marcus is completely bowled over when Olivia performs fellatio on
him on their first date. Strangely, Marcus's sexual initiation with Olivia
takes place in a cemetery, where he has parked the LaSalle he borrowed from his roommate Elwyn for his date. Thus Roth dramatizes
his signature theme of the interplay of Eros and Thanatos in this scene.
As it turns out, another instance of Marcus's sexual hijinks with Olivia,
to which Miss Clement, the nurse at the community hospital, is privy,
becomes one of the reasons for his expulsion from Winesburg College.
Ironically, Marcus dies without consummating his sexual desire, and
even as he lies with his torso and genitals dismembered on the Korean
battlefield, he remembers Olivia as much as he does his parents in his
morphine-induced reveries.

A close reading of *Indignation* reveals that it succeeds in reinventing the Roth protagonist as an existential tragic hero. As in an Attic
tragedy, the novel has a choric structure. Part of this chorus are Marcus's own parents, who become living dead after his death. Jealously
maintaining his independence and refusing to be recruited to others'
versions of truth, Marcus battles indignantly over every infringement
of his personal sovereignty, though, as Alan Cooper argues, such "blind
devotion to truth . . . can be absurd" (Cooper 257). Marcus, whose
name references the Roman god of war, courts danger valiantly, though
he is subliminally aware that life bathetically testifies to "the terrible,
the incomprehensible way one's most banal, incidental, even comical
choices achieve the most disproportionate result" (*Indignation* 231). A

true existential hero, Marcus exhibits a stoic outlook and endures all sufferings patiently. It is not for nothing that Flusser mock-seriously alludes to the stoic philosopher Marcus Aurelius in commenting on Marcus's good upbringing: "You do the right thing in the end, just like Mama Aurelius taught you" (25). Discussing Roth's obsessive reworking of the absurdist worldview in his novels, Joyce Carol Oates, another celebrated contemporary American novelist, specifically identifies *Indignation* as a novel "where the tragic joke is most evident, and most devastating" (224). It is possible that Roth is meditating on how absurd his own destiny could have turned out, considering that he, like Marcus, was both a draftee in the American army and a prelaw student in Newark who sought a transfer elsewhere.[5] Incidentally, Roth moved from Rutgers University's Newark campus to Bucknell University in Lewisburg, Pennsylvania. In an intelligent analysis devoted mostly to discussing Roth's protagonist in *Indignation*, Aldama states, "Marcus is a young man Roth conceives as being both a creature of his time and a vessel for the new understanding and sensibility developing among large segments of the American youth after World War II. This is what makes him such a compelling character. He is neither conformist nor static" (208). Unmistakably, Marcus is alienated by the disgusting jingoism that goes on around him and that co-opts, as Charles Simic puts it, "the lives of the young as if they were toy soldiers." More important, the scene showing an elder in the community speak fulsomely on patriotism and America's founding tryst with the highest of human ideals, as Aimee Pozorski insightfully avers, intensifies the gravity of Marcus's alienation.[6] Perhaps that is how the novel came to incorporate the panty-raid scene and the admonishing speech of President Lentz it necessitates. Be that as it may, Roth's *Indignation* succeeds in presenting a novel conception of heroism that is likely to appeal to youth across generations.

Intriguingly enough, Roth's *Nemesis* makes a radical departure from the rest of the novelist's canon in presenting a protagonist who not only is bereft of irony but also gives up battling against the chaos that living entails. What Victoria Aarons says of characters in Roth's later novels seems to be particularly true of *Nemesis*: "Roth's unhappy characters in the fiction written since the turn of the twenty-first century seem to have lost faith in fiction's talismanic powers of reinvention" (9). For instance, a typical Roth protagonist, more often than not a male, revels in the possibility of counterlives; he is transgressive and bristles to battle the world, unlike the protagonist of *Nemesis*, who is sentimental, timid, and projects a posture of injured innocence. If Roth's protagonist Eugene "Bucky" Cantor is "one-dimensional," as critics claim,[7] then what redeems him as a character is the authenticity of his portrayal, which lies in the plausibility of one's encountering similar human beings in the world. Eugene's characterization, however, is in keeping with Roth's tested methods of depicting characters. As Morris Dickstein observes, "Roth's books can have another kind of protagonist, fundamentally good or simply youthful and innocent, perhaps a devoted son . . . or a conscientious father, the product of centuries of moral discipline." Similar to *Indignation*, Roth's *Nemesis* shows how its protagonist battles an unjust world that continually thwarts all human aspirations and withers every noble and creative impulse.

Eugene Cantor, a twenty-three-year-old young man raised in the Weequahic section of Newark by loving and morally upright grandparents, a graduate of Panzer College of Physical Education and Hygiene in East Orange, is the physical-education instructor at Chancellor Avenue School and director of the nearby playground. Under the tutelage of a hardworking and idealistic grandfather who cherishes athletic robustness and a grandmother who is love and solicitude personified, Eugene successfully puts behind him the trauma of losing his mother as an infant and the vexatious reality of being the son of an irresponsible and notoriously dishonest father. As luck would have it, he inherits his father's poor eyesight, and this biological deficiency kills his dream of fighting in World War II. Declared 4-F, Eugene has to be content with mentoring Newark Jewish children to become physically fit and brave. Despite his regrets about being disqualified from service, he enjoys an idyllic existence, blessed as he is with the love of his widowed grand-mother, the worship of his pupils, and, more important, his romantic involvement with Marcia Steinberg, his colleague at Chancellor Avenue and the daughter of a successful doctor.

The polio epidemic that ravages the Newark neighborhood in 1944 challenges the heroic ideals Eugene has internalized, though initially he rises to the challenge it poses. Saving his wards from polio without depriving them of their regimen in the playground becomes his major concern. But his efforts are mocked, as it were, by a malignant fate that unleashes a series of polio fatalities, beginning with Alan Michaels, his favorite pupil. When the overwrought parents accuse him of gross neglect, his ideals are shaken, and in his frenzy, he ascribes the devastation of polio to the callousness of God as much as to his own moral ineptitude. With his moral resolve weakening in a moment of panic, Eugene gives in to hamartia in accepting the job offer of waterfront director of a camp for Jewish children at Indian Hill in Pennsylvania's Pocono Mountains, where Marcia is serving for the second year in a row as the head counselor. The realization that he has reneged on his commitment to the welfare of the Weequahic children makes his soul writhe in agony. Sooner rather than later, he discovers that it is not possible for him to ever elude polio, as he has already become infected and has become the cause of misery and mayhem in both Weequahic and Indian Hill. Eventually, polio devastates his body and mind, leaving him a ghost of his former self. If he rails at a malignant God, he is far more merciless with himself for having unwittingly been the messenger of death. Bemoaning his fate, Eugene finds that the only way he can salvage his integrity as a human being is by sparing Marcia the sentence of being married to a cripple like himself. His somber vision of life, informed by the horrors he has lived through, qualifies him as an existential tragic hero.

Germane to the present discussion of Roth's heroic ideal in *Nemesis* is a review of the critical reception of the novel. While most reviews of the novel were mixed,[8] a few took particular issue with the novelist for failing to portray a convincing protagonist. A discerning reader would be alert to the novel's narrative point of view, which itself is fairly critical of Eugene Cantor's misplaced sense of responsibility. If Roth's protagonist strikes the reader as bland with no sense of irony, this is simply his characterization as the novelist wills it. It seems to me that Roth is trying to revive a certain heroic ideal modeled on Attic tragedy and mediates it through an existential vision. Perhaps the novelist has not entirely succeeded in this project, though it attests to Roth's continuing experimentation with character making and narrative point of view. For instance, Kakutani dismisses Eugene thus: "He is not torn, as so many Roth heroes famously are, between responsibility and transgression, tradition and rebellion" ("Newark"). In much the same way, Tim Parks rejects Roth's protagonist: "Eugene Cantor in *Nemesis*, however, is a young man who is never more than worthy, entirely lacking the charisma that animates Roth's more typical protagonists." Intriguingly, however, unlike the earlier Roth novels, *Nemesis*, much like *Indignation*, makes a low investment on the transgressive hijinks and instead privileges bourgeois aspirations that draw on the provenance of the superego. In an illuminating review of *Nemesis*, Deresiewicz captures this new turn in Roth's characterization: "Roth's prose, that magnificent voice of his, has always fed off the twin passions of lust and rage; Marcus and Bucky's personalities revolve around the need to keep those emotions suppressed." It is clear that Roth, in trying his hand at creating a heroic ideal different from his earlier versions, deploys a novel narrative point of view. As Leah Cohen aptly observes, "Roth achieves something strange and good here with point of view. From the outset, the narrative is evocative of a Greek chorus, at once communal and all-knowing." Not only is *Nemesis* modeled on Attic tragedy, it also subscribes to a Camusian vision of life.

The pronounced existential worldview of Roth's *Nemesis* is signaled distinctly by the plague motif that underwrites it. In ravaging the world of *Nemesis*, the polio epidemic thrusts to the foreground the issues of fate and freedom that impact human destiny. Reviewing the novel, J. M. Coetzee tellingly notes that Roth "plac[es] himself in a line of writers who have used the plague condition to explore the resolve of human beings and the durability of their institutions under attack by an invisible, inscrutable, and deadly force." Significantly, by placing his protagonist Eugene in a polio-ridden world that severely tests his moral ideals, Roth brilliantly connects the fortunes of his protagonist to the Greek idea of the tragic hero being pursued by Nemesis, the goddess of retribution, to warp his destiny beyond repair. Rendered an exile in his own land, much like the Greek hero Oedipus, Eugene raves against the unjust punishment meted out to him and his community by a bloodthirsty God. In an intelligent review of *Nemesis*, Dickstein discusses Roth's allegiance to the existentialist thinkers, among others: "This stark outlook, so far from the comic turns of the earlier Roth, goes back to the existentialists who were in vogue when Roth was young but also much further back to the protesting and suffering hero of the Book of Job, on which *Nemesis* is a series of variations." Modeling his novel on Attic tragedy while showing with merciless clarity how his protagonist pathetically falls short of what constitutes a true tragic hero, Roth superbly captures Eugene's supreme sense of responsibility, which, if not always directed to enabling ends, drives him to estrange himself from his girlfriend and thus spare her living with him. Roth's *Nemesis*, if it does not rise to the exuberance and virtuoso performance of the American trilogy (*American Pastoral*; *I Married a Communist*; *The Human Stain*), is a work that meditates on the heroic ideal to show how far human dignity and nobility can thrive in our own disfigured contemporary times.

Growing up under the nurturing care of a grandfather who taught him that "a man's every endeavor was imbued with responsibility" (*Nemesis* 22), Eugene, grateful for having been spared the horrors of orphanhood, is earnestly and even excessively committed to making himself useful to others. Permanently deprived of the love of his mother, who died right after he was born, and the guidance of his father, who was too mired in his own criminality to bother about him, Eugene, despite the affections and protection given him by his grandparents, becomes prone to experiencing moments of existential vacancy. Often Eugene cannot help reflecting thus: "He best understood how precarious his footing in the world was when adults bestowed upon him the look that he despised, the pitying look that he knew so well, since he sometimes got it from teachers too" (123). Weaned on idealism, his first moment of triumph occurs as a ten-year-old when he kills a rat singlehandedly at the back of his grandfather's grocery store. Elated, his grandfather nicknames him "Bucky" to cherish the boy's "obstinacy and gutsy, spirited, strong-willed fortitude" (24). Ever trying to live up to his grandfather's high estimation of his worth, Eugene is rudely shocked when the draft board rejects him for his poor vision, blasting his dream of fighting as an American soldier in World War II. The crushing realization that he can never hope to be a war hero informs his sense of deprivation as much as the reality of his being a near-orphan. As Deresiewicz notes, "Because of those eyes he inherited from his worthless father, a kind of congenital taint, Bucky's missed his chance to be a real hero."

Resigned to the reversals that plague his life, Eugene throws himself completely into mentoring young Jewish boys and girls in his role as the playground director at Newark in the summer of 1944. He is worshipped by his wards, and his moment of supreme heroism arrives when he resists and sends packing the ten Italian boys from the neighborhood who come spitting and threatening to spread polio among the Jewish children of Weequahic. The reader is told that "after the incident with the Italians he became an outright hero, an idolized, protective, heroic older brother, particularly to those whose own older brothers were off in the war" (17–18). His fortunes crash down, however, when polio claims several of his Jewish wards in quick succession. Blamed by the children's parents for being negligent and uncaring, Eugene is suddenly seized by the fear that he himself will become a victim of polio. Despite his deep commitment to protecting the children from harm, he gives in to Marcia's urging and accepts the position of waterfront director in the summer camp at Indian Hill, partly out of a need "to flee from the unceasing awareness of the persistent peril" (115) caused by the polio epidemic and partly tempted by the romantic prospects with Marcia the relocation ensures. Unhinged by the devastation he had witnessed, Eugene is "struck by how lives diverge and by how powerless each of us is up against the force of circumstance. And where does God figure in this?" (154). Much to his chagrin, polio pursues him to the summer camp to maim and kill. He is wrecked completely by learning that he himself is a polio carrier. Railing at an unjust God and torturing himself with guilt, Eugene decides to estrange himself from Marcia so that she can be spared living with him, a "human blight" (120), akin to Horace "the moron" (40), who used to wander into the playground at Weequahic. Of course Arnie Mesnikoff, the narrator, would put a different gloss on Eugene's sacrifice through his tongue-in-cheek comment that "his heroism consists of denying his deepest desire by relinquishing her" (274). What better exemplifies the code of the existential hero than Eugene's supreme sacrifice?

Unmistakably, Roth's existential worldview in *Nemesis* is much more pronounced and coherent than the one found in the author's earlier novel *Indignation*. If Eugene is like a less charismatic and more stolid older brother of Marcus, he is nonetheless a spirited naysayer, taking on the gods for their cruelty in inflicting untold suffering on the hapless and the innocent. Enraged with God and plagued by self-guilt, Eugene slips into an exilic consciousness characteristic of an existential hero. Sayeau puts the issue in perspective, commenting, "The way Cantor understands himself and the events that he encounters through a narrative of divine abandonment and personal failure is the thematic heart of *Nemesis*" (19). Reminiscent of Sophocles' protagonist Oedipus, Roth's hero Eugene suffers a tragedy that seems to be the handiwork of a cruel and perverse providence. Further, Deresiewicz argues that *Nemesis*, "like *Indignation*, . . . is a kind of Attic tragedy in prose: hubris, hamartia, nemesis; spare plot, fallen hero, endless suffering." Eugene's litany of complaints against God and the guilt he harbors for not being able to serve in World War II and for deserting the Jewish children in Weequahic leave him teetering on the brink of madness. Blinded by "the gravest meaning" (*Nemesis* 273) he reads into the story of his life, he heartlessly turns down Marcia, though, as he admits, her memory continues to haunt him. The narrator dismisses Eugene's quarrels with God as originating in "stupid hubris" rooted in a "childish religious interpretation" (265). Of course, the reader is likely to empathize with Eugene's heartrending admonition of God following Alan's death: "How could there be forgiveness—let alone hallelujahs—in the face of such lunatic cruelty?" (75). But the reader also grows impatient with Eugene for luxuriating in grief and would rather see him affirm life. Fellow polio survivors Arnie Mesnikoff, Eugene's one-time ward and also the novel's narrator, and Franklin D. Roosevelt, America's much-revered president, exemplify a more enabling way of living with the reality of polio. It would be good to remember, though, that the judgments the reader brings to bear on the novel's protagonist are not binding on Roth. For the novelist, Eugene is a specimen in the vast gallery of men and women he has created and has as much claim on his sympathy as any other character of his.

What is it in Eugene's temperament that contributes to the blighting of his life? His is an object lesson in what the excessive "embrace of conscience" (Kakutani, "Newark") can lead to. He incapacitates himself with guilt attendant on letting his life be driven by superego. Refusing to see the polio-related deaths as tragic occurrences for which nobody needs to be held accountable, he makes both God and himself scapegoats. In Arnie's take, Eugene is guilty of "convert[ing] tragedy into guilt" (265). Given that he conceives of God as "a sick fuck and an evil genius" (264–65) and is no more forgiving toward himself for the tragic deaths of his wards, he embraces a philosophical position that is perhaps much more paralyzing than the polio he has suffered. "Bucky's real hamartia," Deresiewicz points out, "is the delusion that he belongs to a morally coherent universe, a world of good and evil and guilt and punishment. Something went wrong, so someone must be to blame, and that someone is him." Perhaps Eugene Cantor is not a forceful naysayer like Herman Melville's Ahab, but the reader hardly needs to be convinced that in defying the gods, he keeps, in Coetzee's words, "an ideal of human dignity alive in the face of fate, Nemesis, the gods, God."

Philip Roth's late style, noticeable in *Indignation* and *Nemesis*, curiously reinvents the novelist's conception of character and narrative point of view. Revisiting the eras of the 1940s and 1950s, the novelist nostalgically mines America's cultural unconscious and discovers concerns that speak to the twenty-first century. Roth's tragic existential vision locates at the heart of life annihilating forces that can trigger bloodthirsty wars or death-dealing epidemics. No matter whether the threat to life comes from war or an epidemic, human beings have always shown supreme powers of endurance and idealism in battling such ravaging forces to assert the power of humanity. Roth's Marcus Messner and Eugene Cantor, though conventional youths of their eras, turn into moral rebels to defy the authority of religion and even challenge God. Unmistakably death-driven, Marcus dies fighting as a private in the Korean conflict, while Eugene, rendered paralyzed in body and mind thanks to polio, lives as an exile, brooding over how life has simply passed him by. Both these novels embrace an existential vision that attests to how chance events can completely transform one's life. Dramatizing how fate impacts the lives of his protagonists, Roth clearly invests these novels with the properties of Attic tragedy. The overt deployment of Greek tragic overtones in *Nemesis* not only counteracts and deflects the dismissive attitude of the narrator toward Eugene's decision to estrange himself from all life-enhancing acts, but also subtly suggests the possibility of the protagonist achieving the status of a cultural hero such as Hercules or Odysseus, if only the fates had been benign. Even as the twilight shadows deepen and darken Roth's vision in these late novels, the works swirl with the energy of superb artistry that conjures a new avatar of the irresistible Roth hero in tandem with vivid narrative strategies. In the Roth canon, *Indignation* and *Nemesis*, blending the subtlety of his earlier fiction with the exuberance and amplitude of his later work, stand out for the novelist's exploration of a unique heroic ideal.

Notes

1. Robert Hanks, in reviewing *Indignation*, observes that it is "a novel about the way [death] haunts youth" (88). Saturated as their consciousnesses are with the idea of death and doom, the protagonists of *Indignation* and *Nemesis*, if idealistic, are clear eyed in envisioning evil without. Commenting on *Indignation* in their epistolary essay, David Yaffe and Daniel Torday moot the case for the evolving heroic ideal in the late Roth: "Maybe if there's one thing that *Indignation* has going for it that *Goodbye, Columbus* the novella didn't[, it] is a kind of world-weary recognition that what comes to matter more is the world outside Marcus Messner's circumscribed existence—where Neil Klugman was just starting to see that that larger world existed at all, Marc has had that world forced on him to the death" (234).

2. In reviewing *Nemesis*, J. M. Coetzee touches upon the etymological parallels that underwrite both this novel and *Indignation*: "*Nemesis* (the noun) exactly translates the Latin word *indignatio*, from which we get the English 'indignation'; and *Indignation* happens to be the title of a book Roth published in 2008."

3. For instance, finding Marcus's character unconvincing, Michiko Kakutani dismisses *Indignation* as a minor novel that "possesses neither the ambition nor the scope of the author's big postwar trilogy" ("Dead Man"); James Wolcott finds it "the most schematic and set-piecey of Roth's recent novels, a parable of instant karma with an ironic coda that is almost Updikean in its pertness"; and Carlin Romano characterizes the novel as "comic-book logic pretending to be a tragedy." John Banville, however, in his generous review, notes, "But in this new novel [Roth] has regained his poise and subtlety of his earliest work and produced a late masterpiece." David Gates also praises the novel: "And of all Roth's recent novels, it ventures farthest into the unknowable."

4. Derek Royal and Frederick Aldama, among others, laud *Indignation* for its superb deployment of narrative strategies. For example, according to Royal, "*Indignation* demonstrates Philip Roth's ongoing attempts to push the envelope of narration" (130). Similarly, Aldama praises the novel for deploying innovative narrative strategies, commenting, "That is, the narrative asks that readers go to the outer edge of realist *vraisemblance* and do the impossible: overhear another person's full range of recollected emotional and cognitive experiences organized in a delicate and coherent manner" (215).

5. Jay Rogoff's take establishing a purported autobiographical strain in the absurd turn of Marcus's destiny in *Indignation* is germane to my own reading of Marcus as an existential hero. Roth "has reimagined his own youth as a series of ridiculous, disastrous choices Roth himself had the wit and good judgment to reject, and spun out a terrible tragicomedy in which death comes not inevitably but as a sinister pratfall, tripping up his indignant, self-absorbed hero" (Rogoff 515).

6. Pozorski establishes a resonant connection between the Korean War and the intergenerational divide in the 1950s of America to contextualize Marcus's harrowing sense of alienation at Winesburg College. According to Pozorski, "Marcus dies, after all, after failing to heed his father's advice and going off to fight

the Korean War, a war that, in many cases, divided generations, was tied to the rhetoric of the founding ideals, and venerated with lofty rhetoric, as personified in the speech made by the president of a Midwestern university that had succeeded, at every turn, in alienating Marcus" (150).

7. Both Kakutani and Deresiewicz fault Roth for failure of characterization. Kakutani, for instance, sees this failure hampering the plot development of *Nemesis*: "That Bucky is such a one-dimensional character makes for a pallid, predictable story line in which the random workings of fate and the fate of temperament— rather than genuine free choice—are the narrative drivers" ("Newark"). Commenting on Roth's characters in *Nemesis*, Deresiewicz likewise notes, "All of them are one-dimensional, what-you-see-is-what-you-get kinds of figures, lacking the internal tension of substantially realized fictional characters." In contrast to Kakutani and Deresiewicz, Edward Docx ascribes a more coherent valence to Roth's protagonist in *Nemesis*: "For, at the deepest level, *Nemesis* is not really about Cantor's war with polio but his war with himself: the war between a man's idea of duty and decency and the shirking of this for the facilitation of his more immediate happiness."

8. Reviewing *Nemesis*, Coetzee detects a waning of Roth's creative powers. Thus he notes, "Nowhere does one feel that the creative flame is burning at white heat, or the author being stretched by his material." Kakutani, Deresiewicz, and Parks, among others, fault Roth for creating an unconvincing protagonist. The novel has its admirers, however; Leah Cohen observes, "*Nemesis* stands out for its warmth. It is suffused with precise and painful tenderness."

Works Cited

Aarons, Victoria. "Where Is Philip Roth Now?" *Studies in American Jewish Literature* 31.1 (2012): 6–10. Print.

Aldama, Frederick L. "Putting a Finger on That Hollow Emptiness in Roth's *Indignation*." *Philip Roth Studies* 7.2 (2011): 205–17. Print.

Banville, John. Rev. of *Indignation*, by Philip Roth. *Financial Times*. Financial Times, 20 Sept. 2008. Web. 3 Jan. 2013.

"Books Briefly Noted." Rev. of *Indignation*, by Philip Roth. *New Yorker*. Condé Nast, 29 Sept. 2008. Web. 3 Jan. 2013.

Coetzee, J. M. "On the Moral Brink." Rev. of *Nemesis*, by Philip Roth. *New York Review of Books*. NYREV, 28 Oct. 2010. Web. 3 Jan. 2013.

Cohen, Leah Hager. "Summer of '44." Rev. of *Nemesis*, by Philip Roth. *New York Times*. New York Times, 8 Oct. 2010. Web. 3 Jan. 2013.

Cooper, Alan. "*Indignation*: The Opiates of the Occident." *Playful and Serious: Philip Roth as Comic Writer*. Ed. Ben Siegel and Jay L Halio. Newark: U of Delaware P, 2010. 255–68. Print.

Deresiewicz, William. "Portnoy Agonistes." Rev. of *Nemesis*, by Philip Roth. *New Republic*. New Republic, 19 Nov. 2010. Web. 3 Jan. 2013..

Dickstein, Morris."Philip Roth's Extreme Novel." Rev. of *Nemesis*, by Philip Roth. *Daily Beast*. Newsweek/Daily Beast, 2 Oct. 2010. Web. 3 Jan. 2013.

Docx, Edward. Rev. of *Nemesis*, by Philip Roth. *Guardian*. Guardian News and Media, 2 Oct. 2010. Web. 3 Jan. 2013.

Gates, David. "The Student of Desire." Rev. of *Indignation*, by Philip Roth. *New York Times*. New York Times, 19 Sept. 2008. Web. 3 Jan. 2013.

Gross, Theodore L. *The Heroic Ideal in American Literature*. New York: Free, 1971. Print.

Hanks, Robert. "Ruffian on the Stair." Rev. of *Indignation*, by Philip Roth. *New Statesman* 22 Sept. 2008: 86–88. Print.

Hitchens, Christopher. "Nasty, Brutish, and Short." Rev. of *Indignation*, by Philip Roth. *Atlantic*. Atlantic Monthly, Oct. 2008. Web. 3 Jan. 2013.

Kakutani, Michiko. "A Dead Man Tells of His Too Short Life." Rev. of *Indignation*, by Philip Roth. *New York Times*. New York Times, 16 Sept. 2008. Web. 3 Jan. 2013.

___. "Newark, 1944, When Polio Disrupted the Playground." Rev. of *Nemesis*, by Philip Roth. *New York Times*. New York Times, 4 Oct. 2010. Web. 3 Jan. 2013.

Oates, Joyce Carol. "Philip Roth's Tragic Jokes." *In Rough Country: Essays and Reviews*, by Oates. New York: Harper, 2010. 216–25. Print.

Parks, Tim. "The Truth about Consuela." Rev. of *Nemesis*, by Philip Roth. *London Review of Books*. LRB, 4 Nov. 2010. Web. 3 Jan. 2013.

Pozorski, Aimee. *Roth and Trauma: The Problem of History in the Later Works, 1995–2010*. New York: Continuum, 2011. Print.

Robson, Leo. Rev. of *Nemesis*, by Philip Roth. *New Statesman*. New Statesman, 14 Oct. 2010. Web. 3 Jan. 2013.

Rogoff, Jay. "Philip Roth's Master Fictions." *Southern Review* 45.3 (2009): 497–515. Print.

Romano, Carlin. "New Novel Takes Philip Roth Back to College." Rev. of *Indignation*, by Philip Roth. *WVAS*. WVAS, 9 Oct. 2008. Web. 3 Jan. 2013.

Roth, Philip. *Indignation*. London: Cape, 2008. Print.

___. *Nemesis*. Boston: Houghton, 2010. Print.

Royal, Derek Parker. "What to Make of Roth's *Indignation*; or, Serious in the Fifties." Rev. of *Indignation*, by Philip Roth. *Philip Roth Studies* 5.1 (2009): 129–37. Print.

Sayeau, Michael. "Smaller than Life." Rev. of *Nemesis*, by Philip Roth. *Times Literary Supplement* 29 Oct. 2010: 19. Print.

Searles, George J., ed. *Conversations with Philip Roth*. Jackson: UP of Mississippi, 1992. Print.

Simic, Charles. "The Nicest Boy in the World." Rev. of *Indignation*, by Philip Roth. *New York Review of Books*. NYREV, 9 Oct. 2008. Web. 3 Jan. 2013.

Wolcott, James. "The Fatal Handjob." Rev. of *Indignation*, by Philip Roth. *New Republic*. New Republic, 22 Oct. 2008. Web. 3 Jan. 2013.

Yaffe, David, and Daniel Torday. "We Are All Here to Be Insulted: An Epistolary Exchange on the Work of Philip Roth." *Literary Imagination* 11.2 (2009): 228–37. Print.

"Just as He'd Feared from the Start": The Treachery of Desire in Philip Roth's *Nemesis*_____

Victoria Aarons

A quarter of a century having passed since that terrible, lethal summer of 1944 when the polio outbreak in Newark, New Jersey, was feverishly escalating and the furies of war were raging uncontrollably in Europe, Bucky Cantor, the defeated protagonist of Roth's *Nemesis* (2010), will rail against the God he knows to be without conscience or mercy, a god who knows "no limits" (105). In a parody of Job's cry of outrage against the injustices wrought upon him, Bucky, years after contracting the disease that would dramatically unhinge his life, indicts God at the novel's close. He holds God accountable for the tragic misfortunes and barbarity of an era. Here Bucky denounces a vindictive God, a malevolent being "who spends too much time killing children," a fiendish demiurge with sinister motives, for who but "a fiend could invent polio. . . . Only a fiend could invent World War II. Add it all up and the fiend wins. The fiend is omnipotent" (260, 264). And in his obstinate insistence on assigning blame and demanding accountability from some higher, inimical force, Bucky stubbornly fails to acknowledge the obvious evidence before him: "irrefutable historical proof, gleaned during a lifetime passed on this planet in the middle of the twentieth century" (264). Bucky should know better: that one's cries are wasted, not only in the face of all-too-human malice, but when up against any of the vagaries and contingencies of this uncontainable and volatile life. Yet Bucky Cantor, in full retreat mode, will point an accusing finger at God, indulging the delusion of an absolute enemy to pathologically justify suffering. Bucky will surrender history for theology, reason for irrationality, and happiness for self-imposed misery. He will intractably attack God, whom he can only see as an intrusively wicked, anthropomorphized adversary—"a sick fuck and an evil genius"—as a way of deflecting his own acute sense of failure and transgression (265). In blaming God, Bucky excessively, compulsively blames himself, through a stubbornly persistent act of projection. His fears will be fulfilled. And Bucky's attempts to reinvent himself ultimately will be ambushed by the treacheries of desire in the exposing ironies of the Rothian counterlife.

Roth's Bucky Cantor, the once virile, javelin-throwing athlete of the Chancellor Avenue playground, will become, in a moment of unrestraint, the self-appointed carrier of disease and contagion. In response, Bucky will rail against a God he manufactures to be the mastermind of his own failures, the invented golem of misery, as a way of displacing, as Roth's Everyman knows to his core, all his own "ineradicable, stupid, inescapable mistakes" (*Everyman* 158). In his quest to find someone—something—to blame, in recasting the burden of responsibility onto some force beyond human intervention or design, Bucky will martyr himself, not unlike the protagonist of Roth's *The Humbling*, "impaled" on his own biography (138). But, as Roth makes ironically clear, to occupy a place out of history is, of course, impossible. Like the host of Roth's characters who have made his fiction an improvised masquerade of the self, Bucky Cantor, in an attempt to reinvent himself, to walk out of one life and into a fantastical theater of possibility, will find himself finally only to be himself. Constrained by his own character and history, like Roth's Everyman, Bucky is who he is, "just as he'd feared from the start" (*Everyman* 182).

Nemesis opens in Newark in that "poisonous summer" of 1944 that finds Bucky Cantor and his playground boys in the midst of the escalating terror of polio, a terror that insidiously arises against the backdrop of the war in Europe (267). The combination of events, exacerbated by growing American anti-Semitism, sets the stage for the fear and apprehension that will catapult all of Newark and in particular its Weequahic Jewish section, into a state of anxious dread and defensive impulses. Roth's Bucky Cantor, "one of the few young men around who wasn't off fighting in the war," is woefully exempt from enlisting because of "poor vision that necessitated his wearing thick eyeglasses" (10). For that deficiency, he is left behind and instead fights a different war: "the war being waged on the battlefield of his playground . . . fighting their fear of polio alongside his endangered boys (173). Bucky, the newly appointed physical education teacher at Chancellor Avenue School and its summer playground director, is a master of compensatory self-refashioning. Standing "slightly under five feet five inches tall . . . his height, combined with his poor vision . . . prevent[ing] him from playing college-level football, baseball, or basketball," Bucky becomes Weequahic's childhood fantasy of the mythic Greek hero Hercules, the "first javelin thrower" and "the great warrior and slayer of monsters" (11, 276).

Bucky Cantor is the motherless child abandoned by a ne'er-do-well father and raised by his stalwart, working-class, Jewish maternal grandparents in the close quarters of an airless tenement. Because of this inauspicious start in life, he will imagine it his responsibility to protect and defend his boys not only against the virulent spread of polio but also against anti-Semitic bullies, against weakness, and against the contagion of fear itself. For Bucky has been raised to believe that sheer strength of will and character can overcome both nature and inheritance, nourished on the well-cultivated ethical creed of his resolute grandfather, whose lessons were gleaned from his early immigrant years on the streets of Newark: "to stand up for himself as a man and to stand up for himself as a Jew, and to understand that one's battles were never over and that, in the relentless skirmish that living is, 'when you have to pay the price, you pay it'" (25). Indeed, this is a tenet Bucky will take to heart, a precept around which he will build his life and his steeled character. Bred on "ideals of truthfulness and strength . . . ideals of courage and sacrifice," Bucky will propel himself into the life that was bequeathed to him, thrusting forward like the javelin he eloquently hurls, "dancing," "in a high, sweeping arc over the field" (278–79).

However, neither Bucky's steadfast resolve to be the good soldier, nor his unswerving commitment to do the right thing, to live the right life, can withstand the seductive force of desire. In Roth's universe, such elaborately constructed will is a guarantee of ruinous debacle. Indeed, Roth's wily description of Bucky, with the "cast-iron, wear-resistant, strikingly bold face of a sturdy young man you could rely on," is as surely as anything a setup in Roth's fictive worlds for disappointment, disillusionment, and even disaster (12). For in one moment of impetuous erotic desire, an extravagant moment in which he perceives the possibility of hastening the fulfillment of his longing, Bucky will, in an irreversible act, relinquish his hold on restraint, discipline, and resolve. He will, in fact, abandon the well-rehearsed "three D's" of his upbringing: "determination, dedication, and discipline" (278). All such principles collapse in the face of that insidious alliterative rival: desire. Roth makes it clear that Bucky has no real choice. And so Bucky will forsake the structures and scaffolding of his self-made life for the fleeting collateral of pleasure and the promise of a future that holds the simplest of wishes: romance, marriage, family, "the security and predictability and contentment of a normal life lived in normal times" (135). But such a wish, in Roth's critically ironic conception of life and human agency, is nothing if not preposterous. Nevertheless, the heedless Bucky, rushing headlong into the arms of passion and Marcia Steinberg, will yield to the force of desire. Like all of Roth's hapless, reckless characters, he will attempt to create an imagined life in which he might become his fantasized self, the self he might have been, if only—as the protagonist of *Indignation* acerbically puts it: "if only this and if only that, we'd all be together and alive forever and everything would work out fine" (*Indignation* 229). Bucky falsely believes himself to be autonomous, self-determined, and thus able to set the conditions for his life, which, as for all of Roth's characters, is always a real mistake.

In a desperate attempt to live out the "counterlife," Bucky will flee disease-stricken Newark, its suffocating heat and contagion and fear, for the "beguiling" fortunes of Marcia Steinberg and Camp Indian Hill, a retreat tucked away in the Poconos, a sanctuary "atop a secluded mountain, concealed from the world at the far end of a narrow unpaved road and camouflaged from the air by a forest of trees" (179, 173). Both, for Bucky, offer the "premonition of that phantom, future happiness" he so long desired (179). Happily ensconced at Indian Hill, Bucky will wonder at the vagaries of circumstance and his own remarkable turn of fortune,

> struck by how lives diverge and by how powerless each of us is up against the force of circumstance. And where does God figure in this? Why does He set one person down in Nazi-occupied Europe with a rifle in his hands and the other in the Indian Hill dining lodge in front of a plate of macaroni and cheese? Why does He place one Weequahic child in polio-ridden Newark for the summer and another in the splendid sanctuary of the Poconos?" (154)

But such a question is both puerile and irrelevant. And neither Indian Hill nor the seductive promise of a future with Marcia Steinberg can alter the course of history or contingency. "Stunned by so much happiness," Bucky will be struck down (252). Even the Edenic Camp Indian Hill is not isolated enough to prevent the trespass of war and fear and contamination. It is inevitable that the novel's twinned contagions of polio and anti-Semitic fascism will find them there; polio will "hunt them down," just as, with equal certainty, the Nazi machinery, with relentless, virulent fervor will hunt down Europe's Jews (229). In this way, "the tyranny of contingency" is here rivaled only by the inevitability of disaster (242).

Thus Bucky's longing to "flee from the unceasing awareness of the persistent peril" of a Newark under siege will plummet him into even more peril (115). Given the chance, Bucky will flee the menace of polio-infested Newark and the mounting numbers of infected children, numbers that were, in anyone's calculus, increasingly "disheartening and frightening and wearying" (131). But, for Bucky, these weren't the impersonal numbers one was accustomed to hearing on the radio or reading in the paper. . . . These were the terrifying numbers charting the progress of a horrible disease . . . corresponding in their impact to the numbers of the dead, wounded, and missing in the real war. Because this was real war too, a war of slaughter, ruin, waste, and damnation, war with the ravages of war—war upon the children of Newark. (131–33)

Here Roth posits a ruined landscape where Bucky must measure his responsibilities against his desire to escape. Bucky is a pawn in this game of chance. "Sometimes you're lucky and sometimes you're not. Any biography is chance," discloses the narrator of *Nemesis*, one of the playground boys during that noxious summer of sweltering heat, fear, infection, death, and yearning (242). Surrounded by threatening conditions beyond his control—of both human and natural intervention— Bucky is exposed daily to disease, suspicion, fear, and that other peril, the ongoing annihilation of Europe's Jews, and the numbers maimed or killed on both fronts. Such conditions posed a genuine threat, as the narrator with weary nostalgic irony for the nemeses of old suggests, at a time "when it seemed that the greatest menaces on earth were war, the atomic bomb, and polio" (244). But, as always with Roth, the real nemesis here, the peril that will unhinge Bucky and alter the course of his life forever, is Bucky himself, his own worst antagonist and adversary. For Bucky will attempt to run from history-in-the-making, the peril of contagion and of his own inadequacies.

Bucky's exhilaration and relief upon exiting disease-ridden Newark and the daily reminder of the havoc being wreaked upon his neighborhood are short-lived. Bucky's life heretofore has been confined to the circumference of urban Newark and, even more constricting, to the Weequahic section of the city, and—more constricting still—to the suffocating tenements, where he dwells in the stifling company of "twelve families on Barclay Street off lower Avon Avenue, in one of the poorer sections of the city" (19). Bucky's foray to Camp Indian Hill marks his wished-for entry into the promised land, a sojourn that creates in him an exaggerated anticipation of a new life; traveling by train, the city rapidly receding, Bucky experiences "an epic dimension to gliding past a landscape wholly unfamiliar to him, a sense . . . that a future new and unknown to him was about to unfold" (140). Indian Hill, its lush countryside, its cool, beckoning waterfront, the "mild warmth of the sun—a sun that seemed benign and welcoming . . . the flickering luster of the lake and the green mesh of . . . growing things," "the harmless clean air," becomes nothing less for Bucky—as the narrator, Arnie Mesnikoff, comes to realize—than the "irreclaimable homeland, the beloved birthplace that was the site of his undoing" (149–50,157, 245). Here, Bucky will be part of a new covenant, one of the chosen. He will rewrite his own history. And, indeed, Camp Indian Hill comes with its own scripture, its "bible," *The Book of Woodcraft*, filled with Indian lore and lush descriptions of forest flora, fauna, and all varieties of woodland creatures. And as for God? As the narrator tells us, "It was easy to think kindly of Him in a paradise like Indian Hill. It was something else in Newark—or Europe or the Pacific—in the summer of 1944" (177).

Of course, such an Edenic new beginning—a prelapsarian paradise—is always "irreclaimable," since it exists in fantasy alone. Bucky is, however, a believer in new beginnings, buttressed by the infantile belief that if he does the "right thing," he will get a reprieve from the life he was somehow erroneously handed. But Bucky's exhilaration—"the bursting feeling of 'I live! I live!'"—will collapse extravagantly in the face of the realities of his time, of happenstance, and of his own exaggerated sense of accountability (145). For Bucky, everything—both his happiness and his misery—is always extreme, overdone, exaggerated, overblown. Bucky's magnified happiness, his initial elation that he had escaped and had implausibly created a counterlife, is radically tempered by his heightened, bloated sense of duty. Basking in the bountiful, life-affirming properties of his hideaway in the Poconos, Bucky is soon brought up short by the sure conviction that he does not belong there. He is, after all, only Bucky, not one to be privileged, but only the playground director of Chancellor Avenue.

But Bucky is plagued by conflicting identities, and in both cases he is wrong. On the one hand, Bucky believes that he is unworthy of happiness; on the other hand, he measures his value, as the narrator acknowledges, on the basis of "the historical saga of our ancient gender" (279). And so Bucky, before being stricken with the disease that will claim his limbs and his manhood, willfully believes himself to have abdicated his responsibilities to stay with his boys and suffer the stifling summer heat and fear in Newark:

> the war whose troops he had deserted for Marcia and the safety of Indian Hill. If he could not fight in Europe or the Pacific, he could at least have remained in Newark. . . . Instead he had chosen to leave Newark for a summer camp—and doing what there? Playing with children. And happy at it! And the happier he felt, the more humiliating it was. (173)

Bucky is torn between his fantasy of protector and his long-held and well-endowed sense of being the *other*, of being on the outside looking in. Thus Bucky, his own worst critic and adversary, can only chastise himself for his failure to measure up. Rather than remaining faithful to the mature, responsible, and manly creed by which he had been raised, Bucky opts instead for a childish, regressive, self-protective, and cowardly escape. But, as Roth implies, the real problem here is not that Bucky acts in his own defense by seizing the opportunity to leave the "war zone" at the height of the polio outbreak, but rather that he naïvely holds onto the childish fantasy of self-refashioning—and will ultimately be undone by it (176).

Not long after Bucky's arrival in the promised land, the initial quiet, peace, and serenity of Camp Indian Hill are broken by the intrusion of the disease that will shatter the false security of the camp; as Bucky has predicted, "In the end it's going to get every last child" (115). But of course, not everyone will be affected; only those unlucky enough to fall prey to the calamities of fortune will contract polio, and with utter predictability, Bucky will be one of its victims: "And finally the cataclysm began—the monstrous headache, the enfeebling exhaustion, the severe nausea, the raging fever, the unbearable muscle ache, followed in another forty-eight hours by the paralysis" (238). For his "fall," Bucky, clumsily, unimaginatively, casts blame on himself, because "what he no longer had was a conscience he could live with" (174).

Roth shows how the cataclysmic events of that terrible summer radically alter the course of both collective and personal histories; the collective consciousness of the times is defined by "an era of national suffering and strife when men were meant to be undaunted defenders of home and country" (246). The indiscriminate advance of polio and the repercussions of the war both in America and abroad provoke a reassessment of social and political stability and an acute realignment of ethical reckoning and accountability. But for Bucky Cantor, the combustible consequences of that volatile period, fueled by his sense of failure and culpability, become his great undoing. And, indeed, the explosive collapse of the idyllic haven of Camp Indian Hill and the awareness of the vulnerability of those who fled there will bring to a close, not only the central events of Roth's novel, but the naïve and misguided belief in security, innocence, neutrality, isolation, and protection that aligned the psyche of Jewish Newark before this summer of its unraveling.

Thus Roth's novel will shift to the year 1971, almost three decades after the events of that shattering summer. We find Bucky, "disfigured and maimed," exiled in the Newark outpost of his self-imposed misery (240). Thirty years later, Bucky unveils his life—his motivations and his actions—to Arnie Mesnikoff, the previously unnamed narrator of this tale of overwhelming woe and one of the Chancellor playground boys who idolized Bucky. Arnie's inside knowledge of a simpler, more amenable past inspires Bucky to disclose the course of his life since contracting the disease that left him with "a withered left arm and useless left hand" and "a dip in his gait" requiring a leg brace (243). It's to Arnie, who also contracted polio and now maneuvers through life with the help of a crutch and cane, that Bucky, with a kind of self-vindicating candor, for the first time tells "the whole of the story, from beginning to end," in "a pouring forth that before long he could not control" (245). Bucky will embrace and replay, in considerable detail, the minutiae of his inglorious history. His confession is less an unburdening for Bucky than it is a reconfirmation of all that he had and all that was taken from him, a corroboration of his own miserable failures joined by those of a God who, when given the chance, with no little enthusiasm "sticks His shiv in their back" (254).

In so confessing, Bucky will show himself to be both judge and executioner, a self-appointed arbiter of disabling culpability. For Bucky's plight and the wreckage of the lives of those in his charge confirm all his worst fears about himself. Bucky must believe that his punishment for abandoning his family, his neighbors, and his playground boys in Newark, his punishment for seeking happiness with Marcia Steinberg and his longed-for future, indeed, his punishment for wanting a reprieve from being Bucky, was not only to be stricken by polio but to be the carrier, "the Typhoid Mary of the Chancellor playground . . . the playground polio carrier . . . the Indian Hill polio carrier" (248). And despite the lack of tangible or even credible evidence that he was, indeed, the carrier, there is, as Bucky doggedly points out to the astounded Arnie, "no proof that I wasn't" (248). Determined to punish himself, as if contracting polio alone were insufficient, Bucky will deny himself all that he desires: He will cast away the devoted Marcia Steinberg, "the virtuous young woman he dearly loved"; he will act deliberately against his own self-interests; he will, as Arnie protests, "make things worse by scapegoating" himself; and, in an act of skewed, principled uprightness, he will rob himself of all that remains, since "the only way to save a remnant of his honor was in denying himself everything he had ever wanted for himself" (262). If no one else will hold him accountable, then he will willingly take on the burden. His deeply entrenched self-loathing won't let him accept what he can't possibly deserve, despite Marcia's insistence that "you could never put things at the right distance . . . always holding yourself accountable when you're *not*" (260). But Bucky's perspective has always been hyperbolized; he has always felt that he must compensate for not being good enough by forming an exaggerated character, inaptly reinventing himself, as Nathan Zuckerman once put it, "out of character for the character I'd become" (*Exit Ghost* 15).

Bucky, his world and the world around him in ruins, must find someone to blame. As Arnie, struggling to reconcile the broken, bitter man before him with the virile, potent champion of his youth, concedes that "the havoc that had been wrought . . . seemed to [Bucky] not a malicious absurdity of nature but a great crime of his own, costing him all he'd once possessed and wrecking his life" (273). He can't accept mere chance as a cause, for the Jew in him rebels. Assaulted by the conditions of his time, assailed by disease and disappointment and his own punishing superego, Bucky will "convert tragedy into guilt" (265). To do otherwise is to cast himself into an arbitrary universe, to decry intentionality. Unable to accept arbitrariness or determinism, he rejects the Greek notion of tragedy in favor of the Hebraic embrace of the tensions played out between an omniscient God and imperfect human beings. There is, for Bucky, too much history, a lineage of affliction, an inheritance of suffering from which he must draw meaning, even if that meaning points to his own disobedience and the retribution of God—a God whom, paradoxically, as Arnie reminds him, "you disparage" (264). In a kind of ironic echoing of Freud's *Moses and Monotheism*, Bucky, obsessively, in response to guilt, will embrace a religious interpretation of events, will team up with God, despite Marcia's surprisingly perspicacious accusation: "Your attitude toward God—it's juvenile, it's just plain silly" (260). For Freud, the ancient Hebrews create God out of a sense of guilt for killing Moses; for Roth, Bucky turns to a reinvented God out of the need to retain his guilt-ridden persona in the face of the obliteration of everything else he valued. Indeed, in his stubborn resistance, in all the intervening years of "silent suffering," like Job, "a man who was himself the least deserving of harm," Bucky looked to Arnie Mesnikoff like a man who "had lived on this earth seven thousand shameful years" (271). Like Job, disfigured, afflicted, bereft, Bucky will rail against God. Like Job, Bucky, "this maniac of the why," must find a reason for his misery (265). Like Job, Bucky "has to find a necessity for what happens. . . . That it is pointless, contingent, preposterous, and tragic will not satisfy him. . . . Instead he looks desperately for a deeper cause . . . and finds the why either in God or in himself or, mystically, mysteriously, in their dreadful joining together as the sole destroyer" (265). But unlike Job, Bucky willingly, deliberately gives up that which he loves best and gives it up for "moral" reasons. And unlike Job, Bucky takes a perverse pleasure in his misery, in "castigating" himself" to produce punishing, immiserating remorse (*Nemesis* 259).

Bucky, caught up in a whirlwind of self-reproach, will compulsively enlist God in this great debacle. But Bucky is, as Arnie points out, confused: "If it's God who's the criminal, it can't be you who's the criminal as well," he tells him (264). This is, indeed, the conundrum for poor, misguided Bucky, who, in looking for a "reason" for his misery shows himself to be utterly unreasonable and utterly dependent on his image of himself as guilty. This is where Arnie gets it right: Bucky shows himself to be in a juvenile, regressive muddle about who, ultimately, should be blamed for all the misery of that fateful summer. Bucky should know better. As Roth's Everyman comes to learn, "God was a fiction" and religion "a lie . . . all religions offensive . . . their superstitious folderol meaningless" (*Everyman* 170). Where Arnie gets it wrong, however, is in his equally simplistic assessment that "chance is what . . . Mr. Cantor meant when he was decrying what he called God" (243). For chance—unnamed fate—is something that Bucky cannot accept. In an act of tangled transference, Bucky will invoke and blame God in order to align himself with God. Here the conception of God is shown to be an easy, far too simplistic projection of not only Bucky's failures and limitations, but of his compensatory will, his desire to overcome the odds, his desire for mastery. In attempting to construct God as the omnipresent architect of evil intent, Bucky will, with a cynically Rothian predictability, misguidedly cast himself as co-conspirator. But, as Hebraic myth would have it, God and human beings have always been complicitous in this muck-up of a world. And thus, in striking out, Bucky will, inevitably, turn inward, exposing his own misguided attempts to liberate himself from himself, to be, in other words, not Bucky, but rather some refashioned, self-invented impersonation of himself. As Roth's Nathan Zuckerman long ago told us, "in the absence of a self"—and Bucky has, by the end of the novel, clearly lost his carefully constructed, improved upon, sense of self—"one invents one's meanings, along with impersonating one's selves" (*The Counterlife* 370). So Bucky will impersonate both himself and God, not uncomically becoming something of a "medical enigma," as he offhandedly tells Arnie, by both suffering at the hands of God and creating the very divine will that allegedly doles out the suffering (264).

Thus Bucky's surrender of the woman he loves and a future of possible happiness, as well as his return to the very neighborhood from which he longed to escape, working a "desk job with the post office downtown," is not without its self-flagellating gratification (241). Is Bucky, like the delusional Lear on the heath, "a man more sinned against than sinning"? Not in Roth's calculus. For Roth, there is no divine retribution, no theological or ontological or even teleological relation between sin and punishment. In taking on the responsibility for the spread of polio, Bucky grants himself far too much importance, deluded by grandiose notions of agency and authority, the power to control the outcome of events. Bucky can't listen to reason, as Arnie beseeches him to do, for reason challenges Bucky's carefully defended, precariously but perniciously erected image of himself. Bucky's insistence that he is setting Marcia free for her own good is simply an excuse for his self-aggrandizing and self-satisfying punishment, a sentence that Arnie admonishes is "much too harsh," but one that, nonetheless, suits Bucky's sense of martyrdom (249). Roth has a long career of showing that such acts of atonement are never selfless. Bucky unconsciously wants to be applauded for his sacrifice; in releasing Marcia from her promise, Bucky wants her gratitude: "A day would come, and not far in the future, when she would find herself grateful to him for his having so pitilessly turned her away—when she would recognize how much better a life he had given her by his having vanished from it" (262). Ever the good soldier, Bucky will ostensibly sacrifice his future for the woman he loves and condemn himself to a life of deprivation. How much loss can one person bear? For Bucky, enough is never enough. As if not wounded sufficiently already, Bucky will make of himself not only *a* victim, but *the* victim. For, ultimately, as Arnie comes to recognize, "there's nobody less salvageable than a ruined good boy" (273).

Unlike Roth's infuriated narrator of the novel *Indignation*, who will ask "How much more of my past can I take?," Bucky is in it for the long haul (*Indignation* 57). Is there anything cathartic in subjecting Bucky to such prolonged self-imposed suffering? Roth thinks not. Held captive by his punitive superego and his fixations, Bucky takes himself far too seriously—always a problem in Roth's fictive universes. Bucky is a man singularly without perspective, lacking the comic and ironic distance that might be said to save Roth's characters from themselves, from their delusional fantasies of self-aggrandizement and self-absorption. Finally, Bucky is shown to be "largely a humorless person, articulate enough but with barely a trace of wit, who never in his life had spoken satirically or with irony, who rarely cracked a joke or spoke in jest—someone instead haunted by an exacerbated sense of duty but endowed with little force of mind" (273). The lack of ironic good humor coupled with "little force of mind" is never a good combination for Roth.

Is Bucky, as Arnie Mesnikoff concedes, "one of those people taken to pieces by his times" (274)? Perhaps. But Arnie's narrative guidance is not entirely without self-interest and self-protection either. Arnie, in many ways a foil to Bucky's decision to live a life of misery, is the "successful" polio victim, the sufferer who made something out of his misfortune. Arnie, forced "to locomote" haltingly because of the polio that he contracted as a boy, goes on to marry and have a family, acknowledging pointedly to Bucky that "a damaged man is sometimes very attractive to a certain type of woman," and to open a business with another polio victim "specializing in architectural modification for wheelchair accessibility" (*Nemesis* 255). Arnie is the polio victim who adjusts to what Bucky sees as the reduced circumstances of his life. And Roth doesn't give us many options in this regard: The polio-stricken Pomerantz, Arnie's roommate in college and "a brilliant scholarship student, high school valedictorian, pre-med genius," commits suicide; Arnie resigns himself to his lot, recognizes his great luck in reconstructing his life and devotes himself to helping the afflicted; and Bucky martyrs himself, resigning himself to defeat, and in so doing, "perniciously magnified his misfortune" (268, 273). For Bucky, the equation is simple: "Whatever I did, I did. What I don't have, I live without" (249). But it's Bucky's response to the disease and to his perceived loss of manhood that threatens Arnie's consciously reconstituted life and sense of self. Arnie is not entirely in the clear here; he has his own interests to protect and thus accepts his limitations. And so he sees Bucky as he must, as martyr to no cause but his own self-invented artifice of appalling, sinister design. Such a person, Arnie concedes, "is condemned. Nothing he does matches the ideal in him. He never knows where his responsibility ends. He never trusts his limits because, saddled with a stern natural goodness that will not permit him to resign himself to the suffering of others, he will never guiltlessly acknowledge that he has any limits" (273–74).

For Roth, of course, the suffering of others is a given, as is one's own suffering. So finally Bucky will be outdone by his own lack of imagination and courage, his uninspired and largely unoriginal inability to make something of this life. In his protracted need for atonement, all his regressive, childish impulses emerge. In large part, Bucky's fall is precipitated by his delusional and wishful attempt to remake himself, to reinvent himself and have an agency in the unfolding script of his life. To be sure, Bucky will change. No longer the muscled, unassailable man of his youth, Bucky, having lost "that athletic, pigeon-toed stride . . . the sharp planes of his face . . . padded by the weight he'd gained" (244). Forever altered, his "original face was now interred in another. . . . No trace of the compact muscleman remained" (244). Indeed, Bucky's dreams to be reinvented perversely turn on him. Wanting to be someone else, desiring to be more than himself, Bucky will lose rather than gain. In his fantasy, imagining himself to be in control of his destiny, Bucky will lose all he had and more. In Roth's fiction, one always needs to be careful about what one wishes. For, desiring to be other than who he is, Bucky will, at the novel's end, know that "I'll never be me as I was in the past" (267). This is a refashioning, to be sure, but one steered by the treacherous, cunning hand of a self-deluding will.

Works Cited

Roth, Philip. *The Counterlife*. 1986. Rpt. New York: Farrar, 1988. Print.
___. *Everyman*. Boston: Houghton, 2006. Print.
___. *Exit Ghost*. Boston: Houghton, 2007. Print.
___. *The Humbling*. Boston: Houghton, 2009. Print.
___. *Indignation*. Boston: Houghton, 2008. Print.
___. *Nemesis*. Boston: Houghton, 2010. Print.

RESOURCES

Chronology of Philip Roth's Life_____

1933	Philip Roth is born in Newark, New Jersey on March 19 to Bess and Herman Roth.
1950	Graduates from Newark's Weequahic High School.
1951	Attends the Newark extension of Rutgers University and transfers to Bucknell University.
1954	Graduates from Bucknell University with a BA in English
1955	Earns an MA in English from the University of Chicago and serves briefly in the US Army.
1956	Begins a two-year post as composition instructor at University of Chicago.
1957	Roth's short story "Defender of the Faith" appears in the *New Yorker*.
1959	*Goodbye, Columbus and Five Short Stories* is published. Roth marries Margaret Martinson Williams.
1960	*Goodbye, Columbus and Five Short Stories* earns the National Book Award; Roth begins his teaching career with a two-year position as visiting lecturer at the University of Iowa Writers' Workshop.
1962	Begins a two-year position as writer in residence at Princeton University; *Letting Go* is published.
1963	Legally separates from Margaret Williams; begins a ten-year relationship with the Yaddo Artists' Community in Saratoga Springs, New York.
1965	Meets Claire Bloom.
1967	*When She Was Good* is published.

1968	Margaret Williams dies in a car accident.
1969	*Portnoy's Complaint* is published.
1970	Elected to the National Institute of Arts and Letters.
1971	*Our Gang* is published.
1972	*The Breast* is published.
1973	*The Great American Novel* is published; Roth takes a farmhouse in Connecticut as his permanent residence.
1974	*My Life as a Man* is published, introducing the character Nathan Zuckerman; Roth inaugurates and serves as general editor of the Writers from the Other Europe Series published by Penguin Books.
1975	*Reading Myself and Others* is published.
1976	Moves in with Bloom.
1977	*The Professor of Desire* is published.
1979	*The Ghost Writer* is published.
1981	*Zuckerman Unbound* is published.
1983	*The Anatomy Lesson* is published.
1985	*Zuckerman Bound: A Trilogy and an Epilogue* is published.
1986	*The Counterlife* is published; Roth earns the National Book Critics Circle Award.
1988	*The Facts: A Novelist's Autobiography* is published.
1989	Herman Roth dies of a brain tumor; Roth ends his position as editor of Writers from the Other Europe Series.

1990	*Deception* is published; Roth marries Bloom.
1991	*Patrimony* is published; Roth earns the National Art Club's Medal of Honor for Literature and the National Book Critics Circle Award for *Patrimony*.
1992	Roth retires from teaching comparative literature at the University of Pennsylvania.
1993	*Operation Shylock: A Confession* is published.
1994	Roth divorces Claire Bloom; earns the PEN/Faulkner Award for *Operation Shylock*.
1995	*Sabbath's Theater* is published; Roth earns the National Book Award for Fiction.
1997	*American Pastoral* is published.
1998	*I Married a Communist* is published; Roth earns the Pulitzer Prize for *American Pastoral* and the Ambassador Book Award of the English-Speaking Union for *I Married a Communist*; earns the National Medal of Arts.
2000	*The Human Stain* is published.
2001	*The Dying Animal* is published; Roth earns the PEN/Faulkner Award for *The Human Stain* and the Gold Medal in Fiction from the American Academy of Arts and Letters.
2002	Earns the Medal for Distinguished Contribution to American Letters from the National Book Foundation.
2003	Receives an Honorary Doctor of Letters from Harvard University.
2004	*The Plot against America* is published; the Philip Roth Society announces the inaugural publication of *Philip Roth Studies*.
2005	Roth earns the Sidewise Award for Alternate History and the James

Fenimore Cooper Prize for Best Historical Fiction; the Library of America begins to publish the definitive edition of Roth's collected works, edited by Ross Miller.

2006	*Everyman* is published; Roth earns the PEN/Nabokov Award for lifetime achievement.
2007	*Exit Ghost* is published; Roth earns the 2007 PEN/Faulkner Award and the 2007 PEN/Saul Bellow Award for Achievement in American Fiction.
2008	*Indignation* is published.
2009	*The Humbling* is published.
2010	*Nemesis* is published.
2011	Roth earns the Man Booker International Prize for *Nemesis*.
2012	Roth earns the Prince of Asturias Award for Literature; appoints Blake Bailey as his official biographer; quietly announces his retirement in a French magazine.

Works by Philip Roth

Fiction

Goodbye, Columbus and Five Short Stories, 1959

Letting Go, 1962

When She Was Good, 1967

Portnoy's Complaint, 1969

Our Gang (*Starring Tricky and His Friends*), 1971

The Breast, 1972

The Great American Novel, 1973

My Life as a Man, 1974

The Professor of Desire, 1977

The Ghost Writer, 1979

A Philip Roth Reader, 1980

Zuckerman Unbound, 1981

The Anatomy Lesson, 1983

Zuckerman Bound: A Trilogy and Epilogue, 1985

The Counterlife, 1986

The Facts: A Novelist's Autobiography, 1988

Deception: A Novel, 1990

Patrimony: A True Story, 1991

Operation Shylock: A Confession, 1993

Sabbath's Theater, 1995

The Prague Orgy, 1996 (first published in *Zuckerman Bound*, 1985)

American Pastoral, 1997

I Married a Communist, 1998

The Human Stain, 2000

The Dying Animal, 2001

The Plot against America, 2004

Everyman, 2006

Exit Ghost, 2007

Indignation, 2008

The Humbling, 2009

Nemesis, 2010

Nonfiction

Reading Myself and Others, 1975

Shop Talk: A Writer and His Colleagues and Their Work, 2001

Bibliography⎯⎯⎯⎯⎯⎯⎯⎯⎯⎯⎯⎯⎯⎯⎯⎯⎯⎯⎯

Monographs

Baumgarten, Murray, and Barbara Gottfried. *Understanding Philip Roth*. Columbia: U of South Carolina P, 1990.

Brauner, David. *Philip Roth*. Manchester, England: Manchester UP, 2007.

Cooper, Alan. *Philip Roth and the Jews*. Albany: State U of New York P, 1996.

Gooblar, David. *The Major Phases of Philip Roth*. New York: Continuum, 2011.

Halio, Jay L. *Philip Roth Revisited*. New York: Twayne, 1992.

Lee, Hermione. *Philip Roth*. New York: Methuen, 1982.

Masiero, Pia. *Philip Roth and the Zuckerman Books: The Making of a Storyworld*. Amherst, NY: Cambria, 2011.

McDaniel, John N. *The Fiction of Philip Roth*. Haddonfield, NJ: Haddonfield House, 1974.

Milowitz, Steven. *Philip Roth Considered: The Concentrationary Universe of the American Writer*. New York: Garland, 2000.

Nadel, Ira. *Critical Companion to Philip Roth: A Literary Reference to His Life and Work*. New York: Facts on File, 2011.

Posnock, Ross. *Philip Roth's Rude Truth: The Art of Immaturity*. Princeton: Princeton UP, 2006.

Pozorski, Aimee. *Roth and Trauma: The Problem of History in the Later Works (1995–2010)*. New York: Continuum, 2011.

Rodgers, Bernard F., Jr. *Philip Roth*. Boston: Twayne, 1978.

Safer, Elaine B. *Mocking the Age: The Later Novels of Philip Roth*. Albany: State U of New York P, 2006.

Searles, George J. *The Fiction of Philip Roth and John Updike*. Carbondale: Southern Illinois UP, 1985.

Shechner, Mark. *Up Society's Ass, Copper: Rereading Philip Roth*. Madison: U of Wisconsin P, 2003.

Shostak, Debra. *Philip Roth: Countertexts, Counterlives*. Columbia: U of South Carolina P, 2004.

Singh, Balbir. *The Early Fiction of Philip Roth*. New Dehli: Omega, 2009.

Singh, Nandita. *Philip Roth: A Novelist in Crisis*. New Delhi: Classical, 2001.

Wade, Stephen. *The Imagination in Transit: The Fiction of Philip Roth*. Sheffield, England: Sheffield Academic P, 1996.

Zeng, Yanyu. *Towards Postmodern Multiculturalism: A New Trend of African-American and Jewish American Literature Viewed through Ishmael Reed and Philip Roth*. Xiamen: Xiamen UP, 2004.

Edited Collections

Bloom, Harold, ed. *Philip Roth: Modern Critical Views*. Rev. ed. New York: Chelsea House, 2003.

___, ed. *Portnoy's Complaint: Modern Critical Interpretations*. New York: Chelsea House, 2004.

Halio, Jay L., and Ben Siegel, eds. *Turning Up the Flame: Philip Roth's Later Novels*. Newark: U of Delaware P, 2005.

Ivanova, Velichka D., ed. *Reading Philip Roth's* American Pastoral. Toulouse: Presses Universitaires du Mirail, 2011.

Milbauer, Asher Z., and Donald G. Watson, eds. *Reading Philip Roth*. New York: St. Martin's Press, 1988.

Parrish, Timothy, ed. *The Cambridge Companion to Philip Roth*. Cambridge: Cambridge UP, 2007.

Pinsker, Sanford, ed. *Critical Essays on Philip Roth*. Boston: Hall, 1982.

Royal, Derek Parker, ed. *Philip Roth: New Perspectives on an American Author*. Westport, CT: Greenwood-Praeger, 2005.

Shostak, Debra, ed. *Philip Roth:* American Pastoral, The Human Stain, The Plot against America. New York: Continuum, 2011.

Siegel, Ben, and Jay L. Halio, eds. *Playful and Serious: Philip Roth as a Comic Writer*. Newark: U of Delaware P, 2010.

Special Issues of Journals

Aarons, Victoria, ed. *Philip Roth and Bernard Malamud*. Spec. issue of *Philip Roth Studies* 4.1 (2008): 1–106.

Franco, Dean J., ed. *Roth and Race*. Spec. issue of *Philip Roth Studies* 2.2 (2006): 81–176.

Gooblar, David, ed. *Roth and Women*. Spec. issue of *Philip Roth Studies* 8.1. (2012): 1–120.

Halio, Jay L., ed. *Philip Roth*. Spec. issue of *Shofar* 19.1 (2000): 1–216.

Pozorski, Aimee, and Miriam Jaffe-Foger, eds. *Mourning Zuckerman*. Spec. issue of *Philip Roth Studies* 5.2 (2009): 151–301.

Royal, Derek Parker, ed. *Philip Roth's America: The Later Novels*. Spec. issue of *Studies in American Jewish Literature* 23 (2004): 1–181.

Special thanks to the Philip Roth Society for providing this information.

About the Editor_____

Aimee Pozorski is associate professor of English at Central Connecticut State University, where she teaches contemporary literature and trauma theory. She received her PhD in English from Emory University. She is author of *Roth and Trauma: The Problem of History in the Later Works (1995–2010)* (Continuum, 2011) and editor of *Roth and Celebrity* (Lexington, 2012). She coedited, with Miriam Jaffe-Foger, the "Mourning Zuckerman" issue of *Philip Roth Studies*, and, with Stephanie Wall, the "Trauma Issue" of the *Connecticut Review*. She has published articles in *MELUS*, *Hemingway Review*, *ANQ*, *PMC*, *Paideuma*, and *Philip Roth Studies*, among others, and serves as book review editor of *Philip Roth Studies*. She has served as president of the Philip Roth Society since 2009 and is at work on a monograph about representations of "The Falling Man" in September 11 literature (under contract with Continuum, 2014).

Contributors_____

Aimee Pozorski is associate professor of English at Central Connecticut State University, where she teaches contemporary literature and trauma theory. She received her PhD in English from Emory University. She is author of *Roth and Trauma: The Problem of History in the Later Works (1995–2010)* (Continuum, 2011) and editor of *Roth and Celebrity* (Lexington, 2012). She coedited, with Miriam Jaffe-Foger, the "Mourning Zuckerman" issue of *Philip Roth Studies*, and, with Stephanie Wall, the "Trauma Issue" of the *Connecticut Review*. She has published articles in *MELUS*, *Hemingway Review, ANQ, PMC, Paideuma*, and *Philip Roth Studies*, among others, and serves as book review editor of *Philip Roth Studies*.

Pia Masiero is an assistant professor of American literature at the University of Venice, Ca' Foscari. She has previously worked and published on African American literature in the twentieth century and William Faulkner's short stories. Her research and teaching focus on Hawthorne and the American Renaissance, literary theory and narratology, and contemporary American fiction. She is the author of the book *Philip Roth and the Zuckerman Books: The Making of a Storyworld* (Cambria, 2011).

Christopher Gonzalez is assistant professor of English at Texas A&M University–Commerce. He is at work on two book projects: The first traces the arc of post-1960s Latino/a literature in the United States by investigating the relationship between authorial decisions related to the creation of narrative storyworlds and the willing readerships that enable or constrain such authorial decisions. The second is a contribution to the *Contemporary Latino Writers and Directors* series (Ohio State) on the Pulitzer Prize–winning American author Junot Díaz. Gonzalez is also the managing editor of *Philip Roth Studies*, and he has recently published or has forthcoming essays on the author Edward P. Jones, the comics artist Jaime Hernandez, and filmmakers Alex Rivera and Robert Rodriguez.

Maggie McKinley is assistant professor of English at Harper College in Chicago. She is revising for publication her book manuscript Violence and Masculinity in American Fiction, 1950–1975, which addresses works by Richard Wright, Norman Mailer, Saul Bellow, James Baldwin, and Philip Roth. In 2012 an essay of hers appeared in *Roth and Celebrity*, published by Lexington Press. She was also the 2011 recipient of the Philip Roth Society's Siegel-McDaniel award for her essay on Roth's *My Life as a Man*.

Patrick Hayes is a fellow and tutor in English at St. John's College, Oxford, where he teaches literature in English from 1740 to the present day. His current research explores the relationship between fiction and cultural criticism in postwar America. He is working on a book entitled *Portnoy's Politics: Philip Roth, Literature, and Cultural*

Criticism, which considers Roth's ongoing quarrel with public moralists and the ways in which literature is evaluated in the public sphere. His book *J. M. Coetzee and the Novel: Writing and Politics after Beckett* (Oxford, 2010) explores the inventive ways in which Coetzee has responded to the tradition of the novel, focusing on a range of figures from Cervantes, Defoe, and Richardson, to Dostoevsky, Kafka, and Beckett.

Velichka Ivanova holds a PhD in English and comparative literature from the University of Paris 3–Sorbonne Nouvelle in France. She is the author of *Fiction, utopie, histoire: Essai sur Phillip Roth et Milan Kundera* (L'Harmattan, 2010) and editor of the collection *Reading Philip Roth's American Pastoral* (Presses Universitaires du Mirail, 2011). She is working on an edited collection titled *Philip Roth: Transatlantic Perspectives* (Cambria, forthcoming).

Miriam Jaffe-Foger is assistant director of the writing program at Rutgers University. She previously coedited with Aimee Pozorski the *Philip Roth Studies* special issue "Mourning Zuckerman." She is working on a project titled *The Death of Philip Roth* and an essay on Philip Roth's relevance as a twenty-first century author.

Michael Kimmage is associate professor of history at the Catholic University of America. He is the author of *In History's Grip: Philip Roth's Newark Trilogy* (Stanford, 2012) and *The Conservative Turn: Lionel Trilling, Whittaker Chambers, and the Lessons of Anti-Communism* (Harvard, 2009). He is also the translator of Wolfgang Koeppen's 1959 travelogue, *Journey through America* (Berghahn, 2012).

Debra Shostak is professor of English at the College of Wooster in Ohio. She is the author of *Philip Roth: Countertexts, Counterlives* (South Carolina, 2004) and editor of *Philip Roth: American Pastoral, The Human Stain, The Plot against America* (Continuum, 2011). Her articles on contemporary American novelists, including Paul Auster, Jeffrey Eugenides, John Irving, Maxine Hong Kingston, and Philip Roth, have appeared in *Contemporary Literature*, *Critique*, *Modern Fiction Studies*, *Shofar*, *Studies in the Novel*, and *Twentieth Century Literature*. She also writes on film and is currently working on cinematic adaptations of contemporary American novels.

Namoi Desrochers served in the United States Marine Corps before attending Central Connecticut State University, achieving a bachelor of science degree in secondary English education and a master's degree in English. She has served as poetry editor of the *Helix*, a literary arts magazine, and has done extensive research on the pastoral as a literary genre. She aims to gain a teaching post in a secondary school and to complete a PhD program in the near future.

Gurumurthy Neelakantan is a professor of English and the Rahul and Namita Gautam Chair at the Indian Institute of Technology Kanpur. He is the author of *Saul Bellow and the Modern Waste Land* (Indian Publishers, 2000), in addition to articles on a range of modern and contemporary American novelists.

Victoria Aarons is O. R. & Eva Mitchell Distinguished Professor of Literature and chair of the English Department at Trinity University in Texas. She is the author of *A Measure of Memory: Storytelling and Identity in American Jewish Fiction* (University of Georgia, 1996) and *What Happened to Abraham? Reinventing the Covenant in American Jewish Fiction* (University of Delaware, 2005), as well as numerous articles on American Jewish and Holocaust literatures in books and scholarly journals. She is a contributor to *The Cambridge Companion to Philip Roth* and the collection *Playful and Serious: Philip Roth as a Comic Writer*, edited by Ben Siegel and Jay Halio, and she is the guest editor of a special issue of *Philip Roth Studies* devoted to Saul Bellow, Bernard Malamud, and Philip Roth.

Index